The Search
for Wider Horizons

Arne C. Wiprud

THE SEARCH
FOR WIDER HORIZONS

By

Arne C. Wiprud

1970

Printed in the United States of America by
The William Byrd Press, Inc.,
Richmond, Virginia

Distributed by The Williamsburg Press, Inc.
Williamsburg, Virginia 23185

To my wife,

BEATHA MARY WIPRUD

whose unfaltering patience and
assistance supported me in the
writing of this book.

Foreword

THE RESISTANCE to change in a rapidly changing world is a phenomenon that, despite the efforts of a comparatively few in private and public life to understand and meet the challenge of change, is troubling our land. As a result, a multiplicity of economic, social, and cultural problems of magnitude that might have been foreseen and constructively dealt with, but were not, confronts the Nation.

There appears to be no easy solution to many of these accumulated problems, yet they must be solved. Promises of future progress will no longer suffice. The Nation can no longer temporize with these pressing problems, for they will not solve themselves. If timely action is not taken to develop enduring solutions to these problems, the result may be even greater problems that could be extremely costly to the Nation, its industries and businesses, and its people.

The resistance to change in major areas of public concern as related in this book, may be a shocking story to whose who believe in the American tradition of free, competitive enterprise. It shows the consequences of the failure or the refusal of those who own and manage some of the great institutions and industries in our land to understand and meet the need for change in their ancient methods and practices. The purpose of the book, however, is not to denounce anyone. It is rather to document and record for history, and thus inform the public about the struggles of outstanding leaders in private and public life who understood and constructively met the challenge of change. The hope expressed is that those who succeed in the ownership and management of our great institutions and industries may benefit by their example. Unless they learn that resistance to constructive change is the first step towards catastrophe, then the future of our tradition of free, competitive enterprise is in doubt.

This could be a vain hope. Current and relevant happenings in the field of mergers and acquisitions are threatening the continued existence of free, competitive enterprise in the United States. Dominant private groups have converted their organizations into so-called "conglomerates." As conglomerates they are taking over companies, large and small, on a gigantic scale. Thus, by eliminating all meaningful competition they are concentrating their economic control and power over the Nation's economy.

The facts, scope and implications of this amazing development—unhindered by effective action that could be taken by Congress and its regulatory agencies to protect the public interest—is related in Chapter X. The nature of this development can best be understood when contrasted with the work of those dedicated men who solved some of the major domestic problems of our country *in the public interest,* as related in this book.

Since my work dealt in large part with opposition to some of the major policy decisions and activities relating to the problems of change by those who control private companies operating public transportation services, some of which in later years I helped to solve, I was surprised to receive from Walter J. Tuohy, then President of the Chesapeake and Ohio Railway Company, a letter dated March 11, 1965, which reads in part as follows:

The transportation industry has been and will always be in your debt for the many years of devoted service you have given it. And most assuredly, my friend, you more than anyone I know strengthened the free enterprise system in the industry. You have set a record which is almost impossible to emulate.

It will be clear to the reader that outstanding men in private and public life gave me the opportunities for the services to which Mr. Touhy referred. If other major problems of national concern were approached by men equal to these in understanding, ability, and determination, solutions to these problems will be found. Thus, the horizons of all our people would be widened.

In the 1960's, major groups in the railroad industry appear to have turned away from the traditional American free enterprise system. In the name of "private enterprise" they propose to eliminate all meaningful competition in transportation by establishing cartels. Further, by the device discussed herein, they would subordinate the transportation function by creating railroad-based conglomerates for the purpose of acquiring non-transportation companies which, as railroad companies, the law forbids without the approval of the Interstate Commerce Commission. It should be noted that the ownership of large and perhaps controlling blocks of stock in the railroads of the United States is not known. It may be that only an *informed citizenry* can prevail against the few powerful groups controlling the railroad industry and thus preserve our railroads as private enterprises and protect the public interest. The events related in this book sustain this view.

It was the people on our farms and in our towns and cities, *being informed,* that provided their leaders with the support essential to establish a national rural credit system at a critical time in our history over the opposition of financial groups that sought to maintain the *status quo* and thus preserve their costly method of making farm loans.

It was the people of the upper Mississippi valley who, *being informed,* actively supported the program of their leaders in private and public life that unlocked a vast landlocked area of the United States. This program included a project to improve, in modern terms, the upper Mississippi River for reliable commercial navigation, which was achieved over the opposition of powerful groups who sought to maintain the *status quo* in railroad transportation.

It was a man of the people, with the support of the people, who, despite all obstacles, conceived and brought into being the first transcontinental land transportation system in the United States.

It was the people who sustained a dedicated Postmaster General in his efforts to modernize the transportation of mail over the strange hostility of the organized railroad industry.

It was the people to which "a fabulous person" turned in seeking to bring the railroad industry into the twentieth century over the opposition of the organized railroad industry.

It was the people, and a concern for their welfare, who inspired a Governor to publicly and effectively outline for the Federal government's regulatory agency a sound policy to replace its ancient, piecemeal, and ineffective policy in railroad merger cases, cases that involved the restructuring of the nation's obsolete railroad network.

It was a compassionate concern for the poor and neglected people in many lands that motivated a prominent industrialist to devote his life to improving their economic, social, and cultural well-being by helping them to help themselves.

Against this background, it is clear that our people, *being informed,* will strongly oppose policies and programs that are detrimental to the public interest, and will actively support those policies and programs that serve the public interest. Applying this view to the major programs of powerful groups in our nation, programs that would so enlarge and concentrate their control over the Nation's economy as to threaten the continued existence of the American free enterprise system, the primary duty of our representatives in Congress and in the Executive Department of the Federal government is to fully inform the people about the nature and implications of such programs. In so doing they will have the support essential to take alternative action to preserve our heritage, the freedom of opportunity in a free society for all our people.

I trust this book will prove helpful to those who seek an understanding of the growing problems of the Nation, and their causes, and the importance of an informed approach to their solution; and that it also will be of value to students of business, government, foreign affairs, and American history.

ARNE C. WIPRUD

Williamsburg, Virginia
August 6, 1970

Acknowledgements

MANY OF the outstanding and dedicated men with whom I have been associated over the years in solving major problems of public concern expressed the hope that our struggles to meet the challenges of change, and how they were solved—those that were successful and others that laid the foundation for later success—should not be forgotten because others may benefit therefrom. This hope was encouraged by Joseph C. Scheleen, Editor of *Traffic World*, Dr. Fraser Neiman, Head of the Department of English and Literature at the College of William and Mary, and Mrs. Stella D. Neiman, his wife, who assisted in editing the manuscript.

While the years of research and writing were of course my own, many supplied documented information that assisted in bringing the statistical and other material up-to-date. They include the published material supplied by the Farm Credit Administration, the United States Army Corps of Engineers, The Greyhound Corporation, the Ways and Means Committee and the Committee on Banking and Currency of the House of Representatives of the United States, the Antitrust Division of the Department of Justice, the United Nations Development Programme, and a few non-governmental published articles, all of which are credited in the text.

It is of course understood that these acknowledgements in no way constitute endorsement of the views expressed herein. I assume full responsibility for the views expressed in this work.

ARNE C. WIPRUD

Illustrations

Contents

The Search
for Wider Horizons

CHAPTER I

Wider Horizons for
the American Farmer

> Government is a combination of people of a country to effect certain objects by joint effort.
>
> The legitimate object of government is to do for the people what needs to be done, but which they cannot, by individual effort, do at all, or do so well, for themselves.
>
> ABRAHAM LINCOLN

IN 1917, some said it was an impossible dream—the idea of farmers cooperating to create a mechanism for transforming investment capital into agricultural production. But, for reasons set forth in this chapter, they persisted. By 1968, with the initial financial assistance of the Federal government, which has been repaid in its entirety to the United States Treasury, the American farmers built and now own a national Farm Credit System that is the largest cooperative rural credit system in the world! In its 51 years of existence, the System has provided over $100 billion in loans to farmers and ranchers of the nation on a basis that met their needs.

In the early years there were some dark days for the Federal land banks, times of crises. As an official of the Federal Land Bank of St. Paul, I participated in their solutions. The outcome has been called a great American saga,—a gigantic achievement

3

for agriculture and for the nation's economy at a critical time in our history.

After years of "hard and painful fighting" the farmers of the United States obtained the enactment by Congress of the Federal Farm Loan Act of 1916. This Act established twelve cooperative Federal land banks in the United States, which formed the Federal Farm Loan System, to supply the farmers need for long-term, amortized loans on reasonable terms and at low rates of interest. Such loans, not theretofore available, would enable them to repay their loans from the earnings of their land, and to develop and expand their farm operations on a sound, business-like basis.

Privately-owned financial institutions made farm loans for periods of from three to five years, often at high interest rates, although in most cases it was impossible for the farmer-borrower to repay his loan from the earnings of his land within so short a time. The farmer could, of course, renew his three-to-five year loan when it fell due, but he would run the risk of the money market being unfavorable at the time, and even if he did renew there would be additional costs, such as renewal commissions, recording charges, abstract fees, registration taxes, etc., incident to such renewal. These institutions failed to recognize that long-term, amortized loans on reasonable terms were essential to the growth and development of the agricultural industry, a basic industry in the nation's private enterprise economy.

In this situation, to paraphrase Lincoln, the Federal government, in establishing the Federal Farm Loan System, did for the farmers what needed to be done, but which they could not, by individual effort, do at all.

The initial task of the Federal Farm Loan Board, in which the control of the entire Federal Farm Loan System was centralized, was of lasting consequence. Continental United States was divided into 12 loaning districts and a Federal land bank established in each district, with its principal office located in a city within the district designated by the Board.

Shortly after the twelve Federal land banks were organized and in operation, their continued existence was threatened, first, by suspending the flow of funds from private sources essential to their operation and, then, by court proceedings challenging the constitutionality of the Federal Farm Loan Act. The obvious purpose was to maintain the *status quo* in the field of farm mortgage banking, and thus preserve the long established and costly method of making farm loans which had placed such a heavy and increasingly unbearable burden on the American farmer. For a time, it appeared that these attacks might achieve their purpose.

To understand the conditions and the events that threatened the continued existence of the Federal Farm Loan System, it must be noted that the lending operations of the Federal land banks were dependent upon the continuous issuance and sale of their bonds, termed Federal farm loan bonds, to private investors. Aside from the original capital, the banks obtained funds for lending purposes only by the sale of their bonds in volume.

Federal farm loan bonds are not obligations of the Federal government. As provided in the Farm Loan Act, the security underlying farm loan bonds consists in the first instance of mortgages on farm lands, carefully selected according to reliable and uniform standards. These mortgages, pledged as collateral, are secured by the personal undertaking of the borrowers; by the security of the mortgaged land at least double the value of the amount of the loan; by the capital, reserves, and earnings of the local farm loan association endorsing the loan; and by the liability of the members of the endorsing association to double the amount of stock held by them. In addition to the security of all the mortgages held by all of the land banks, at least equal in amount to the outstanding bonds, every farm loan bond is secured by the capital, and earnings of the eleven other land banks. Manifestly these are adequate safeguards.[1]

While the security underlying Federal farm loan bonds could

[1] National banks and State member banks of the Federal Reserve System may invest in Federal Land Bank bonds, which are not subject to the statutory limitations and restrictions generally applicable to investment securities. The bonds are lawful investments for Federal credit unions and Federal savings and loan associations and for fiduciary and and trust funds under the jurisdiction of the United States Government, and are eligible as security for Government deposits. Under the laws of various states, including New York and Massachusetts, these bonds are also legal investments for savings banks, trust companies, and trust funds.

not be questioned, the Federal Farm Loan Board, in which, as stated, the control of the entire System was centralized, was of the opinion that they were unknown to the American investor. For this reason, principally, the Board entered into negotiations for a contract with certain bond houses, "with large 'clienteles' of investors and an established reputation for dealing in conservative investments," to sell these bonds.

These bond houses obtained an opinion from a leading attorney, Charles Evans Hughes, who years later became Chief Justice of the United States, advising them that the Federal Farm Loan Act was constitutional, that Federal farm loan bonds would be, when issued and paid for, valid securities constituting instrumentalities of the United States government, and that they would be exempt from Federal, state, municipal and local taxation.[2] The bond houses then signed the contract and formed a syndicate for the purpose of introducing Federal farm loan bonds on the American bond market. The first issue of these bonds, totaling $30,000,000, bearing interest at the rate of $4\frac{1}{2}$ percent, was sold through this syndicate, which issue was substantially oversubscribed.

The lending operations of the Federal land banks also require a comparatively large commitment on loans prior to the bond sale. This commitment constitutes firm promises to farmers to make loans to them in order that mortgages would be readily available as collateral security for the bonds sold. This procedure was, of course, known to the banking syndicate handling Federal farm loan bonds. Therefore, in view of the earlier demand for these bonds, the officers of the Federal land banks assumed that the Federal Farm Loan Board's contract with the banking syndicate would be renewed without question. They were amazed when the announcement was received from the Federal Farm Loan Board on November 30, 1917, *one day* before the expiration of its contract with the banking syndicate, that it would not be

---

[2] Federal Land Bank bonds and the income from them are exempt from State, municipal, and local taxes. Interest on the bonds is subject to Federal income taxes, and gain from their sale or other disposition, or their transfer by inheritance, gift, etc., is subject to Federal and State taxes. (The Congress made Federal Land Bank bonds subject to Federal income tax in 1941.)

renewed. The syndicate gave no warning of its action and suggested no alternative to meet the situation. The reason assigned by the syndicate was brief—adverse market conditions.

Consternation reigned throughout the Federal Farm Loan System, for each of the Federal land banks had commitments to farmers far in excess of their immediate money supply; in fact, the total commitments of the twelve Federal land banks exceeded $100,000,000. The only way of meeting these commitments under existing law was through the sale of bonds which these banks issue. The establishment of a bond selling agency within the Federal Farm Loan System to sell the amount of Federal farm loan bonds within the time sufficient to care for this situation was not feasible. What to do?

I should state here that I am more than a transmitter of reported facts about this crisis of the Federal land banks. As a land bank official, I had a part in its solution, so I write from first-hand knowledge of the facts. In the fall of 1916, E. G. Quamme, President of the Federal Land Bank of St. Paul, Minnesota, one of the land banks then in the process of organization, offered me the position as his secretary. I set aside my plans for the private practice of law and accepted. As the organizational work progressed, and at the direction of Mr. Quamme, I worked on the bank's legal as well as its administrative problems. To more effectively perform my tasks, I was promoted to Assistant to the President. This was before the crisis. After the crisis, I was elected Executive Vice President of the St. Paul Federal Land Bank.

Well do I remember the day when Mr. Quamme asked me to join him on a trip to Washington, D. C. The purpose was to do something about the crisis which seemed to have stunned the government and land bank officials involved into inaction. Enroute we worked out our strategy. On arrival in Washington, after calling at the offices of the Federal Farm Loan Board, where a "what can we do" attitude prevailed, Mr. Quamme telephoned the Secretary of the Treasury, William G. McAdoo, and arranged for an appointment.

Upon arrival at his office, Secretary McAdoo greeted us cordially and asked what he could do for us. Apparently, he had not heard about the crisis that had so suddenly confronted the officials of the Federal land banks. Mr. Quamme explained the situation:

"Mr. Secretary, following the recent and successful sale of Federal farm loan bonds by the banking houses that formed the syndicate to market these bonds, they served notice one day before the expiration of their contract with the Federal Farm Loan Board that their contract with the Board would not be renewed. The land banks have $100,000,000 in firm commitments to the farmers of the country. In view of the action of the bond syndicate, these commitments cannot now be met. The members of the bond syndicate know how the land banks must operate, yet there was no warning given for their negative action. There is insufficient time to establish a bond-selling agency within the Federal Farm Loan System to meet this crisis. I believe that such a bond-selling agency should be established as soon as possible after we solve this crisis.

"Mr. Secretary, if the Federal Farm Loan System is destroyed for want of an effort to preserve it, the result will not only be a fatal blow to the nation's farmers, but it will adversely affect the economy of the country. The farmers know that this new rural credit system, a major accomplishment of the Wilson Administration, meets their long-term credit needs, a need that the private farm-mortgage bankers and other financial institutions making farm loans have failed to provide."

Mr. Quamme then proceeded to detail the plight of the land banks and the farmers, and concluded: "This is an emergency, Mr. Secretary, and immediate action must be taken to meet the situation."

Secretary McAdoo said: "Gentlemen, there can be no question about the emergency. What suggestions have you to meet it?"

Mr. Quamme replied: "To care for the present situation, I suggest a Congressional appropriation of $100,000,000 with which to purchase an equal amount of Federal farm loan bonds, and the authorization of an additional and similar amount to be

The first officers and directors of The Federal Land Bank of St. Paul, Minnesota (1917) *Left to right:* A. C. Wiprud, Executive Vice President; E. G. Quamme, President; H. K. Jennings, Secretary; W. S. Harris; A. H. Turrittin, Treasurer; F. W. McLean, Registrar; and B. F. Faast, Vice President.

established as a revolving fund to assure us that such a situation cannot happen again."

Secretary McAdoo used his pencil for several minutes, then asked: "Who would you have sponsor this bill?"

"We suggest Senator Knute Nelson of Minnesota, with the Administration's endorsement," Mr. Quamme replied.

"All right," Secretary McAdoo said, "I will get you the Administration's O. K. Go ahead."

When we arrived at his office, following our telephone call for an appointment, Senator Nelson received us promptly. He listened intently to Mr. Quamme's detailed account of the developments that led to the crisis in the Federal Farm Loan System, and the proposal approved by the Administration to meet the situation. The Senator made some notes in response to his questions, and, then, when asked by Mr. Quamme whether in his opinion such a bill could be passed immediately as an emergency measure, the Senator slowly reached into his pocket for a plug of his famous chewing tobacco, took a generous bite, and said, simply and emphatically, "YEP." That "yep" spoke volumes.

Leaders in the Senate and House of Representatives were called to the Senator Nelson's office and advised of the emergency confronting the Federal Farm Loan System. A short time thereafter, a bill amending the Federal Farm Loan Act was passed by Congress authorizing the Secretary of the Treasury to purchase from any Federal land bank, at par and accrued interest, Federal farm loan bonds issued by that bank, such purchases not to exceed in the aggregate $100,000,000 in each of the fiscal years ending June 30, 1918, and June 30, 1919. With the signature of President Wilson, the amendment became law January 18, 1918. Mr. Quamme was given the pen with which the President signed the emergency bill that enabled the Federal land banks to meet their first major crisis.

Under the authority of this legislation, the Treasury Department bought a total of $183,035,000 of Federal farm loan bonds. They subsequently were redeemed by the Federal land banks.

In view of the emergency legislation, supported by the Wilson Administration and enacted by Congress as herein related, it soon appeared that no difficulty was experienced in selling Federal farm loan bonds through the same syndicate of bond houses that handled the first bond sale.[3] Between the third and fourth Liberty Bond sales in 1918, there was a period of four months within which to conduct a sale of Federal farm loan bonds. Under contract with the Federal Farm Loan Board, the syndicate, within that period, sold an issue of $56,000,000 of farm loan bonds in 16 days. The selling commenced on May 20 and closed on June 5, 1918. Following the Federal government's Victory Bond sale, the syndicate, in June, 1919, sold another issue of farm loan bonds, totaling $54,000,000, in 10 days. These sales of Federal farm loan bonds by the syndicate makes it clear that, while government financing of the war was a factor to be considered, the marketing of these bonds (which commanded a substantial premium on the market) was only a question of timing.

During the two years following the enactment of emergency legislation to meet the crisis, the Federal land banks grew by leaps and bounds. The long-term credit needs of the agricultural industry were cared for in a businesslike manner, at the lowest possible cost, as the credit needs of other industries were cared for through the Federal Reserve System.

It should be noted here that during the late 1920s and the early 1930s, the so-called dust-bowl years in the midwestern states, the Federal land banks of Witchita, Spokane, and St. Paul were designated as financial agents of the United States for the purpose of making seed-grain loans to farmers in the drought-stricken areas served by these banks in an amount not to exceed $5,000,000.

While constructive work was going on throughout the Federal Farm Loan System, another and perhaps more serious crisis threatened the continued existence of the System. The long-ex-

---

[3] The Federal Farm Loan Board did not look with favor on this arrangement for selling Federal farm loan bonds as a permanent one. The Board stated: "It is our belief that in harmony with the other cooperative features of the Act, the sale of bonds directly by the banks to the investors should be stimulated in every possible way." In March, 1923, the Board established a Fiscal Agency for the Federal land banks to handle the sale of consolidated Federal farm loan bonds to the investing public. This arrangement proved eminently successful.

pected lawsuit of opponents of the Federal Farm Loan System to contest the constitutionality of the Federal Farm Loan Act was instituted. The suit was begun in August, 1919, in the form of an equity proceeding in the United States District Court for the Western District of Missouri. Following a hearing on October 30 and 31, 1919, the complaint was dismissed by order of the court and the validity of the Federal Farm Loan Act sustained. An appeal was taken by the opponents to the United States Supreme Court.

The case was heard in the United States Supreme Court on January 6, 1920 and reargued on October 14 and 15, 1920. On February 28, 1921, the Court upheld the constitutionality of all provisions of the Federal Farm Loan Act.[4] The validity of the Act could no longer be assailed. The financing of the Federal land banks then became a problem of marketing, on the most favorable terms, and unexcelled security. Thus, the Federal Farm Loan System survived its second major crisis.

During the period of the conflict in the courts, which lasted for over one year, the System was virtually at a standstill. At the suggestion of Dr. Norman S. B. Gras, professor of economics at the University of Minnesota, I took this opportunity to write a book which I entitled *The Federal Farm Loan System in Operation*. I had lectured at the Minnesota Union to students of the University on this new rural credit system.

A few months after the Supreme Court decision was rendered upholding the constitutionality of the Federal Farm Loan Act, I called on the former Secretary of the Treasury, William G. McAdoo, at his law office in New York City. The purpose of my call was to ask him if he would write an introduction to the book I had just completed on the Federal Farm Loan System. This he agreed to do a few weeks later after reading the manuscript. Mr. McAdoo concluded his introduction as follows:

This new agricultural credit system, the Federal Farm Loan System, is a genuine blessing to the farmers of the United States. It will prove its usefulness more and more as it grows and develops. We must see to it that neither selfish nor designing interests, nor subservient or

[4] 255 U. S. 180(1921).

crooked politicians, shall be permitted to emasculate or weaken or destroy it. What the farmers have gotten after years of hard and painful fighting, they must keep. . . .

A wonderful beginning has been made, and with sympathetic and intelligent administration by the Farm Loan Board and friendly cooperation on the part of the Congress and the President of the United States, this great system of agricultural credit will become a very rock of Gibraltar for agricultural prosperity.

That Mr. McAdoo's views and hopes for the Federal Farm Loan System, thus expressed, were justified finds support in the record of growth in the years since its organization in 1917. During these years, the System was to experience other crises, particularly the crisis created by the Great Depression that had its beginnings in the early 1920s and then broke suddenly in all its fury on an unprepared nation in 1929. The System not only weathered the storms of these years, and the years that followed, but helped American agriculture to survive and emerged as the largest cooperative farm mortgage credit system in the world. The services of the System have been made available to the agricultural community in fifty states and Puerto Rico.

As stated, there were those engaged in making farm loans who opposed the Federal Farm Loan System during the critical early years. They feared that the success of this new, cooperative rural credit system would endanger their interests. They were unwilling or unable to meet the pressing need for credit on a basis essential to the growth and development of the agricultural industry, so they resisted change in an effort to maintain the *status quo*. In the light of events of the succeeding years, the consequences to the agricultural industry and to the national economy had they succeeded might have been disastrous if the Federal government had not helped American farmers establish the Federal Farm Loan System. It should be added, as hereinafter noted, that the fears of these financial institutions that change would endanger their legitimate interests were unfounded.

This new rural credit system not only pioneered long-term, amortized loans for the American farmer on a nationwide basis, but low, uniform interest rates made possible by standardization, not only of the credit granted but also of the security placed on the market. It also introduced the practice of permitting the farmer to pay off his loan at any time without penalty; the practice of basing loans on normal agricultural values of farms instead of the current market value, or other temporary levels of value; and the adaption of its services to the changing needs of farmers, such as increasing the maximum size of land bank loans, thus reflecting the continuous trend towards larger farms and the necessity for modern machinery. The system undoubtedly benefits all farmer-borrowers regardless of where they obtain their funds because lenders have followed its leadership, lowered their interest rates, and otherwise improved their services.

The original capital stock of the Federal land banks, $750,000 for each of the twelve banks, was practically all subscribed by the United States Treasury Department. In accordance with the provisions of the Farm Loan Act, the Federal land banks became farmer-owned in 1947, the year when all capital stock subscribed by the Federal government—both in the initial stage and during the depression years of the 1930s—was returned to the United States Treasury. Each of the land banks is now owned by its stockholders, the Federal land bank associations (formerly called national farm associations) in the bank's district,[5] which associations, in turn, are completely owned by member-borrowers.

The combined net worth of Federal land banks and the Federal land bank associations, which comprise the Federal Land

---

[5] Federal land bank associations are local organizations of farmers upon which the cooperative Federal Land Bank System (formerly the Federal Farm Loan System) is based, and through which the land banks carry on their loaning operations. These associations do not lend money to their members. Their function is to enable members to meet certain requirements and thus obtain loans from the land banks. In addition to the work of appraising a member's property offered as security, transmitting papers and documents to the land bank, and other work incident to closing a loan, the association contributes to a member's security by endorsing the borrow's mortgage note. A member-borrower is required to subscribe 5 percent of his loan to stock in the association and the association, in turn, subscribes an equal amount to stock in the land bank of the district in which the association is located. This is the financial machinery which over a period of 30 years—1917 to 1947—has brought into being the largest cooperative rural credit system in the world.

Bank System, as of June 30, 1968, totaled $867.2 million. Because the System is owned and operated by and for the farmers, the earnings of the System represent savings. After using a portion of these savings to build and maintain reserves needed to keep the banks and associations strong, the remaining savings are passed back to the users of the System. Savings thus returned to member borrowers as dividends have the effect of reducing the cost of credit. From July 1, 1943, to June 30, 1968, the Federal Land Bank System's savings passed back to member-borrowers in the 664 Federal land bank associations totaled $131 million.

Farmers, through the Federal Land Bank System, have obtained over two million loans for about $15.9 billion from the organization of the land banks in 1917 to June 30, 1968. According to estimates of the United States Department of Agriculture, on January 1, 1968, the Federal Land Bank System held 21.8 percent of the farmers' real estate mortgage loans. The balance of 78.2 percent was held by insurance companies, commercial banks, Farmers Home Administration, individuals and others. *Clearly, then, the Federal Farm Loan System, which met the needs of the farmers at a critical time, also preserved the legitimate interests of financial institutions engaged in making farm loans.*

The Federal land banks have become the senior elements in an expanded cooperative Farm Credit System. The basic principles embodied in the original Federal Farm Loan Act which established the land banks were followed in legislation that created other parts of the expanded System.

The Federal Intermediate Credit Banks

The serious agricultural depression which began in the 1920s, caused by the decline in post-war prices for farm products, was a difficult time for the American farmer. With inflated values in industry, the spread between what the farmer paid for his supplies and the prices received for his products widened to a point where farm income was virtually reduced to a "point of no return." Further, many farmers found that railroad freight rates to market were so high that the freight bill often exceeded the price received for their products.

The plight of the farmer was compounded by the fact that the demands of industry increasingly restricted the volume of short-term credit available to him. An attempt was made to make notes of farmers having a maturity up to 6 months, and secured by staple agricultural products and live stock, eligible for rediscount at Federal reserve banks. As the crisis deepened, Federal reserve banks, with some exceptions, refused to accept farmers' notes for rediscount which bore a maturity of more than 30 days. As a result, farmers had great difficulty in borrowing from commercial banks to meet their short-term credit needs. This situation caused great distress and chattel liquidations.

Emergency measures were launched by the Congress and the President of the United States to meet the increasingly critical agricultural situation which extended into the 1930s. As important and helpful as these measures were, the urgent need of the farmer was for short- and intermediate-term credit on a basis which would enable him to repay his loan from the earnings of his enterprise—his farm. A simple illustration will suffice. The farmer cannot repay a 30-day loan for the purpose of raising hogs when it takes at least 120 days or so long as necessary to prepare the hogs for market.

In 1923, Congress enacted the Agricultural Act which created the Federal intermediate credit banks. The initial capital stock of these banks was subscribed by the Federal government. Under the provisions of this Act, the Federal Farm Loan Board was authorized to charter 12 Federal intermediate credit banks, one in each of the 12 cities in which a Federal land bank is located, to serve the territories of those banks. Their supervision was placed under the direction of the officers and directors of the 12 Federal land banks.

The Federal intermediate credit banks do not make loans direct to farmers. The banks were intended to discount or purchase short- and intermediate-term notes of farmers and ranchers given to private lending institutions, commercial banks and agricultural credit cooperatives. As noted by R. B. Tootell, Governor of the Farm Credit Administration, in a statement made public on December 31, 1968,

Agricultural lenders [private lenders making farm loans] did not use the Federal intermediate credit banks to the extent expected and were not able to adequately provide the production credit needs of agriculture. During this period farmers could provide neither the leadership nor the capital to organize their own credit institutions to use the facilities of these banks.

In 1933, Congress enacted the Farm Credit Act which authorized the creation of farmers' cooperative production credit associations to supplement the services of the Federal intermediate credit banks and make them available to farmers and ranchers throughout the country. The Act also provided for the initial capital and special staff to assist farmers in organizing these cooperatives. The financial institutions, including the production credit associations, are unconditionally liable for the payment of their obligations to the credit banks.

Production credit associations have been established to serve every agricultural county in the United States. On June 30, 1968, there were 453 such associations. A farmer or rancher becomes a member when he takes out a loan. Each member of the association is required to own voting stock in the association equal to $5 on each $100 of his loan. The control of the association is in the hands of the farmers and ranchers who use it.

The maturity dates on production credit association loans are arranged for a time when farmers will have something to sell. Therefore, they are made for the length of time needed to soundly finance a particular operation. For example, a farmer can get a loan to cover a period of time from the day he plants his crop through harvest and until he sells his products in an orderly manner. Likewise, a dairyman can arrange his repayment program so that it is geared to his monthly milk checks, if he so desires. Interest rates on credit association loans are comparable to those other businesses pay.

The Federal intermediate credit banks have been characterized as credit wholesalers for production credit associations and other financial institutions. As such they require funds in large amounts, which have reached a total of more than $4 billion a year, to finance their operations. This sum is raised through the sale of short-term bonds, designated by law as "consolidated collateral trust debentures," to investors. These debentures are issued against collateral security in an amount at least equal to the debentures issued. In addition, all 12 credit banks are jointly and severally liable for the payment of the principal and interest of the debentures.[6] The aggregate amount of consolidated debentures issued for the benefit and account of any credit bank may not exceed 10 times the surplus and paid-in capital of such bank.

These credit bank debentures command a wide market among purchasers of high-grade securities, though the Federal government assumes no liability for these obligations. They are legal investments for banks, insurance companies, and trust funds in most states. National banks may invest in these debentures without regard to statutory limitations on amount involved. They are lawful investments for all fiduciary, trust, and public funds held under the authority of the United States and are approved as security for deposits in postal savings banks. The bulk of these debentures are bought by commercial banks, corporations, and other institutional investors such as insurance companies and trust funds.

As stated, the initial capital stock of the Federal credit banks and the production credit associations was subscribed by the Federal government. Beginning in 1957, the stock owned by the members of the production credit associations began to accumulate and their reserves build up. Under provisions of acts of Congress, the associations then began to acquire stock in these credit banks. In the December 31, 1968, statement above referred to, R. B. Tootell, Governor of the Farm Credit Administration, announced that the remaining stock of the Federal government in the Federal intermediate credit banks, totaling $126 million, was retired. These credit banks are completely owned by the farmer-users of these banks, members of the production credit associations.

The combined net worth of the credit banks and associations which comprise the Federal Intermediate Credit System, totaled

---

[6] See f.n. 2, above, for tax exemptions which are also applicable to Federal intermediate credit bank debentures.

$976 million as of June 30, 1968. Of this amount, the net worth of the credit banks was $337 million.

Through the services performed by the Federal intermediate credit banks for their affiliated production credit associations, and other financial institutions which use the credit banks' services, farmers and ranchers, as of June 30, 1968, have obtained $79.6 billion in loans since these credit banks were established in 1923. From 1934, the year the first production credit association began operations, to June 30, 1968, the loans and discounts made by the credit banks to the credit associations totaled $69.1 billion. (Of this $69.1 billion, $56.4 billion was loaned by the production credit associations to the farmers and ranchers and the balance to other financing institutions.) Thus, the credit associations account for over 90 percent of the credit extended by the credit banks.[7]

On January 1, 1968, production credit associations held 15 percent of the total non-real estate loans outstanding from all lenders, according to the estimate of the United States Department of Agriculture. If individuals, merchants and dealers are excepted, thus leaving only the institutional lenders, production credit associations held 25.6 percent of the total.

The Banks for Cooperatives

By early 1933, the Great Depression had taken a heavy toll in terms of foreclosures and bankruptcies in agriculture as well as in the general economy. On March 4, 1933, the day that President Franklin D. Roosevelt was inaugurated, the commercial banks that had been able to keep going were compelled by Presidential decree to close temporarily to prevent disastrous runs on their funds. Most businesses were in desperate straits, but historians of that period agree that farmers generally, as prime producers, were, if possible, in even worse financial condition. Great emphasis was placed on farm credit as a means of meeting the crisis.

The Farm Credit Act of 1933, created not only the produc-

---

[7] Production credit associations are subject to taxes as is any other corporation doing business as these associations do.

tion credit associations, but the Banks for Cooperatives to provide specialized services to farmers' marketing, supply and service cooperatives.

As provided in the Act, 13 banks for cooperatives were chartered by the Farm Credit Administration, an agency hereinafter described, one in each of the 12 cities in which a Federal land bank is located to serve the same territories as those banks. A thirteenth bank, called the Central Bank for Cooperatives, was established with headquarters in Washington, D. C. The district banks were designed to serve the needs of cooperatives in their respective territories, and the Central Bank "gave the system the means of financing large cooperatives whose credit requirements were too large to be handled with the financial structure available to any of the individual district banks." These 13 banks constituted another major branch of the Farm Credit System.

Congress in enacting legislation for the banks for cooperatives followed the same pattern it developed for other parts of the Farm Credit System. It provided the initial capital in the form of government-owned stock in these banks. Congress also made it possible for the users of these banks to buy stock in connection with their loans, plus providing the means of going to the investment markets for loanable funds.

By Act of August 23, 1954, Congress authorized the 13 banks for cooperatives to issue "consolidated debentures in the manner and form and on terms approved by the Farm Credit Administration." These debentures, too, are not obligations of the Federal government. The Act provided further that the notes of the borrowing cooperatives could be included in the collateral behind such debentures, which would be joint and several obligations of the 13 banks and limited in amount to 8 times the net worth of the banks.

The consolidated debentures of the banks for cooperatives are prime investments for national banks, insurance companies, fiduciary and trust funds to the same extent as are the consolidated bonds of the Federal land banks and the consolidated debentures of the Federal intermediate credit banks.[8]

---

[8] Banks for cooperatives are generally subject to taxes as is any other corporation doing business as these banks do.

The provisions of law and the policies of the banks for cooperatives relating to the determination of the rate of interest to be
paid on their debentures, which, in turn, determines the rate of
interest the farmer cooperative must pay on loans, as well as the
method of allocating the earnings of the banks, are similar to
those applicable to the Federal intermediate credit banks.

The banks for cooperatives make loans only to farmer-owned
and farmer-controlled cooperative marketing, purchasing, and
business services in the United States and Puerto Rico. From
1933 to 1968, they have made loans to farmer cooperatives in
the amount of $19.1 billion, about 60 percent of the credit used
by these cooperatives. On June 30, 1968, there were 3036 farmer
cooperatives.

On June 30, 1968, the consolidated net worth of the banks
for cooperatives was $275 million.

The original capital stock of the banks for cooperatives was
subscribed by the Federal government in the amount of $110
million. The peak investment of the government in the banks'
stock was $178.5 million. In his statement of December 31, 1968,
R. B. Tootell, Governor of the Farm Credit Administration,
announced,

Today, with payments to the U. S. Treasury by the farmer-oper-
ated Farm Credit System to retire $148 million of Government-owned
capital, farmers became the sole owners of this $12 billion credit re-
source. This ends a significant phase of the partnership between farmers and their Government in building this 51-year-old system—an
almost impossible dream come true. . . . with the faith, determination
and dedication of more than 20,000 farmer-members of boards of directors of cooperatives—the land bank and production credit associations
and marketing, purchasing and business service cooperatives.

Supervision of the Farm Credit System

The Farm Credit Administration, an independent agency
within the Executive Branch of the Federal government, has
general regulatory and supervisory authority over the 37 credit
banks and the 1,100 credit associations in the 12 Farm Credit
Districts that make up the Farm Credit System. These responsibilities were given to the Farm Credit Administration by Con-

gress "to provide uniformity in policies throughout the System, and to assure that the basic objectives of the applicable acts of Congress are being achieved and the operations conducted in the interest of the public."

The Federal Farm Credit Board, a 13-member, part-time policy-making board, directs, supervises, and controls the Farm Credit Administration. Twelve of the members of the Board, one from each Farm Credit District (formerly called Federal Land Bank District), are appointed by the President of the United States with the advice and consent of the Senate. The President is required by law, in making these appointments, to consider nominations from each Farm Credit District made by Federal land bank associations, production credit associations, and farmer marketing, purchasing and business service cooperatives who are stockholders of the district bank for cooperatives. The Secretary of Agriculture designates the 13th member of the Board who serves at the Secretary's pleasure.

The organizational structure of the cooperative Farm Credit System is graphically shown in the accompaning chart.

The 37 Farm Credit Banks jointly employ a full-time fiscal agent (originally established in 1923 for the Federal land banks), with offices in the financial district of New York City. This agency handles all transactions for the credit banks in the sale of their bonds and debentures. The fiscal agent also performs related financial services for the banks, such as sales and purchases of securities for investment by the credit banks or associations.

As of June 30, 1968, the farmers, ranchers and their cooperatives had a total of $872 million invested in the Farm Credit System. In addition, the System's net worth reserves, which protects the farmers' capital in the System, totaled $970 million. The peak investment of the Government in the capital of the Farm Credit System was $638 million in 1939. The net worth of the completely farmer-owned System is over $2 billion.

Since the Federal land banks, the pioneers of the System, were established in 1917, to June 30, 1968, a total of $100.2 billion has been loaned to farmers and their cooperatives by the Farm Credit System.

It has been truly said that this rural credit system constitutes

how farmers share in control of the farm credit system

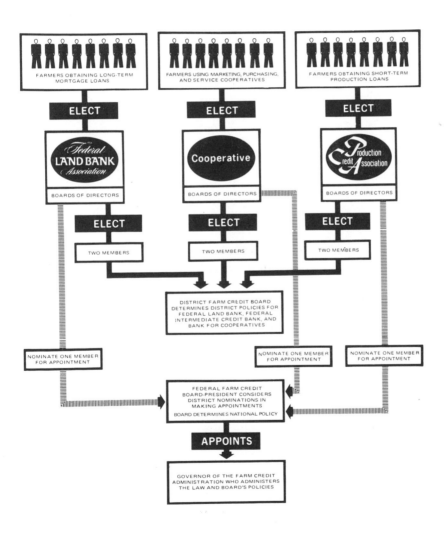

FARMERS OBTAINING LONG-TERM MORTGAGE LOANS

FARMERS USING MARKETING, PURCHASING, AND SERVICE COOPERATIVES

FARMERS OBTAINING SHORT-TERM PRODUCTION LOANS

ELECT

ELECT

ELECT

Federal LAND BANK Association

Cooperative

Production Credit Association

BOARDS OF DIRECTORS

BOARDS OF DIRECTORS

BOARDS OF DIRECTORS

ELECT

ELECT

ELECT

TWO MEMBERS

TWO MEMBERS

TWO MEMBERS

DISTRICT FARM CREDIT BOARD DETERMINES DISTRICT POLICIES FOR FEDERAL LAND BANK, FEDERAL INTERMEDIATE CREDIT BANK, AND BANK FOR COOPERATIVES

NOMINATE ONE MEMBER FOR APPOINTMENT

NOMINATE ONE MEMBER FOR APPOINTMENT

NOMINATE ONE MEMBER FOR APPOINTMENT

FEDERAL FARM CREDIT BOARD-PRESIDENT CONSIDERS DISTRICT NOMINATIONS IN MAKING APPOINTMENTS
BOARD DETERMINES NATIONAL POLICY

APPOINTS

GOVERNOR OF THE FARM CREDIT ADMINISTRATION WHO ADMINISTERS THE LAW AND BOARD'S POLICIES

Presentation of the Federal Land Bank Medal to the author. *Left to right:* Dr. Kenneth R. Williams, President, Florida Atlantic University, Arne C. Wiprud, and Doyle E. Abbott, regional supervisor, Federal Land Bank of Columbia, South Carolina.

a unique mechanism for transforming privately invested capital into agricultural production. The farmers' underlying collateral supporting their credit needs has been presented in its most attractive form, to the benefit of the farmers, the lenders, and the nation. Their future now depends in large measure on their imaginative, sound and continuing use of credit as a productive tool.

The Farm Credit System has not only widened the horizons of the farmers and ranchers who have obtained loans from the System, but the horizons of all farmers and ranchers, for as a large factor in the farm- and ranch-loan business the System has had, and continues to have, a direct and significant influence on agricultural policies of all types of agricultural lending institutions. Thus, this cooperative Farm Credit System has become not only a part of the Nation's system, but an important part of the Nation's private enterprise economy at a critical time in its history.

Fifty years after the Federal land banks were established, I was presented with the Federal Land Banks Golden Anniversary Medal, with the following inscription:

50th ANNIVERSARY MEDAL

Authorized by Congress and the

President of the United States

Awarded in 1967 to

ARNE C. WIPRUD

For Outstanding Contributions to American Agriculture

Presented by the

FEDERAL LAND BANK OF ST. PAUL

My work as the executive vice president of the Federal Land Bank of St. Paul, Minnesota, during its early years of crises, was a strenuous but interesting and broadening experience. But I still hoped for a professional career in law. I was able to realize this ambition in 1921 upon the completion and publication of my book on the Federal Farm Loan System which I was encouraged to write by the officers of the St. Paul Federal Land Bank with the approval of the Federal Farm Loan Board, Washington. D. C.

CHAPTER II

The Landlocked
Upper Mississippi Valley

FOLLOWING MY RESIGNATION as an officer of the Federal Land
Bank of St. Paul, I practiced law in Minneapolis, Minnesota,
and later in New York City.

In May, 1925, at the request of Glenn W. Traer, Vice President of Lane, Piper and Jaffray, Inc., a leading investment banking firm in Minneapolis, Minnesota, I accepted his offer to
become counsel of that firm.

One day, early in November, 1925, Palmer Jaffray, a vice
president of Lane, Piper and Jaffray, asked me to take his place
on a delegation of businessmen designated by the Governor of
Minnesota, Theodore Christianson, to attend the annual convention in St. Louis, Missouri, of the Mississippi Valley Association. I of course agreed.

On the train enroute to St. Louis I learned from members of
the delegation that the upper Mississippi valley shippers and
businessmen were seeking to revive water transportation on the
Mississippi River above St. Louis. The immediate reason was a
report of an Interstate Commerce Commission hearing examiner
in the so-called *Indiana Rate Case* which stated that there was not
even potential water competition on the upper Mississippi River
and therefore recommended that the existing water-compelled
rail rates be raised to a "dry-land level." This report and recommendation aroused shippers, including leaders in business and
agriculture, in the upper Mississippi valley from Hannibal, Mis-

souri, to the Twin Cities of Minneapolis and St. Paul, because, if approved by the Commissioner, it meant substantially higher railroad freight rates which could adversely affect their interests. They organized the Upper Mississippi Waterway Association to meet this threat and launched an all-out effort to restore water transportation on the upper Mississippi River. This they would do with modern towboats and barges, not with river steamboats of bygone days.

In the morning, as our train was approaching St. Louis, I discussed the matter with the leader of the upper Mississippi valley delegation, S. S. Thorpe, a prominent realtor in Minneapolis. He appeared discouraged because Federal government officials had taken the position that the barge operation of the Inland Waterways Corporation, then owned by the Federal government and operated by the Secretary of War as a demonstration project to encourage private operation of modern inland water transport on the nation's inland waterways, could not legally be extended on the Mississippi River above St. Louis to the Twin Cities. This was so, these officials contended, because a condition in "the applicable law" provided that the United States Supreme Court must first render its decision in a pending case involving a fleet of towboats and barges leased by the Inland Waterways Corporation to a private barge operator, a fleet which the corporation sought to recover in that proceeding. The implication appeared to be that the condition would be met only if the Court's decision was favorable to the Inland Waterways Corporation. The offer of the shippers and businessmen of the upper Mississippi valley to build a new fleet of towboats and barges to be operated by the Corporation on the upper Mississippi River did not change the position of these Federal government officials.

The contention of these officials interested me as a lawyer. I could not conceive that an Act of Congress would so condition the powers of the executive branch of the United States government or one of its corporations.

When we arrived in St. Louis, and I had registered at the headquarters of the convention, I proceeded to the nearest law library to study the question as presented to me by Mr. Thorpe. By late afternoon I had the answer. Contrary to the contention of the government officials, I found no condition in "the applicable law" as they had contended or any reference therein to the Inland Waterways Corporation's pending case before the United States Supreme court; on the contrary, I found a specific provision in the Inland Waterways Corporation Act that placed a mandate on the Secretary of War, as the operator of the Inland Waterways Corporation, to extend the corporation's operations to the upper Mississippi River from St. Louis to the Twin Cities of St. Paul and Minneapolis!

I prepared and submitted to Mr. Thorpe a written opinion of my findings and my conclusion. He promptly called a meeting of the upper Mississippi valley delegation. The ensuing discussion of my opinion created a new spirit within the delegation. The next morning, the entire delegation appeared before a special session of the Advisory Board of the Inland Waterways Corporation which, after a thorough presentation and discussion of the matter, voted unanimously to recommend the extension of the Corporation's operations on the Mississippi river from St. Louis to the Twin Cities. This action proved conclusive. When the convention ended, I returned to Minneapolis and my work with the investment banking firm of Lane, Piper and Jaffray.

A few days later, Charles C. Webber, president of Deere and Webber Company, a prominent businessman in Minneapolis and one of the truly great men associated with the effort to inaugurate barge transportation on the upper Mississippi River, called on the president of Lane, Piper and Jaffray, George B. Lane. Mr. Webber requested Mr. Lane to make my services available for six months to negotiate a contract with the Secretary of War for the operation by the Inland Waterways Corporation of a fleet of towboats and barges to be built by the Upper Mississippi Barge Line Company. This company was incorporated by the businessmen and shippers of the upper Mississippi valley for this purpose. Mr. Lane agreed.

It was on a Monday, January 11, 1926, when I arrived in Washington to meet the staff of the then Secretary of War,

Dwight W. Davis. The following three days, members of the Secretary's staff, and I as a representative of the businessmen and shippers in upper Mississippi valley, sat across the desk from Secretary Davis for a half hour each afternoon, discussing the terms of the contract between the Inland Waterways Corporation and the Upper Mississippi Barge Line Company.

The terms of the contract were finally agreed upon at our meeting with Secretary Davis on Thursday afternoon, January 14, 1926. In summary, the contract provided that the Upper Mississippi Barge Line Company, organized by the shippers and businessmen of the upper Mississippi valley, would finance and build a fleet of towboats and barges, especially designed for operation on the six-foot channel of the upper river, and leased for this purpose to the Inland Waterways Corporation.

Approval of the contract by the President of the United States, as required by law, was given on January 15, 1926, and thereupon the Secretary of War also affixed his signature to the contract. General Thomas Q. Ashburn, president of the Inland Waterways Corporation, brought the contract to Minneapolis on January 20, 1926, where at a public ceremony it was formally completed by the signature of S. S. Thorpe, president of the Upper Mississippi Barge Line Company. This contract assured barge transportation on the upper Mississippi River, providing an all-water outlet from the Twin Cities of Minneapolis and St. Paul to St. Louis and on to the Gulf of Mexico. This was the first step toward unlocking the land-locked upper Mississippi valley, which has been described as a great inland domain as large as the European nations of Germany, France, Italy and Great Britain combined.

A few months later, the leaders among the businessmen and shippers in the Twin Cities decided to call on President Coolidge at the White House and thank him, on behalf of the people of the upper Mississippi valley, for approving the contract that brought barge operation to the upper river. The appointment was made for five persons, Mr. Thorpe, Mr. Webber, Horace M. Hill, president of Janney, Semple, Hill & Company, of Minneapolis, Richard P. Warner, vice president of Griggs, Cooper & Company, of St. Paul, and myself.

When we were ushered into the President's office, the President was writing at his desk, while smoking a cigar in a paper holder. The right-hand top drawer of his desk was drawn out, and there, in plain sight, was an open box of W. and D. cigars. When he finished writing, and without looking up—we, of course, were all standing at attention—the President reached into his pants pocket, pulled out a bunch of keys, selected one, carefully reached over and closed the cover on the box of cigars, then closed the drawer, locked it, tried it to be sure it was securely locked, then stood up and said in his well-known Yankee twang, "Good morning, gentlemen, I am glad to see you." It appeared that he was not going to waste any of his cigars on total strangers!

While it may come as a surprise to many, as it did to us, the "taciturn" President Coolidge was a most talkative man in a private conference. We had difficulty in getting a word in "edgewise." But, finally, Mr. Thorpe managed to express the appreciation of the people of the upper Mississippi valley for his action in authorizing the restoration of commercial navigation on the upper Mississippi River. The President seemed pleased.

The conservative Yankee character of President Coolidge was again in evidence at a meeting with him in the summer of 1928 when he was vacationing at the Cedar Island Lodge on the Brule River in Wisconsin. A summer White House had been established for the President's convenience in the high school at Superior, Wisconsin.

The senior United States Senator from Minnesota, Henrik Shipstead, who proved to be a most effective public official for the upper Mississippi valley people in their struggle to establish barge transportation on the upper river, suggested at a luncheon meeting of businessmen and shippers in Minneapolis in June, 1928, that it would be appropriate if they or their representatives called on the President while he was in the area and expressed their appreciation for his continued interest in their problems.

The group attending the meeting acted immediately. A com-

Yours Sincerely

Henrik Shipstead

mittee of four was appointed, consisting of Mr. Webber, Mr. Hill, Mr. Warner, and myself. As directed, I had a hand-lettered, highly-illumined parchment scroll prepared, signed by the leaders in the upper Mississippi valley, expressing the appreciation of the people for the President's assistance and continued interest in matters of vital importance to the economy of this important region of the United States. I then arranged for our conference with the President at his summer White House in Superior.

Our meeting with the President was in the morning of June 29, 1928. Mr. Webber, who was our spokesman in the absence of Mr. Thorpe who was abroad, had prepared a five-minute speech preliminary to the presentation of the scroll to the President, which he tried on me at least five times enroute by train from Minneapolis to Superior. On arrival, we found some of the larger offices at the high school in Superior had been renovated for the President and furnished with new, red-leather-upholstered furniture.

When we were ushered into the President's office, and after shaking hands with us, the President started talking. In essence, what he had to say was that he doubted if water transportation could ever be successfully revived on our rivers! He quoted, among others, Owen D. Young, a nationally known business executive. The expression of these views took some time, and of course we did not interrupt him. The President finally concluded by stating that despite his doubts, he was willing to make the experiment, as evidenced by his approval of the upper Mississippi River barge contract.

As the President stopped speaking, Mr. Webber quickly began his five-minute speech of appreciation, at the conclusion of which he handed the President the parchment scroll. The President expressed his thanks, then asked us to join him in front of the high school summer White House for a photograph, giving specific directions to all of us where to stand and telling Mr. Webber to again present the scroll to him at "the picture taking," as if he were presenting it for the first time.

On our return trip to Minneapolis, we pondered the realities

President Calvin Coolidge at the Summer White House, Superior, Wisconsin, June 29, 1928. *Left to right:* aide, the author, Charles C. Webber, President Coolidge, R. P. Warner, and Horace M. Hill.

and the myths about the public image of President Calvin Coolidge as "Silent Cal." This was not in the spirit of irreverence but rather of wonderment. We were sincerely grateful to the President for his timely and powerful support in this all-out effort to protect and improve the economy of the upper Mississippi valley.

The doubts expressed by President Coolidge at our conference about the successful revival of water transportation on the nation's rivers were also discussed on our return to Minneapolis. We concluded that he may have had in mind the uncertainties of river navigation during the nineteenth century. That century of navigation on the upper Mississippi River was summarized in a brochure by the United States Army Corps of Engineers as "A Glimpse at the Past," published in August 1962, which preceded a presentation of the great strides forward "in engineering knowledge and techniques that were to bring commerce flowing back to many of the nation's inland waterways."

The upper Mississippi has long served man—it has borne the Indian canoe, the explorer's pirogue, the pioneer's keelboat, and later during the golden age of the river steamer, the romantic paddlewheelers, so vividly recalled in song and story. The upper river until recent times, however, had been a rebellious and undependable servant, and navigation had been forced to accommodate to its capricious whims—deep-flowing, but turbulent in time of flood; placid, but shallow to the point of non-navigability in time of drought. Swift and treacherous rapids occurred in several reaches; in others, submerged rocks and boulders lay in wait for the unwary riverman. Each storm built up new, uncharted shoals and sand bars and washed hundreds of overhanging trees into the stream to form the "snags," so deadly to the oldtime wooden-hulled river boats. Considering the many perils which beset navigation, it is not surprising that the life of a steamer on the upper river during the nineteenth century was usually very short.

During the nineteenth century efforts were made by the Federal government to improve navigation on the upper Mississippi River by removing snags, shoals, sand bars, dynamiting and excavating rocks in some rapids to clear passages, and by-passing the more obstructive rapids by constructing short lateral canals with navigation locks. In 1907, Congress authorized a comprehensive project to maintain a six-foot channel on the upper Mississippi River. This depth was to be maintained mainly by the construction of hundreds of rock and brush "wing dams." These dams were built by the Army Engineer Corps and described as "low structures extending radially from the shore into the river for varying distances to further restrict low water flows."

My six-month leave of absence as counsel for the investment banking house of Lane, Piper and Jaffray developed into an arrangement to give my full time to the struggle of the leaders in business and agriculture in the upper Mississippi valley to establish modern commercial barge transportation on the upper river. In addition to acting as general counsel of the Upper Mississippi Waterway Association, I had become secretary, treasurer, and general counsel of the Upper Mississippi Barge Line Company. As an official of the latter company, I arranged for the employment of naval architects to design the towboats and barges that could operate in the 6-foot channel of the upper Mississippi River, the awarding of contracts for their construction, the inspection (with independent and Federal government engineers) of the work as it progressed, and for all payments to the contractors on certified inspections, all of which was subject to the approval of the board of directors of the barge line company.

The two towboats built by the Upper Mississippi Barge Line Company were named the "S. S. Thorpe" and the "C. C. Webber," in honor of the two outstanding businessmen, leaders in the campaign to restore water transportation on the upper Mississippi River. These towboats were built by the Dubuque Boat and Boiler Works, Dubuque, Iowa, under competitive bidding and launched on March 24 and 26, 1927. Mr. Thorpe was at the launching but Mr. and Mrs. Webber were in Paris, France. I cabled Mr. Webber as follows: "Towboat C. C. Webber successfully launched today." I had an acknowledgement, with an expression of appreciation from this strong and usually unemotional man, but later Mrs. Webber told me that when he received the cablegram, tears streaked down his cheeks.

In the years that followed restoration of transportation on the upper Mississippi River, Mrs. Wiprud and I enjoyed many delightful trips on the river. Some of those trips extended from Minneapolis, past Red Wing and Winona, Minnesota, LaCrosse, Wisconsin, to Dubuque, Iowa, and then on south to Cairo, Illinois. Nowhere is the scenery more beautiful or the trip more restful. The accommodations and the food aboard the towboats were surprisingly good. In the evening, we would sit in the pilot house listening to the older rivermen spinning their yarns as the big barge tow, 600 feet long, was skillfully navigated on the winding river. On the front barge—the towboat pushed a number of barges which were fastened together with steel cables into a barge tow—a riverman would take soundings, calling back through a megaphone in the language of the river people that reminded us of the stories by Mark Twain, his soundings of the depth of the river channel to guide the pilot. These were unforgettable experiences.

CHAPTER III

The Larger Role for
the Upper Mississippi River

IN THE SUMMER OF 1926, the Secretary of Commerce of the United States, Herbert Hoover, delivered an address at Kansas City, Missouri, outlining his program for developing a vast integrated inland waterways system in the United States for commercial navigation, with a minimum channel depth of nine feet. He envisioned this system as extending up the Mississippi River from New Orleans to St. Louis, up the Ohio River to Pittsburgh, up the Illinois River to Chicago, and up the Missouri River to Kansas City. Secretary Hoover, known throughout the world as a great humanitarian and highly respected as a public figure and an outstanding engineer, was widely acclaimed for this concept of utilizing and preserving one of the nation's great natural resources.

Secretary Hoover omitted any reference to the Mississippi River *above* St. Louis to the Twin Cities as a part of his program and made no reference to the beginning of barge operation thereon in his Kansas City address. This disturbed the leaders in business and agriculture in the upper Mississippi valley because the barge operation on the upper river during the extreme drought of the late 1920s had clearly demonstrated the unreliability of the existing so-called six-foot channel. They reasoned that since a minimum nine-foot channel depth, with suitable widths for long-haul barge service, had been achieved in segments of the Secretary's proposed national inland waterways system by a series of navigation dams, notably on the Ohio River and some of its tributaries, it seemed logical that a similar result could be achieved by the same means on the Mississippi River between St. Louis and the Twin Cities of St. Paul and Minneapolis.

In this view, the Secretary's omission in his Kansas City address proved to be the spark for an all-out effort by these leaders for the canalization of the upper Mississippi River by the construction of a series of navigation dams that would raise the water level to a minimum channel depth of nine-feet, with suitable widths. Thus, the upper Mississippi River would become an integral part of the Nation's great inland waterways system envisioned by Secretary Hoover.

A few weeks after his Kansas City address, Secretary Hoover indicated a desire to correct his omission of any reference to the upper Mississippi River in that address. Apparently, he had not been informed of the new barge operation on the upper river which had been inaugurated by the Inland Waterways Corporation, with the substantial and effective cooperation of the people of the upper Mississippi valley. An invitation was promptly extended to the Secretary by the waterway leaders in the Twin Cities to speak in St. Paul and Minneapolis on the subject. I was requested to go to Washington, D. C., and advise the Secretary of the arrangements that had been made for his visit and to accompany him and members of his staff to the Twin Cities.

Secretary Hoover, two members of his staff, and I left Washington for Chicago on the Baltimore & Ohio Railroad's finest passenger train, the "Capitol Limited." After dinner aboard the train, Secretary Hoover suggested we continue our discussion of inland waterways in the club car. When our discussion on this subject was concluded, I asked the Secretary if he would tell us about some of his experiences in China. The Secretary agreed. Reminiscing about his years in that strange, vast country seemed to relax him. He was a most interesting conversationalist. The recounting of his experiences and views on China was, for me at least, almost a post-graduate course on the subject.

To A.C. Wiford,
With Kind Regards of
Herbert Hoover

The following evening, on the Milwaukee Railroad's finest passenger train, the "Pioneer Limited," from Chicago to the Twin Cities, an opportunity was presented to ask Secretary Hoover about some of his experiences in Russia. We listened eagerly. Again, it was a most informative as well as an interesting account of another strange and vast land. I have often thought about these informal talks by the Secretary in the light of world events that followed.

Secretary Hoover spoke in St. Paul, at noon, to an audience that filled the main dining room of the St. Paul Athletic Club. As was usual for him in those days, the Secretary wore a high, starched collar, and as he spoke, concentrating on his subject, his chin would drop lower and lower and his voice would become weaker and weaker. The result was that he could hardly be heard the width of the dining room, let along its length.

When the Secretary had completed his rather technical address on inland waterways, I hurried to Minneapolis and urged Mr. Thorpe and Mr. Webber to have amplifiers installed in the large banquet room of the Nicollet Hotel in Minneapolis where the Secretary was scheduled to deliver an address on inland waterways to over one thousand leading citizens from the upper Mississippi valley; otherwise, I said, it would be impossible for those beyond the front rows to hear the Secretary's address in this large room. Amplifiers were not common in those days, but after considerable effort, one was obtained and installed in time. The result was quite remarkable. Every person in the audience could hear every word the Secretary uttered. The Secretary made a masterful presentation.

After his address, the Secretary, who had gone to his suite in the hotel, sent for me. Several prominent people were there with him. When I entered, he called to me and said he was told that I was responsible for the "loud-speaker" and indicated how grateful he was. I was a little flustered, but I managed to congratulate him on his address on a subject that was so important to the people and the economy of the valley.

In retrospect, I believe that every economic and engineering fact and argument supporting the upper Mississippi River nine-foot channel project advanced by the shippers, and the leaders in business and agriculture, in their long struggle for the approval and construction of that project was set forth in, or stemmed from, Secretary Hoover's speech that evening in Minneapolis.

Early in December, 1928, a few days before Secretary Hoover, President-elect of the United States, left on a trip to South America, Mr. Webber, Mr. Warner and I were invited to meet with him at his home in Palo Alto, California. Upon arriving in San Francisco, we proceeded by auto down the Santa Clara valley to Palo Alto. Secretary Hoover's house was situated on a hillside, a large picture window in his library overlooking that beautiful city and valley. As we discussed the progress that had been made in the development of the vast inland waterways system that Secretary Hoover had envisioned for the United States, we felt added confidence in our struggle for the improvement of the upper Mississippi River for commercial navigation.

Our visit that day was a most interesting experience, and Secretary Hoover made it delightful with his characteristically gentle humor. We returned that afternoon to San Francisco by auto over the skyline drive, after a brief visit to Stanford University, and then by train to Minneapolis.

The extreme drought of the 1920s in the midwestern part of the United States, to which I have referred, continued into the early 1930s. As a consequence, the water table was reduced to a point where the mighty Mississippi River, in its upper reaches, was little more than a large creek. Navigation in this area of the river, even with towboats and barges drawing only three and a half feet, was virtually at a standstill.

This situation caused businessmen and agricultural leaders to increase their efforts to obtain the approval by Congress of the upper Mississippi River nine-foot channel project.

The opposition to the Congressional authorization and the construction of a series of dams that would insure a minimum depth of nine feet in the upper Mississippi River was led by powerful railroad and related interests. But the leading business and agricultural leaders stood firm.[1] Faith in their leaders was evidenced by the action of people in the cities on the upper river in voting funds for the construction of river-rail terminals, not only for the benefit of their communities but the hinterland that they serve.

A study was made and a report was prepared under my direction for the Upper Mississippi Waterways Association supporting Congressional authorization of the nine-foot channel project to be constructed by the United States, under the supervision of the Army Corps of Engineers. This report, as required by law, was first presented to the Army district engineer at Rock Island, Illinois. On February 23, 1929, following a hearing, the district engineer rejected the recommendation in the Association's report on the ground that the benefits from such a project would extend only to the cities and towns along the upper Mississippi River and that these benefits would not justify the cost.

As provided by law, an appeal was taken by the Upper Mississippi Waterway Association to the Board of Engineers for Rivers and Harbors in Washington, D. C., based on facts, which were detailed and documented, that under through routes and joint rates with connecting railroads, the benefits from the completion of the nine-foot channel project would extend far inland, as had been demonstrated on the lower Mississippi River and the Ohio River.

Following a hearing on April 22, 1929, the Board of Engineers for Rivers and Harbors reversed the findings and recommendation of the district engineer and recommended Congressional authorization of the proposed upper Mississippi River nine-foot channel project. On February 15, 1930, the Secretary of War transmitted this report to Congress.

[1] They included such outstanding men as S. S. Thorpe, C. C. Webber, H. M. Hill, W. W. Morse, J. L. Record, J. S. Clapper, E. J. Ellertson, and A. R. Rogers of Minneapolis; R. P. Warner, Colonel George C. Lambert, E. B. Ober, and William Hamm of St. Paul; B. F. Peek, Moline, Ill., H. J. McConnon, Winona, Minn., H. W. Seaman, Clinton, Ia., J. A. Kerper, Dubuque, Ia., J. S. Ahern, Quincy, Ill., Fred C. Anderson, Bayport, Minn., Ralph W. Cramm and Geo. M. Cummins, Davenport, Ia., R. A. Jacobson, Rock Island, Ill., Chas. McLean, Dubuque, Ia., F. J. Riling, Burlington, Ia., W. A. Sheaffer, Ft. Madison, Ia., Geo. M. Titus, Muscatine, Ia., R. H. Watkins, Winona, Minn., A. J. Weber, Keokuk, Ia.

In April, 1930, hearings were held on the report of the Board of Engineers for River and Harbors before the Commerce Committee of the Senate and the Interstate and Foreign Committee of the House of Representatives, in Washington, D. C. The presentation of the case for the upper Mississippi valley before these committees was under my direction. After the hearings, being somewhat apprehensive of the outcome, in view of the nature of the opposition, I remained in Washington.

A few days after the committee hearings, I met George E. Akerson, a member of President Hoover's Secretariat, and a former Washington correspondent for the Minneapolis *Tribune.* I asked him about the attitude of the Administration towards the upper Mississippi River nine-foot channel project. He answered, "If you think that President Hoover is going to approve the expenditure of $165,000,000 to construct dams on the upper Mississippi River during this depression, you are wrong."

In view of the President's earlier advocacy of the project as essential to the economic welfare of the upper Mississippi valley, I was so amazed at his statement that I asked for a conference with the President on the matter. After further discussion, he grudgingly said I could see the President for a few minutes at eleven o'clock the following Monday morning. I then said to him, "George, I do not want this meeting for myself but for five leading shippers and businessmen in the upper valley." And, of course, I named them.

In response to my urgent telephone calls, Mr. Webber, Mr. Hill, Mr. Warner, Arthur R. Rogers, President of the Rogers Lumber Company, Minneapolis, and William J. Murphy, President of the Minneapolis *Tribune* arrived in Washington Monday morning. I briefed them on the situation before they met with the President at eleven o'clock that morning. After the conference, they returned to my hotel, the Carlton, utterly discouraged at the President's change in attitude toward river development. The President, they said, seemd to be overwhelmed by the severity of the depression which he, and many others in high places, had not foreseen.

During an extended discussion with these men, I suggested

that I remain in Washington and try to find out what, if anything, could be done to improve the prospects for the upper Mississippi River nine-foot channel project. They agreed, but one added that he thought nothing could be done in the light of the attitude of the President. Undoubtedly, the others were of the same view.

In the late afternoon of April 25, 1930, a river and harbors bill was reported by the House Interstate and Foreign Commerce Committee. Just as I feared, the bill as reported included a provision for the upper Mississippi River that failed to authorize the nine-foot channel project. Apparently, a spokesman for the opposition from the Twin Cities had assured the committee members that a mere reference to the upper river project as being desirable in the future would satisfy the shippers and businessmen in the upper Mississippi valley.

I conferred immediately with Senator Shipstead. In view of the widespread public support for the project, I suggested to him that a petition be signed by members of the Senate from the entire Mississippi valley, directed to the Senate Commerce Committee, urging inclusion of the upper Mississippi River nine-foot channel project in the river and harbors bill pending before that committee. The Senator twice rejected the suggestion, but finally he told me to prepare the petition.

When the Senator determined that the petition had been signed by a representative number of Senators from the Mississippi valley, he acted quickly. At his request the Senate Commerce Committee was reconvened at eleven o'clock in the morning of May 25, 1930. He asked me to come to his office that morning and wait for him. At about noon, the acting chairman of the Senate Commerce Committee, Senator Gerald P. Nye, of North Dakota, telephoned me at Senator Shipstead's office to come over to the committee room. When I arrived, he said, "I think you are entitled to know first. The upper Mississippi River nine-foot channel project has been approved by the committee and is now in the rivers and harbors bill."

Senator Shipstead was standing by Senator Nye, smiling as happily as I was. I thanked Senator Nye, as I did Senator Shipstead whose all-out effort and high standing in the Senate made authorization of the upper Mississippi River project a reality. I learned later that Senator Shipstead had obtained signatures on the petition from twenty-one senators, representing sixteen midwestern and western states, supporting the inclusion of the upper Mississippi project in the Senate rivers and harbors bill.

The bill, as reported, authorized the construction of 26 locks and dams to provide a navigation channel of nine-foot depth, with a minimum width of 400 feet, embracing the section of the river between the mouth of the Missouri River and Minneapolis. The bill passed the Senate and the House of Representatives and, with the signature of the President of the United States, became law on July 3, 1930.

In November, 1931, the Chicago, Burlington & Quincy Railroad Company instituted a suit in the United States District Court for the Western District of Wisconsin to restrain the Secretary of War and his subordinates, including the United States Army Corps of Engineers, from constructing a navigation dam across the Mississippi River at Alma, Wisconsin, because, as alleged, the Army Corps of Engineers did not propose to construct the dam at the *exact* location tentatively designated in its report. In short, there was no leeway; if the Army Corps of Engineers determined that a better location would be fifty or one hundred yards south of the location tentatively selected, they were without authority to move the site.

Following arguments before the United States District Court in Madison, Wisconsin, in which the Upper Mississippi Valley Association participated as *amicus curiae*, the Judge, on December 5, 1931, granted the injunction sought by the railroad company and thus seemingly effectively stopped the construction of the upper Mississippi River nine-foot channel project. On January 13, 1932, an appeal was taken by the United States to the United States Circuit Court of Appeals for the Seventh Circuit from the decree granting the injunction.

After considerable discussion of this unexpected development, and after consultation with the leading business and agricultural leaders in the upper Mississippi valley, Mr. Thorpe and

Mr. Webber directed me to proceed to Washington. My mission was to secure an amendment to the Federal act authorizing the upper Mississippi River nine-foot channel project specifically vesting in the United States Army Corps of Engineers complete discretion in the manner and method of constructing the project.

Upon arriving in Washington, I conferred with Senator Shipstead, and we determined upon a course of action. The Senator and Congressman J. J. Mansfield, of Texas, on February 2, 1932, introduced in Congress a joint resolution vesting in the Chief of Army Engineers discretion in the construction of the upper Mississippi River nine-foot channel project, adding that "all locks below the Twin City Dam shall not be less than the Ohio River standard dimensions." In preparing the joint resolution, we, of course, consulted with the Chief of Army Engineers and his staff.

Fortunately, both the Senate Commerce Committee and the House Interstate and Foreign Commerce Committee were in session. Brig. General George Bigelow Pillsbury, of the office of the Chief of Army Engineers, and I appeared and testified first before the House committee, outlining the emergency. We urged favorable and prompt action on the proposed joint resolution. The House committee approved and reported the joint resolution immediately. General Pillsbury and I then appeared the same day before the Senate Commerce Committee which, after our presentation, took action similar to that taken by the House committee.

The next day was calendar Wednesday in the House of Representatives. The joint resolution could be called up for consideration if there were no objections. Congressman LaGuardia, of New York, objected. When he was advised by Senator Shipstead and Congressman Mansfield of the significance of the joint resolution to a project of great importance to the people of the upper Mississippi valley, Congressman LaGuardia withdrew his objection, and the joint resolution was unanimously approved. Senator Shipstead obtained favorable action that afternoon in the Senate.

The President signed the joint resolution causing it to become law on February 24, 1932. Based thereon, the United

States Circuit Court of Appeals for the Seventh Circuit remanded the cause with direction to the District Court that the injunction be dissolved. Thus, another crisis was met and the Chief of Army Engineers was free to proceed with the construction of dams and related structures for the upper Mississippi River nine-foot channel project. But there were to be other crises.

While in Washington on matters relating to the joint resolution, I received a telephone call from Mr. Webber in Minneapolis. He stated that the Secretary of War, Patrick J. Hurley, and another member of President Hoover's Secretariat, Walter H. Newton, a former Congressman from Minneapolis, had asked for a meeting in Minneapolis with the leaders of the upper Mississippi valley to discuss the nine-foot channel project. Mr. Webber suggested that I return to Minneapolis and be present at the meeting. I returned immediately.

The meeting with Secretary Hurley and Mr. Newton was held at the Minneapolis Club, and the leaders in the upper Mississippi valley who constituted my board of directors were present. The burden of what Secretary Hurley and Mr. Newton had to say was that a Republican Administration was in power, that nothing could be done with the upper Mississippi River project without Administration approval, and that therefore the business and agricultural leaders should discontinue their efforts and leave the matter entirely in the hands of the Republican Administration.

After a general discussion, Mr. Webber, who presided at the meeting, called on me for comment. I stated that the businessmen and agricultural leaders of the upper valley had worked for the nine-foot channel project as a matter vital to the economy of the area, seeking support from all sections of the United States, particularly in the lower Mississippi valley where, with few exceptions, public representatives, businessmen and shippers were Democrats with a capital D. Further, I pointed out that in the State of Minnesota, our most effective advocate and unfaltering supporter was Senator Henrik Shipstead, a Farmer-Laborite. In this situation, I argued, if we now changed our well-known position that the nine-foot channel project is an economic project to aid the people of the upper Mississippi valley and made it a partisan political matter, we would destroy the basis for our local, as well as our nationwide, support for the project. If, as a result of such a change, I continued, the project failed of early completion, we would be condemned by the businessmen and farmers who depended upon us—indeed by all the people of the upper Mississippi valley. And, for good measure, I added that I was raised as a Republican and that my brother-in-law, J. A. O. Preus, whom I greatly admired, was the former Republican Governor of Minnesota, but that did not affect my judgment in this matter.

My board of directors unanimously supported my position, a position that was amply justified by subsequent events. Mr. Webber, a giant among businessmen in the upper Mississippi valley, thanked Secretary Hurley and Mr. Newton for their visit, but cautioned them not to interfere with the efforts of the people of the upper valley to obtain as speedily as possible a nine-foot channel in the upper Mississippi River! They then returned to Washington. Another crisis was met.

River and harbor bills in Congress authorize projects such as the upper Mississippi River project. Authorization, however, is futile unless followed by the appropriation of funds by Congress adequate to complete construction. In the case of the authorization of the upper Mississippi River project, the sum of $15,000,000 of previously appropriated funds for dredging to keep open the old six-foot channel project was made available to begin construction of dams for the nine-foot channel project. This was sufficient to build two dams. The remaining twenty-one dams and larger locks in the three existing dams would, under the long established method of financing river and harbor projects, have to await further action by Congress.

The method of financing river canalization projects in the United States through the piecemeal construction of a series of navigation dams appeared to me to be extremely wasteful. In the case of the Ohio River, for example, funds were provided by Congress for the construction of one or two dams for the authorized project, and when construction was completed, the crew was disbanded and expensive equipment withdrawn. When Congress at some future time appropriated funds for another dam or two, another crew was recruited and equipment obtained. This method of constructing such projects could be compared to constructing a large office building, one story at a time, disbanding the construction crew and taking away the expensive construction equipment each time a story was completed! Nothing could be more unbusinesslike or more extravagant. But also improvident from the standpoint of the shippers of the upper valley was the loss of valuable time before the project could become operational.

After considerable research, I drew up a proposal in the form of a bill, with an explanatory memorandum, to finance the completion of all authorized river and harbor projects, including the upper Mississippi River nine-foot channel project, in an amount not exceeding $500,000,000. This bill, if enacted into law, would permit construction work on all authorized projects to continue, without interruption, to completion, as rapidly as possible.

At the first opportunity, I discussed this proposal with Mr. Webber, who had been elected President of the Upper Mississippi Waterway Association upon the retirement of Mr. Thorpe. Following a telephone discussion with Senator Shipstead, Mr. Webber called a meeting of the business and agricultural leaders who constituted the directors of the Association. After a thorough discussion of the proposal, the directors gave their approval.

Our first move for support was made at the November, 1931, convention of the Mississippi Valley Association held in St. Louis, Missouri. Among our most vocal opponents were the river contractors who appeared to benefit from the piecemeal construction of waterway projects. As floor manager for the upper river forces at the convention, I called on selected leaders from our delegation for their views, followed by an able and vigorous speech on the subject by Senator Shipstead. The convention responded by approving the upper Mississippi River proposal for financing river and harbor projects by acclamation. This action proved to be the first step towards success.

The Great Depression of the 1920's, with its woes, still plagued the nation in 1932. The economy slowed down almost to a standstill. The people were discouraged. The Administration, with the best of intentions, appeared unable to develop an adequate program to alleviate the situation.

There were those in and out of Congress who believed that a large public works program would provide substantial relief. Therefore, in April, 1932, I went to Washington to discuss the proposed comprehensive method of financing river and harbor projects with Senator Shipstead.

After our discussion, the Senator took me to the office of the Speaker of the House of Representatives, John Nance Garner, who had proposed a billion dollar public works program to aid in meeting the urgent needs of the nation's depressed economy. I explained to Speaker Garner the proposed new method of financing river and harbor projects which had been approved by representative organizations in the Mississippi valley. When I finished, Speaker Garner said he would include the proposal in his public works bill to the extent of $500,000,000. At the hearings on the bill, shippers, business and agricultural leaders from all parts of the Mississippi valley appeared and testified in support of the Garner public works bill.

The Garner bill passed the House of Representatives but, due to the opposition of the Administration to increasing Federal expenditures, particularly for public works, to meet depression needs, the bill did not come to a vote in the Senate. Though we did not realize it at the time, all the thought and effort we had put into this new, "revolutionary" method of financing river and harbor projects became the basis for success later.

It was now abundantly clear to the leaders of the upper Mississippi valley that they could expect no further help from the Hoover Administration in carrying forward the nine-foot channel project, at least so long as the depression continued. This was a matter of regret to me personally, for I greatly admired President Hoover as a man, but I could not understand his reasons for a change in policy toward projects that would aid the economy. I knew of course that his Administration, which began with a tax refund for taxpayers, had misjudged the nature and possible extent of the depression; that its principal weapon to meet the deteriorating situation was to reduce Federal expenditures, regardless of their purpose, in an effort to balance the budget; and that when this course did not meet the increasingly adverse effects of the depression, the Administration seemed unable to develop a meaningful alternative.

Despite this turn of events, which I did not fully understand, I shall always remember President Hoover, not only as a great American, but as the man who envisaged a truly national integrated inland waterway system which today is a reality serving the growing economic needs of the vast region known as the Mississippi valley basin of the United States.

CHAPTER IV

Victory for the
Landlocked Upper Mississippi Valley

In SEPTEMBER, 1932, United States Senator Henrik Shipstead, who was then on his vacation at his home near Alexandria, Minnesota, advised me that he had a telephone call from the Governor of New York State, Franklin D. Roosevelt, asking that he, Senator Shipstead, arrange for one or two representatives from the Mississippi Valley to come to Albany, New York, for the purpose of discussing the upper Mississippi River nine-foot channel project with him. Governor Roosevelt was then a candidate for the Presidency of the United States on the Democratic ticket. After a conference between officials of the Upper Mississippi Waterway Association and Senator Shipstead, Theodore Brent, of New Orleans, a leading advocate and authority on inland waterways development, and I were selected to proceed to Albany and present to Governor Roosevelt the facts regarding the project, its status, and its importance to the people of the upper Mississippi valley.

One afternoon a few days later, Governor Roosevelt received us at the Executive Mansion in Albany with a cordial greeting and his famous smile. His radiant personality conveyed the impression that there was no one he would rather meet than Mr. Brent and me. I thought this a wonderful quality to find in a public figure.

I laid a map of the Mississippi River and its principal tributaries on the Governor's desk, and with frequent references to

President Franklin D. Roosevelt

this map, Mr. Brent and I told the Governor about the upper Mississippi River nine-foot channel project, its status, and its importance, particularly as an integral part of the nation's vast inland waterways system. During our discussion, the Governor told us about New York State's Erie Canal, mentioning the 1000-ton barges that plied the canal. When he inquired about barge operations on the lower Mississippi River and its main tributaries, we told him that barge tows of eight to ten barges, fastened together with cables, carrying from 1500 to 3000 tons in each barge, were not uncommon. He seemed quite surprised.

Our conference with Governor Roosevelt was unhurried. When it was concluded, he asked us to tell Senator Shipstead and the leaders of the upper Mississippi valley that he would deliver an address supporting the upper Mississippi River project, and that, if elected President, he would take immediate steps to insure its completion. We expressed our appreciation and assured him that we would give his message to the Senator and to the upper Missisippi valley leaders promptly upon our return to Minneapolis.

I shall never forget the warmth and the charming personality of Governor Roosevelt, even during the farewells, as he thanked us for coming to Albany to visit with him on this important matter. In later years, I found the same qualities in my association with one of his sons, James Roosevelt.

After Governor Roosevelt was elected President of the United States, and upon assuming office on March 4, 1933, he launched a Federal public works program, among other programs, to alleviate the desperate conditions that were the result of the prolonged depression. It was long overdue.

At first, a committee was appointed to administer the public works program. Upon learning of the membership of this committee, I became concerned about the fate of the upper Mississippi River nine-foot channel project. After conferring with my principals, I proceeded to Washington and discussed the matter with the Chief of Army Engineers, General Lytle Brown. From our discussion, I learned that my concern was justified. I telephoned Senator Shipstead, who was still in Minnesota, that a decision by the Public Works Committee on the upper Mississippi River project would be made within three days and that it might be unfavorable unless he came to Washington at once and talked with the President.

Senator Shipstead left immediately for Washington, after having arranged by telephone for an appointment with the President upon arrival in Washington. I met the Senator at the station and from there we rode to the White House. He asked me to wait while he went in for his conference with President Roosevelt.

After waiting for almost an hour, I became somewhat apprehensive. The Senator, I thought, must be having a difficult time. To relieve my growing concern, I took a walk along the semi-circular driveway in front of the entrance to the White House. Halfway around this driveway, I noticed a new Buick sedan. The front windows were open, so I put my head in to get a better view of the interior and the instrument panel. I was absorbed in this inspection when I heard a lady's voice behind me, saying, "It is a beautiful car, isn't it?" I looked up in surprise and some embarrassment, and said, "It is a beautiful car, Mrs. Roosevelt!" After a few pleasantries, Mrs. Roosevelt entered the car and drove away. Later, a guard told me that the car was Mrs. Roosevelt's own and that she often drove it herself.

Another hour passed, and no word from Senator Shipstead. My anxiety increased. After another forty minutes, the Senator appeared and said, "Let us drive up to Baltimore and see Senator Borah who is in Johns Hopkins Hospital there."

On the way to Baltimore, the Senator told me about his two hour and forty minute conference with the President. During the first hour the President discussed foreign affairs with the Senator. During the second hour and some minutes, the President discussed domestic matters, seeking particularly the Senator's views on the farm problem. Then the Senator raised the question of approval of the upper-Mississippi River nine-foot channel project, and in this relation expressed his concern over the composition and possible attitude of the President's Public Works Committee. The President said the project had his approval and would be included in his public works program, adding that the Senator could announce that fact to the press as he left the President's office. The Senator replied that this was a major act by the President to aid the people of a vast area of the United States and that, under the circumstances, it would be most appropriate for the President to make the announcement.

After returning to Washington from Baltimore, Senator Shipstead and I were visiting over the developments of the day at his home when the telephone rang. He asked me to answer because he wanted to avoid the press until the President had made his announcement regarding the upper river project.

The voice said, "Is Senator Shipstead there?" I answered, "Who is calling him?" The voice answered, "This is the White House. The President of the United States." I turned to the Senator and said, "The President wants to speak with you."

The President's voice came through loud and clear: "Henrik, a memorandum has been placed on my desk. It is from a tax organization in Minneapolis which claims that the approval of the upper Mississippi River project will do much to wreck the economy. What is this organization?"

The Senator replied, also loud and clear: "That is a new front organization set up a few months ago by some special interests to defeat the upper river project. It's run by a two-by-four propagandist in Minneapolis."

The President said: "That's just what I thought. Henrik, I am putting the project through on Friday."

The Senator: "Thank you, Mr. President, for all the people of the upper Mississippi valley."

On Friday afternoon, as we were returning to Minneapolis on the Baltimore and Ohio Railroad's "Capitol Limited," the train stopped at Cumberland, Maryland. The conductor brought a telegram to Senator Shipstead from the President stating that he had just publicly announced the inclusion of the upper Mississippi River nine-foot channel project in his public works program. This action of President Roosevelt, following his conference and exchange of views with Senator Shipstead, ensured funds adequate for the construction of the project. Without further incident, the project, so important to the economy of the upper Mississippi valley, proceeded to completion.

On October 26, 1933, the Upper Mississippi Waterway Association held a Victory Dinner celebrating inclusion of the channel project in the Nation's public works program. Senator Shipstead was the guest of honor. Businessmen, industrialists, and other shippers from all sections of the Mississippi valley attended the dinner. Most of them had participated in this all-out effort to bring into being a commercially navigable waterway to the upper Mississippi valley as an integral part of the inland waterways system of the nation.

It was eminently fitting that Senator Shipstead was the guest of honor at the Victory Dinner. If it had not been for his prestige in public life, his unceasing efforts, his zeal and diligence, the upper Mississippi River project might never have become a reality.

Those of us who worked so closely with the late Senator Shipstead during those trying years hoped that the people of the upper Mississippi valley, particularly the people of the State of Minnesota he served so well, who are the beneficiaries of this, one of his greatest achievements for them, will not forget Senator Shipstead. *Even at this late date, it would be most appropriate for them to express their appreciation in a lasting memorial, perhaps at the beginning of the upper Mississippi River nine-foot channel in Minneapolis, Minnesota.* In so doing they would indeed honor themselves.

The horizons of the people living in the upper Mississippi valley, a region which, as I have stated, has been described as a great inland domain as large as the European nations of Germany, France, Italy and Great Britain combined, were immeasurably widened by the completion of the upper Mississippi River nine-foot channel project. The shippers, including leaders in business and agriculture, who had actively supported the project, not only established a permanent "equalizer" for this great region against high and discriminatory freight rates, but brought into being a permanent and reliable all-water outlet to New Orleans and the world for the otherwise landlocked upper Mississippi valley. They realized that no primarily agriculture areas

in the world, and their budding industries, have prospered without access to commercially usable water transport.[1] In 1968, the
Mississippi River ranked first among the nation's waterways in
attracting new construction and expansion of industrial production and service facilities.

A few weeks prior to the Victory Dinner, I learned that the
legal proceedings for the acquisition of lands and easements
along the upper Mississippi River for the nine-foot channel project had bogged down for want of an adequate staff from the
United States Attorney General's office to handle the condemnation cases pending before Federal courts. I ascertained the facts
and then proceeded to Washington to discuss the matter with
Senator Shipstead. Following our discussion, the Senator accompanied me to the office of the then Attorney General, Homer S.
Cummings, with whom he had arranged a conference to discuss
the matter. When I had completed my presentation of the sa-
lient facts, the Attorney General asked me to submit a memorandum to him on the subject, adding that he would personally
see to it that the situation would be corrected promptly.

I prepared and submitted my memorandum to Attorney General Cummings the next day, with a copy to Senator Shipstead
and then returned to Minneapolis.

A few days after my return, I had a telephone call from the
Assistant Attorney General in charge of the Lands Division of
the Department of Justice, George C. Sweeney. He said he was
leaving for Minneapolis and wanted to discuss the upper Mississippi River project condemnation proceedings with me. At the
conclusion of our discussion in Minneapolis, Mr. Sweeney asked
me to accept an appointment as Special Assistant to the United
States Attorney General to aid in expediting the handling of the
many pending condemnation cases relating to the upper river
project. Since this post involved a substantial reduction in

---

[1] The facts regarding the construction and operation of the upper Mississippi River
9-foot channel project, which made the upper Mississippi an integral part of the nation's vast inland waterways system; the resulting rapid growth of commercial traffic on
the upper Mississippi River; and the "extra dividends" in recreational and conservation
benefits afforded since the completion of the project, were prepared by the United
States Army Corps of Engineers and are summarized in Appendix A.

income, and I had a growing family, I hesitated, but after talking to my wife and the men with whom I had been closely associated for so many years, I accepted. My appointment was made official by Attorney General Cummings on October 24, 1933. Senator Shipstead announced my appointment publicly at the Victory Dinner on October 26, 1933.

There was a great accumulation of condemnation cases that urgently required attention, some pending before Commissioners but many more pending in the Federal courts. Among the more interesting cases which I handled were those that involved flowage easements on railroad rights-of-way which extended into the river below ordinary high water mark. One of these cases, involving the Chicago, Burlington and Quincy Railroad, proceeded through the United States District Court for the Western District of Wisconsin and the United States Circuit Court of Appeals for the Seventh Circuit. The decision sustained the railroad's claim for damages to its railroad embankment extending into the river below ordinary high water mark. I recommended an appeal to the United States Supreme Court.

Because of the importance of the Burlington Railroad case, I was called to Washington, D. C., for a conference with Attorney General Cummings and Solicitor General, Stanley Reed, on my recommendation for an appeal. After a thorough discussion of the matter, I was authorized to prepare a petition for a *writ of certiorari* to the United States Supreme Court, but the Solicitor General said he doubted that it would be granted. I expressed surprise, calling his attention to a recent statement of the Chief Justice of the United States that such petitions would be granted in cases where there was a conflict in the decisions of the United States Circuit Courts of Appeal on the legal question presented. The petition was prepared and filed on the question of law involved; it specifically directed attention to the conflict on that question between the Fifth and Seventh United States Circuit Courts of Appeal. The Supreme Court, however, denied the petition.

After three years of almost continuous hearings before Commissioners and trials in the Federal courts, the condemnation cases were brought under control to a point where construction of the upper Mississippi River nine-foot channel project could proceed expeditiously. My tasks for the Federal government as well as for the people in the upper Mississippi valley, which extended over a period of eleven years, were completed.

In the latter part of 1936, Glenn W. Traer, who had been vice president of the investment banking house of Lane, Piper and Jaffray, Inc., became vice president of The Greyhound Corporation, a newly established holding company for the various companies that formed The Greyhound Lines. He offered me a position as attorney in the new corporation's legal department in Chicago. This appeared to be an opportunity to widen my horizons in the transporation field, so I accepted.

After I had returned to private life as an attorney for The Greyhound Corporation, I received a letter from the then Solicitor General, Francis Biddle, advising me that the United States Supreme Court in a condemnation case involving the Chicago, Milwaukee and St. Paul Railroad, which presented the identical question of law as in the Burlington Railroad case, had granted a petition for *writ of certiorari*. In view of the position I had taken as Federal government counsel in the Burlington Railroad case, the Solicitor General stated that he would send me a copy of the government's brief on the merits when it was printed. He added that, if I were in Washington on the day of the argument before the Supreme Court, perhaps I would like to sit with government counsel in that case. I replied, thanking him for his letter and stated that I would be in Washington for the argument.

A courtesy extended to me while in Washington, which I also appreciated, was an opportunity to meet and visit with the Chief Justice of the United States, Charles Evans Hughes, in his chambers. I had always admired him as a great Chief Justice and a great American. Later that same day, I received an autographed photograph of the Chief Justice. It still is one of my prized possessions.

The argument for the government in the Milwaukee Railroad case before the Supreme Court was made by the Assistant Attorney General, Norman Littell. I congratulated him on his

excellent presentation and expressed my thanks for being allowed to sit with him and other government counsel in the case and for his kindness in arranging a meeting for me with Chief Justice Hughes.

Within a month after the argument, the United States Supreme Court rendered its unanimous decision in favor of the government, thus upholding the position I had taken on behalf of the government in the Burlington Railroad case which the Court had refused to hear! In the interval between the disposition of these two cases by the Supreme Court, there had been a substantial change in the membership of the Court. The Court's "change of heart" during the interval lends support to the statement made by the late, great Chief Justice Charles Evans Hughes, that the Constitution is what the judges say it is.

CHAPTER V

The First Transcontinental
Land Transportation System

THE HORIZONS of millions of Americans have been widened by the imagination, the determination, the organizing ability, and the leadership of Eric C. Wickman. From a modest beginning, he, and the talented men who became his closest associates, fashioned a land transporation system that enabled the people of our country to travel, at comparatively low cost, between virtually every city, town, and community throughout the land.

The story of Mr. Wickman and the evolution of his small "jitney" service into a great transcontinental motorbus system is a modern American saga. He achieved with motorbus transportation what the Harrimans, the Hills, and the other empire builders of earlier years were unable to accomplish with railroad transportation.

The Wickman story has been told and retold many times, and inevitably in the retelling there have been many embellishments. In the years when the story was almost completed, I had the privilege of knowing and working for him. From time to time during those years, there were opportunities to discuss with him—at his home, or at his office, or occasionally on a trip—some of the events and experiences of his truly remarkable career. These discussions were usually at my prompting, but he didn't seem to mind.

Eric, as he was called by his many friends and acquaintances, was a plain, unpretentious person who spoke his mind with directness and without vanity or guile. He was a shrewd businessman, with a Midas touch that attracted men to him and his enterprises, seemingly without effort. He was the man who could and did provide the leadership that brought together many motorbus companies and operations scattered throughout the country and welded them into a single entity which became the nationwide Greyhound motorbus system. The discussions I had with him, and with his close associates, form the background of the following brief account of Eric's rapid rise to fame and fortune.

The story began in 1914 when Eric was a diamond-drill operator on the Mesabi Iron Range in Minnesota. His home was in the town of Hibbing on the iron range. Eric tried to sell Hupmobile automobiles "to have something to do during the dull months in mining operations." The Hupmobiles were touring cars, with canvas curtains to be fastened on each side when it rained and during the winter season. They proved inadequate for the bitterly cold winters in northern Minnesota. Therefore, they could not be profitably sold. The question was, what to do with them?

A solution grew out of the fact that the town of Hibbing was built on top of a large body of valuable iron ore which lay close to the surface. This ore could be reached through strip mining methods. It was not long before Hibbing was being encircled by what was to become the world's largest open pit iron mine. Many people moved from Hibbing to a small town called Alice, two miles south of Hibbing. Since there was no public transporation between Hibbing and Alice, Eric decided to put in a "jitney" service with his unsaleable automobiles. The fare for the two-mile trip was fifteen cents one way and twenty-five cents round trip. At first no one seemed willing to ride, so they were offered free transporation. As a result, the "customers" filled the cars, stood on the running boards, and hung on the fenders. When the "customers" became acquainted with the convenient new service, Eric put the fifteen cents one way and twenty-five cents round-trip fares into effect.

Eric C. Wickman, president of the Greyhound Corporation

Eric placed all the money received from his "jitney" operation in a trunk, and when he thought that sufficient funds had been accumulated, he bought his first motorbus, counting out $200 in silver coins as the down payment! The motorbus, hurriedly built, was a comparatively crude affair, with unpainted, wooden-paneled sides. Eric immediately put it into operation between Hibbing and Eveleth, Minnesota, on the Mesabi Iron Range. At the end of each trip, he painted one panel, with the result that when all panels were finally painted, the motorbus, because of dust, rain, or sun on each freshly painted panel, produced the appearance of a varicolored patch quilt.

This was the beginning, and it was financially successful. By 1916, the Mesabi Transportation Company was organized to meet the need for more capital and more drivers. There were five members of the corporation which owned five buses. Each man was a director and each a driver. On one occasion, a waiting farmer on one of the routes from Hibbing to a town on the iron range was passed by a driver who failed to see him. The farmer jumped on the back of the bus and held on to the next stop. Then climbing into the bus, he shook his finger in the driver's face, and shouted, "You passed me by. I am going to tell the president of the company about this."

"Go ahead," said the driver, Eric Wickman, "I am the president."[1]

From Eveleth, Eric extended his motorbus operation to Duluth and from there to the Twin Cities of Minneapolis and St. Paul, Minnesota. These extensions and operations involved a number of transactions, including mergers, purchases, and sales of small motorbus operations and equipment. In 1925, Eric sold a majority interest in Northland Transporation Company, as his motorbus operation was then known, to the Great Northern Railroad Company, which provided needed funds for further expansion. Eric remained its manager. Subsequently, as hereinafter related, this majority interest in the Northland Transportation Company, which later became the Northland Greyhound Lines, was reduced to a minority interest.

[1] *Era of Excellence,* published by The Greyhound Corporation, Chicago, Illinois.

The Legislature of Minnesota and other states soon thereafter passed laws that placed motorbus operators under regulation, requiring them to obtain certificates of public convenience and necessity to conduct their operations. For motorbus operations that were in existence prior to the enactment of such laws, the operators automatically received what were termed "grandfather certificates." This latter provision gave Eric what may be termed "a property right" over the routes he operated as long as he continued operations in accordance with the motorbus laws.

Eric, primarily a motorbus operator, soon associated himself with Glenn W. Traer, vice president of the investment banking house of Lane, Piper and Jaffray, of Minneapolis, a brilliant financier, and Orville S. Caesar, an able mechanic and auto dealer in Superior, Wisconsin. This combination of talent moved with great skill, energy and speed in building, through purchases, unifications, and extension of new lines, the first transcontinental land transportation system in the United States.

Early in their efforts, they adopted the name "Greyhound Lines" for this bus system. This name, as one legend has it, grew out of a remark made one night by a station employee in a Wisconsin town before an official of the company as he saw the motorbus drive away from the station in a snowstorm. "Looks just like a greyhound," the station employee is reported to have said, and out of this chance remark, so the legend goes, Eric's motorbus operations became the Greyhound Lines.

The rapid progress towards success in their great effort was threatened in the early 1930s when Eric and his associates determined to extend the operations of the Greyhound system to the Pacific northwest over the long route that would parallel the existing operations of the Union Pacific Stages, a subsidiary of the Union Pacific Railroad Company. Eric and his associates had succeeded in extending Greyhound's operations to San Francisco and Los Angeles and the Pacific northwest extension seemed promising.

The Union Pacific Stages, however, opposed this extension of operations by the Greyhound system. The competitive struggle became intense and reached a point where the competing operations would run virtually empty buses, cut fares without regard to cost, and, it is reported, for a time carried passengers without charge.

This historic competitive struggle occurred prior to the passage of the motor Carrier Act of 1935 by Congress, an Act that provided for the regulation of interstate routes, operations, and fares of the motorbus companies. Both parties to the struggle knew at the time that the passage of the Act was imminent. The prize sought by them was "grandfather rights," that is, operating rights that would be automatically granted to motorbus operators with *bona fide* services over specific routes when the proposed Act became law. The Union Pacific Stages, certain of being granted such rights because of its existing operations, was determined that the Greyhound system should not succeed in establishing a competing operation that would qualify it for similar rights.

The lack of business due to the continuing depression of the early 1930s reduced the earning power of the Greyhound system, and the financial drain caused by the costly competitive struggle with the Union Pacific Stages for the extension of operations over the long route to the Pacific northwest, weakened the Greyhound system financially to a point where it not only had to give up its proposed Pacific northwest extension but found itself threatened with bankruptcy. Reportedly, a voluntary petition in bankruptcy was prepared, but Eric Wickman refused to sign it, urging that another effort be made to obtain financial assistance to tide Greyhound over this difficult period. This effort proved successful.

As previously stated, my association with the Greyhound Lines grew out of a discussion with my friend, Glenn W. Traer, vice president of The Greyhound Corporation, in November, 1936, during which he offered me a position in the legal department of this new corporation.

It was after I had begun my work for The Greyhound Corporation that I first met Mr. Wickman. He was president of the Corporation. My relationship with him and the other officers of the company during the years that followed was cordial, and my work was interesting and stimulating. Everyone connected with the company was given the widest latitude to use and develop his talents to the fullest extent.

I represented The Greyhound Corporation and a number of its subsidiaries in court cases and regulatory proceedings in many parts of the United States. As commerce counsel, I was able to coordinate much of these far-flung activities.

One of my earliest and most important cases before the Interstate Commerce Commission involved a proposed acquisition of a motorbus company operating between Richmond, Williamsburg and Norfolk, Virginia, by the Richmond Greyhound Lines, a subsidiary of The Greyhound Corporation.

The capital stock of Richmond Greyhound Lines was owned fifty percent by The Greyhound Corporation and fifty percent by the Richmond, Fredericksburg and Potomac Railroad Company. There were also common officers, directors and employees of the two companies, and the offices of Richmond Greyhound Lines were located in the offices of the railroad company.

The key question in the case was whether the railroad's stock interest and other relationships with the Richmond Greyhound Lines constituted an "affiliation," within the meaning of the Interstate Commerce Act, that would enable the railroad to exercise control over the affairs of the applicant, Richmond Greyhound Lines, and thus, if its application was approved, over the motorbus company proposed to be acquired. If so, the acquisition could not be approved by the Interstate Commerce Commission; if not, the Commission could approve the acquisition if it were established that it would be in the public interest.

As the result of my interpretations of the law, the management of the Richmond, Fredericksburg and Potomac Railroad Company reduced its stock interest in the Richmond Greyhound Lines to a minority interest, all common officers, directors and employees resigned, and an independent office and staff was established for the Richmond Greyhound Lines.

Following extensive hearings, the Interstate Commerce Commission ruled that Richmond Greyhound Lines was not affiliated with the Richmond, Fredericksburg and Potomac Railroad Company within the meaning of the Interstate Commerce Act and approved the acquisition of the motorbus operation between

Richmond, Williamsburg and Norfolk, Virginia. This decision set the pattern for similar changes in the relationships between other motorbus subsidiaries of The Greyhound Corporation and their railroad stockholders. The Corporation eventually acquired all of the stock held by railroads in its motorbus subsidiaries.

During the early days of the hearings before the Interstate Commerce Commission in the Richmond Greyhound case, which were held in Washington, D. C., I had a visit with Senator Shipstead. I mentioned to him that Eric Wickman was the first man to establish a transcontinental land transportation system in the United States. Out of our discussion of this historical fact grew the suggestion that the Swedish Government might want to officially recognize this great achievement by one who was born and raised in Sweden and when a young man had emigrated to the United States. A few days later, the Senator and I discussed this thought with the Swedish Ambassador in Washington and suggested that his government might wish to honor Eric Wickman, a Swedish immigrant, with appropriate official recognition of his achievements in the United States that reflected great credit on his mother country and its people. The Ambassador agreed to take the matter up with his government.

As the lengthy hearings in the Richmond Greyhound case were drawing to a close, Eric telephoned me from Chicago, stating that the Swedish Consul in Chicago had just informed him that His Majesty King Gustav V of Sweden had bestowed upon him the Royal Order of Vasa, First Class. Obviously, Eric was much surprised. He asked me to return to Chicago immediately. I was able to wind up the case that afternoon and return to Chicago by plane.

The next day, upon my arrival at the office in Chicago, and after my talk with Eric, I learned that Mr. Traer and Mr. Caesar, vice presidents of The Greyhound Corporation, had been advised of this development, and that they had taken over all preparations for the presentation of this honor to their long-time associate. Prominent people in business, industry and government from all parts of the United States and Canada came to honor Eric at a banquet and the presentation of the decoration by the Swedish Ambassador at the Blackstone Hotel in Chicago.

Eric, after many discussions with me and others about the kind of an acceptance speech he should make, discarded all suggestions and spoke only one sentence in response to the presentation by the Swedish Ambassador. He said, "Please tell the King of Sweden that I am deeply thankful for this great honor."

This was characteristic of the simplicity and sincerity of the man. And from that day on, close friends of Eric often referred to him as "Sir Eric."

A few years and many legal proceedings later, I was asked to represent the Greyhound Lines and the motorbus industry as a witness before the Senate Commerce Committee on legislation that, if enacted, would materially and adversely affect the motorbus industry. Upon examination of the bill, it was clear that it would permit the creation of giant monopolies involving all forms of transportation.

On arrival in Washington, I called on Senator Burton K. Wheeler, Chairman of the Senate Commerce Committee, and stated that I would appear as a witness at the hearings on the bill on behalf of the motorbus industry. He told me that he had introduced the bill as an unwilling author for the consideration of the Committee at the request of the President of the United States. In view of the extensive and well-publicized program of antitrust and antimonopoly prosecutions currently being conducted by the Administration through the Antitrust Division of the Department of Justice, the President's sponsorship of the bill seemed to be a strange contradiction. This prompted me to seek a conference with the Assistant Attorney General, Thurman Arnold, in charge of the Antitrust Division.

When I was ushered into the office of Assistant Attorney General Arnold, I opened the discussion with the statement that I had understood the Administration was opposed to monopolies in any field as being harmful to the American system of private enterprise, but that the President was sponsoring one of the greatest monopoly bills ever introduced in Congress. This statement proved to be an attention getter. I was asked to explain. This I did in some detail, showing the Assistant Attorney General a copy of the bill. After reading the bill, he telephoned the White House for an appointment with the President, which request wound up with an appointment with a Presidential aide, Colonel Watson.

When he completed his telephone conversation, Mr. Arnold turned to me and said, "Well, young man, you may not realize it, but you are a one-man army."

When the Assistant Attorney General and I arrived at the White House, we were promptly ushered into the office of Colonel Watson. He told us that since Mr. Arnold's telephone call he had thoroughly checked the situation and could advise us that the President had not seen the bill to which we referred nor had he endorsed it. We were also told by the Colonel that we could convey this information to Senator Wheeler. We did not inquire whether anyone else in the White House had endorsed the bill.

Upon our return to the Assistant Attorney General's office, he telephoned Senator Wheeler, advising him what Colonel Watson had told us. Senator Wheeler promptly withdrew his authorship of the bill, hearings were cancelled, and nothing further was heard of this proposed legislation.

As I was leaving the Assistant Attorney General's office, he said that he was about to reactivate a transportation section in his Division and asked whether I would consider an appointment as a Special Assistant to the Attorney General to act as chief of the section. Since this might be another opportunity to widen my horizons, I answered that I would be glad to consider such an appointment.

Upon my return to Chicago, I discussed the offer of an appointment in the Department of Justice with my wife, who approved, and then with Eric Wickman and Glenn Traer. They urged me to decline the offer since my income would be reduced and other opportunities in the Greyhound set-up were before me. I answered, it seemed to me that this was an unusual opportunity in government at a national level, and for this reason I had decided to accept. With friendly pats on the back and the "best of good luck" from these two men whom I had come to know and greatly admire, I returned to my office, wrote out my acceptance to Assistant Attorney General Arnold, and began preparations for an entirely new experience which did widen my horizons not only on a national but on an international level.

CHAPTER VI

The Antitrust Laws and Transportation

> The purpose of the Sherman Antitrust Act is to prevent undue restraints of interstate commerce, to maintain its appropriate freedom in the public interest, to afford protection from the subversive or coercive influences of monopolistic endeavor. *As a charter of freedom,* the Act has a generality and adaptability comparable to that found to be desirable in constitutional provisions. [Emphasis supplied]
>
> CHARLES EVANS HUGHES
> *Chief Justice of the United States.*[1]

PART ONE

ON AUGUST 1, 1961, I reported for duty at the Antitrust Division of the Department of Justice, in Washington, D. C. I found its transportation unit virtually dormant. It was clear that my task, as Special Assistant to the Attorney General and chief of the Transportation Section in the Antitrust Division of the Department, was to revive the antitrust laws in the transportation field, laws that had for decades fallen into virtual disuse in this field.

As soon as possible after taking office, I began an analysis of the many complaints of antitrust violations in the transportation field which had accumulated in the Antitrust Division. Also, I

[1] 288 U.S. 344, 359 (1933).

proceeded with the difficult task of recruiting a competent staff. By the end of the year 1941, I had a professional staff of seventeen lawyers and several economists, with adequate stenographic and clerical help, and by the end of 1942 we were handling, in cooperation with the Division's field offices, 208 cases and investigations, including about 40 cases involving the defense of orders of the Interstate Commerce Commission on appeal to the courts.

In my book *Justice in Transportation,* published in March, 1945, I dealt at length with the antitrust laws as they were applied by the Antitrust Division of the Department of Justice to the noncompetitive agreements and activities of private companies performing public transportation services during the years 1941 to 1945. Therefore, many details, however important, are not repeated herein. However, the following summary of major events, some of which are discussed in detail in *Justice in Transportation,* are included because they bear on developments that occured after the year 1945.

The Antitrust Division of the Department of Justice instituted a civil suit against the railroads west of the Mississippi River. The complaint charged violations of the Sherman Antitrust Act by the Association of American Railroads, the officers and members of its board of directors, the Western Association of Railway Executives, two New York banking houses, J. P. Morgan and Company, Inc., and Kuhn, Loeb and Company, forty-seven railroads and their chief executives, and thirty-one other individuals. This suit which challenged, among other alleged violations of the antitrust laws, the group rate-making network of the railroads, was instituted by the filing of the complaint in the United States District Court for the District of Nebraska, at Lincoln, Nebraska, on August 23, 1944. This suit, officially titled the *United States versus Association of American Railroads, et al.,*[2] was commonly called the Western Railroad Agreement Case.

The stated purpose of the Department of Justice in instituting this civil action was to free the railroads from restrictive, noncompetitive practices, which the Department of Justice alleged existed in railroad technology, services and pricing. These

[2] 4 F. R. D. 510 (D. C. Nebr., 1945).

practices proved as injurious to the railroads as they were to the public.

Shortly after the filing of the antitrust suit by the Department of Justice in Lincoln, Nebraska, Governor Ellis Arnall of Georgia filed an original suit in the United States Supreme Court on behalf of his State against the eastern and southern railroads. The complaint of the State of Georgia charged these railroads with a rate-fixing conspiracy detrimental to the economy of the State and the South in violation of the antitrust laws. Governor Arnall made the oral argument for the State before the Supreme Court. He concluded his argument in words I shall never forget:

"When the last shot has been fired and the last boy has died in this war, I want the boys from Georgia who survive to return to their homes in Georgia and be able to make a living for themselves and their families and find a future unhampered by this conspiracy to retard the growth of Georgia and the South."

While the opinion of the Supreme Court was rendered pursuant to hearing on jurisdiction, the Court went further and laid down the law that governed the substantive questions in the case.[3]

The Court held that regulated industries are not *per se* exempt from the Sherman Antitrust Act; that conspiracies among carriers to fix rates are included within the broad sweep of the Sherman Antitrust Act; that none of the powers acquired by the Interstate Commerce Commission since the enactment of the Sherman Antitrust Act relate to the regulation of rate-fixing combinations; that the type of regulation which Congress chose did not eliminate the emphasis on competition and individual freedom of action in rate making; and that the fact that the rates which have been fixed may or may not be held unlawful by the Commission is immaterial to the issue before the Court.

Thus, the Supreme Court sustained the legal position of the State of Georgia and the Department of Justice. Soon thereafter the trials began.

It should be noted that during the years 1941 to 1945, exten-

[3] *Georgia vs. the Pennsylvania Railroad, et al.,* 324 U.S. 439 (1945).

sive hearings were held before the Senate Commerce Committee
and the House Interstate and Foreign Commerce Committee on
bills, sponsored by the transportation industry, to immunize the
railroads and other private companies performing public transportation services from the antitrust laws. My staff and I appeared and testified at all these hearings. These bills failed of
passage by the Congress.

During my administration of the Transportation Section in
the Antitrust Division, Attorney General Francis Biddle would
from time to time call me to his office to discuss transportation
problems as they related to the antitrust laws. One day in mid-
1942 at one of these discussions, he said:

"I am going to be asked many policy questions regarding
international aviation when this war ends, and even before. For
this purpose, I would like you to make a complete factual and
legal study of international aviation as a guide to post-war policy
determinations. I have arranged for you to receive such assistance as you may need from any department or agency of government, and you have authority to obtain whatever information
is available in government. You are also authorized to call on the
airlines for information, if necessary."

Fortunately, I was able to recruit an exceptionally competent
staff for this special task. Further, I was given complete cooperation, not only by the departments and agencies of the Federal
government, but by the airlines operating in the international
field. After extensive research, following exhaustive investigations, including numerous conferences with leaders in public and
private life in the international aviation field, all factual material
developed by my staff was carefully analyzed in the light of
international aviation laws and existing international conven-
tions and agreements. Thus, we were able to make specific policy
recommendations in our report.

The report was submitted to the Attorney General in late
1943. Since much of the material had some bearing on the war
effort, the report was classified, with copies sent only to the
President, the Secretary of State, the Chairman of the Civil
Aviation Board, and the Army and Navy Air Transport
Commands.

Our report became the basis of agreement of the free nations of the world at their First Provisional Aviation Convention, held in Chicago, Illinois, in 1944. I prize the memorandum from Attorney General Biddle stating that the conference chairman, Adolf Berle, wanted me to know how much the international aviation policy study made under my direction had helped him—"that in fact it was really the basis of the final agreement" among the free nations of the world. Recognition of a contribution so important to the solution of a difficult international problem is the real reward one receives for public service.

On one occasion, after I had argued a case on appeal involving an order of the Interstate Commerce Commission before a statutory three-judge court sitting as the District Court of the United States for the Southern District of New York, I prepared an outline of a book that had been on my mind for some time. There was need, I thought, for a book on the importance to the country and the transportation industry of the Justice Department's efforts to revive the antitrust laws in that industry.

During evenings and week-ends over a period of several years, with the encouragement and patience of my wife, I managed to complete the book which I entitled *Justice in Transportation*. Attorney General Francis Biddle gave his approval to the book, and Federal Judge Thurman Arnold, formerly Assistant Attorney General in charge of the Antitrust Division in the Department of Justice, wrote the introduction.

Advance printed copies of the manuscript were sent by the publisher to many prominent persons in public and private life, including the Vice President of the United States, Harry S. Truman. Vice President Truman's endorsement read: "A penetrating analysis of transporation problems. It should be read by everyone."

The Vice President's endorsement was given on March 26, 1945. President Franklin D. Roosevelt died on April 12, 1945, and Vice President Truman became President of the United States.

I became concerned that Mr. Truman, as President, would not wish to say about my book what he was willing to say as Vice President. I immediately asked the publisher to withhold all advertising matter with reference to Mr. Truman's endorsement made as Vice President until Mr. Truman's feelings in the matter could be ascertained. My friends gave varied advice. Finally, I called on my long-time friend, Senator Henrik Shipstead, with the result that he went to see President Truman on my behalf.

After Senator Shipstead explained to President Truman the problem which caused my concern, the President said: "I meant what I said when I gave that endorsement, and I still mean it. You can tell Mr. Wiprud that he can use the endorsement as I gave it."

The President, being rather pleased by the consideration shown him, added: "You know, Senator, it's refreshing to learn that there are still people in the world who do thoughtful things like this."

The act of Mr. Truman in endorsing *Justice in Transportation* when he was Vice President, and confirming that act when he became President of the United States, proved to be an important turning point in my life. For this, I shall always be grateful to him.

For personal reasons, I resigned as Special Assistant to the Attorney General in charge of the Transportation Section, Antitrust Division in the Department of Justice, on July 10, 1945, secure in the knowledge that the antitrust laws, as interpreted by the highest court in the land, had been revived in the transportation industry; and that this accomplishment was in the interest of the public and the future of transportation as a basic industry in our private enterprise economy.

PART TWO

AFTER I HAD RETURNED to private life, I learned that the organized railroad industry again turned to Congress for relief from the antitrust laws, though the antitrust suits instituted by the Department of Justice and the State of Georgia were being tried

Kindest regards to Arne C. Wiprud

Harry Truman

in the courts under those laws as interpreted by the Supreme
Court of the United States.

A bill to accomplish this purpose was introduced by Congressman Alfred L. Bulwinkle which, after a hearing and a favorable
committee report, passed the House of Representatives on December 10, 1945.

Among others, Governor Arnall of Georgia appeared before
the Senate Commerce Committee on the Bulwinkle bill which
was then before that committee. In summary, he testified that on
March 26, 1945, the Supreme Court sustained the jurisdiction of
the State of Georgia against the railroads; that the defendants on
May 26, 1945, filed their motions and answer, and that "made
the issue;" that the Supreme Court had appointed Lloyd K.
Garrison as Special Master to hear all the evidence; and that the
State's evidence had been presented to Mr. Garrison.

Governor Arnall then laid the basis for a presentation of the
evidence of conspiracy alleged in Georgia's case before the committee, as follows: "Now, then, it may please the committee, if
the Senate of the United States is going to try the Georgia case—
and that is what the Bulwinkle does—I want to have the permis-
sion of the committee to acquaint you with the conspiracy we are
talking about and to show you cases of its operation, to show how
it is operated and to show you what will actually happen if the
Bulwinkle bill becomes a law."

Over a period of three days, April 1 to 3, 1946, Governor
Arnall presented documentary evidence in support of his testimony on the conspiracy alleged in the complaint of the State of
Georgia; how the alleged conspiracy was formed by establishing
a nationwide organization of regional conferences and associations
and rate bureaus, headed by the Association of American
Railroads, "the object of which was to establish private domina-
tion and control over freight moving to and from the State of
Georgia by preventing individual railroads from initiating competitive rates in accordance with the provisions of the Interstate
Commerce Act; how the Bulwinkle bill would put the "stamp of
approval" on the operations of the Association of American Railroads and its subordinate conferences, associations, and rate bu-

reaus; how the alleged conspiracy functions, including its lobbying activities in relation to such legislation as the Bulwinkle bill; how other modes of transportation are related to the conspiracy; and the effect on the public interest if this national transportation conspiracy is immunized from the antitrust laws as provided in the Bulwinkle bill.

By letter, dated March 12, 1946, Senator Burton K. Wheeler, Chairman of the Senate Commerce Committee, requested me to appear and express my views on the Bulwinkle bill.

On April 4 and 5, 1946, I appeared as a private citizen and testified in opposition to the Bulwinkle bill. I concluded my testimony with this statement:

"Thus it appears that the Bulwinkle bill may well be the touchstone of our future economic life. If so, we might as well face it. Our free enterprise system will be gone. We will be substituting therefore a cartel economy. This means that our industries will be owned and operated by a few powerful groups—and our boys and girls who fought so valiantly for freedom abroad will have returned to find that they have lost opportunities and free enterprise at home.

"For all of the above reasons, I am constrained to respectfully suggest that this committee recess hearings on this legislation until the trials have been concluded and the courts, including our highest tribunal of justice, have rendered their judgments. That is the way of justice under our democratic form of government."

The Bulwinkle bill was reported by the Committee on June 18, 1946, but did not come to a vote in the Senate.

Five times since the passage of the Sherman Antitrust Act in 1890, the Congress of the United States refused to enact legislation exempting rate-making conferences of private companies performing public transportation services from the antitrust laws. In 1947, a sixth attempt was made. Spearheaded by the organized railroad industry, an all-out drive was launched by all modes of transportation to secure immunity from the antitrust laws for their conference rate making and other group activities.

On January 3, 1947, Congressman Bulwinkle introduced

another bill (H. R. 221), and on January 8, 1947, Senator Clyde M. Reed introduced a similar bill (S. 110), bills that were designed to provide the means of exempting from the Sherman Antitrust Act agreements between private companies performing public transportation service to fix rates collectively, and to engage in other noncompetitive agreements and practices.

The Department of Justice and the State of Georgia contended in testimony before Congressional committees that this legislation, if it became law, would deprive the courts of jurisdiction in the midst of conspiracy trials in the *Association of American Railroads* and the *State of Georgia* cases. The proponents of this legislation assured the committees that this legislation, if it became law, would not be used to deprive the courts of jurisdiction in these cases.

It was becoming evident that the representatives in Congress were beginning to weaken under the relentless campaign of the transportation industry under the leadership of the organized railroad industry.

A brief hearing on bill S. 110 was held in the Senate Commerce Committee on January 21 and February 4, 1947, at which, again on the invitation of Senator Wheeler, I was, as a private citizen, one of the witnesses in opposition to the bill. The Committee reported S. 110 on March 3, 1947, and the bill passed the Senate on June 18, 1947.

At the urgent request of my former associates in the Department of Justice and pursuant to an equally urgent call from Congressman Joseph P. O'Hara of Minnesota, I appeared, again as a private citizen, before the House Committee on Interstate and Foreign Commerce on June 27, and Monday, June 30, 1947, and testified in opposition to the Bulwinkle bill. I was the last opposition witness before the Committee and hence was under severe examination by many of the committee members. Indeed, at one point in my testimony, the Chairman endeavored to stop my testimony, but Congressman Robert Crosser objected, stating:

"Mr. Chairman, I would like to have the gentleman come back if he has some light to give us on this subject. I desire to hear it. We can find time for all of these other things and I think we can find time to listen to this gentleman."

I was permitted to continue my testimony.

Following an analysis of the provisions of S. 110, I concluded my testimony as follows:

"With all the facts before you, I believe you will reject this monopoly bill in favor of a sound program for transportation in the public interest—a program which insures the continuance of public transportation in this country as a legitimate and fruitful field for private enterprise."

Robert R. Young, speaking for the Federation of Railway Progress, which he organized, made the following statement concerning the Bulwinkle bill:

"The Federation of Railway Progress is opposed to the Bulwinkle bill. We recognize for practical purposes the necessity of maintaining rate conferences insofar as they are suitably regulated. However, we are categorically opposed to any attempt to legalize other non-competitive practices. For example, this bill would permit agreements among railroads to control such services to the traveler as air-conditioning, streamlining, flowers on dining car tables, or even the degree of comfort to be provided in a train seat—with I. C. C. approval. We believe that such competitive services and facilities should be left to the individual initiative of each railroad."

Robert W. Purcell, Vice President of the Chesapeake and Ohio Railway Company, after expressing the view that rate making by carriers presents a problem peculiar to the industry, testified:

"As far as our philosophy is concerned, agreements on services and facilities which are of a competitive nature are against the public interest. These are things which bring the railroad industry down to the level of the poorest and lowest, and which are simply against the public interest. . . . I want the committee to know insofar as those features of competitive service and facilities are concerned, I do not think that any legislation is necessary because I believe if those agreements are entered into which are unreasonable restraints that the antitrust laws should apply and that if agreements are entered into which are not unreasonable restraints of trade, then the antitrust laws do not apply . . . I do not understand that the antitrust laws prohibit a carrier from discussing and considering their operating, engineering, and other problems or from entering into agreements or taking other joint action respecting such matters which do not restrain trade or commerce."

These spokesmen within the industry stated the basis upon which private operation of public transportation services can be justified in the public interest.

The House Interstate and Foreign Commerce Committee reported H. R. 221, with amendments, and it was passed by the House of Representatives on May 11, 1948. The Senate refused to accept the House bill and it went to a conference committee. The conference committee report was then agreed to by the Senate and House of Representatives, and as S. 110, known as the Reed-Bulwinkle bill, was sent to President Truman for his approval.

President Truman, on June 1, 1948, in a message to Congress vetoing the Reed-Bulwinkle bill, stated:

"No legislation giving a major industry immunity from the antitrust laws should be enacted unless alternative safeguards are provided in the public interest. This bill fails to provide such safeguards.

"Power to control transportation rates is a power to influence the competitive success or failure of other businesses. Legislation furthering the exercise of this power by private groups would clearly be contrary to the public interest."

The President noted that certain railroad activities subject to the provisions of the bill were being challenged in the courts. In this connection, he stated: "It would not be proper to provide the immunity proposed before the cases are settled."

The President concluded his veto message with the statement: "The bill carries serious potential harm to the public."

At a time when Congress was in a mood to override the President's veto of several other bills passed by Congress, on June 16, 1948 in the Senate and June 17, 1948, in the House of

Representatives it overrode the President's veto of the Reed-Bulwinkle bill.

Contrary to the assurances of its proponents in testimony before Congressional committees during hearings on the Reed-Bulwinkle bill, the immunity from the antitrust laws provided for in the bill was used by the organized railroad industry to obtain the dismissal of the conspiracy cases brought by the Department of Justice and the State of Georgia.

Thus the transportation industry achieved its objective to legalize the cartelization of each mode of transportation in the United States. Will it prove another Pyrrhic victory for those private companies operating public transportation services in our otherwise free, competitive, private enterprise economy?

CHAPTER VII

Private Enterprise in Transportation

PART ONE

IT WAS EARLY IN JULY, 1945, shortly before my resignation as Special Assistant to the Attorney General became effective on July 10, that Judge Thurman Arnold resigned as Associate Justice of the United States Circuit Court of Appeals for the District of Columbia to enter private law practice. He called me to his chambers and proposed that I join him in establishing a law firm. I agreed, and the firm was established under the name of Arnold and Wiprud. My principal contribution to the firm was in the field of transportation.

In a suit instituted by the United States Government before a specially constituted district court of three Federal judges, sitting in Philadelphia, Pennsylvania, Pullman Incorporated, a holding company which owned all of the stock of Pullman-Standard Car Manufacturing Company (manufacturer of sleeping cars) and of The Pullman Company (operator of sleeping cars), was held to constitute a monopoly in violation of the Sherman Antitrust Act.[1] The sleeping car service included a pool of about 6,250 heavyweight sleeping cars of obsolete design, the control and operation of which, under exclusive dealing contracts between The Pullman Company and the railroads, enabled Pullman Incorporated to maintain a complete monopoly of the busi-

---

[1] *United States v. Pullman Co., et al.,* 50 F. Supp. 123 (1943)

ness of manufacturing and servicing sleeping cars for the railroads of the United States.

Pursuant to the trial court's opinion both the Government and The Pullman Company submitted forms of a proposed judgment. The Government urged that Pullman Incorporated should be directed to dispose of the manufacturing business and continue to operate an equipment service pool. On January 22, 1944, the court held, one judge dissenting, that Pullman Incorporated should have the choice as to which one of its two businesses it would continue to operate.[2] On May 8, 1944, the court entered an order requiring the complete and perpetual separation of the manufacturing business and the sleeping car business of the defendants.[3] Pullman Incorporated elected to dispose of its sleeping car business.

Pursuant to this election, from September 1944 to March 1945 plans were formulated and a proposal put forward by Pullman Incorporated to sell the sleeping car business. Not until May 12, 1945, however, was a definite proposition made to sell the stock of The Pullman Company (the sleeping car business) to the railroads. The price was to be about $75,000,000. Instead of taking affirmative action on this offer, a committee representing the railroads proposed a delay of eighteen months from March 22, 1946.

At this stage in these court proceedings, Robert R. Young, Chairman of the Board of the Chesapeake and Ohio Railway Company, on July 26, 1945, asked me if I would be interested in acting as counsel in his effort to purchase The Pullman Company's sleeping car business. I answered in the affirmative on behalf of my new firm.

Working with Mr. Young and his associates in this enterprise, Alan Kirby, and Cyrus K. Eaton and William R. Daley of Otis & Co., we gathered facts from every available source essential to an effective presentation to the court of the offer of the Young-Kirby-Otis group to purchase the sleeping car business of The Pullman Company.

[2] 53 F. Supp. 908.
[3] 55 F. Supp. 985.

On August 27, 1945, Otis & Co., on behalf of itself, Robert R. Young, and Alan Kirby, intervened in the court proceedings and submitted its offer to purchase the stock of The Pullman Company upon substantially the same terms and for substantially the same sum, $75,000,000, as those that Pullman Incorporated had offered to the railroads. That offer conformed in every particular to the decree of the court. It assured not only complete separation of the sleeping car business from any manufacturing interest, but also complete separation of the sleeping car business from those railroad and banking interests which were shown by the record to have joined with The Pullman Company in discriminating against smaller railroads and suppressing the modernization of the sleeping car business.

In its intervening petition Otis & Co. described the stagnation of production and service which the Pullman monopoly had created in sleeping car transportation. It stated that the present fleet of about 6,250 heavyweight Pullman cars was in a deteriorated condition; that in design they were obsolete; that their weight was excessive causing unnecessary expense in fuel cost and roadbed repair and preventing speedy travel. It showed that if the railroads were to compete effectively with air and motor transportation, the entire fleet must be replaced with modern lightweight equipment.

To meet this need to dissipate the effects of the past monopoly, and through competition to restore the expansion of the business which had been halted for years, Otis & Co. proposed to place immediate orders for sleeping car equipment to replace the entire fleet within five years at an estimated cost of $500,000,000. In addition it committed itself and the group it represented to set up a network of agencies over the entire United States to develop, promote and advertise recreational and educational travel.

After Otis & Co. came forward with its offer, the major railroads were faced with the necessity of taking positive steps in their plan to dismember the pool of sleeping cars, a plan which would prevent its modernization and expansion. This was dra-

To Anne C. Wifred
With all good wishes
Robert R. Young

Dorothy Wilding

Robert R. Young

matically shown by the memorandum of W. F. Place, vice president of the New York Central Railroad Company, of record in the Pullman case.[4] After pointing out the ultimate advantages of dismemberment of the pool, he wrote:

While this may be the ultimate situation in the future, the railroads appear to be faced with the necessity of immediate action as the result of the petition by the syndicate of Otis & Co.

Thus it was not the crisis in sleeping car transportation but the crisis caused by the Otis-Young-Kirby offer which compelled the major railroads to take action for the first time in the two and a half years which had elapsed since the decree of the trial court.

Several other bids were then submitted to purchase Pullman's sleeping car business at the same price offered by the Otis-Young-Kirby group, but without a commitment to modernize the old sleeping car fleet. Included among these bids was one from a combination of railroads doing most of the passenger-carrying business in the railroad industry.

Hearings were held by the court and evidence taken with respect to all offers before it. It was my task to present evidence through such witnesses as William R. Daley, President of Otis & Co., Mr. Young, and others, in support of the Otis & Co. offer. Former Judge Thurman Arnold and former United States Senator Robert J. Bulkley made the oral arguments.

Following the hearings on the various offers to purchase Pullman's sleeping car service, the trial court entered its final order and decree on January 4, 1946, approving the offer of the combination of railroads.[5] In so doing the three judges, as a court of equity, held that they could not substitute a judicial judgment for the decision of Pullman Incorporated, the proprietor of The Pullman Company.

An appeal was taken by the United States Government direct to the United States Supreme Court from the final order

[4] Hearing on petition for approval of offer to purchase The Pullman Company, R-2278, 2303.
[5] 64 F. Supp. 168 (1946).

and decree of the trial court, entered January 4, 1946, approving the sale of The Pullman Company to a combination of railroads. Otis & Co. also appealed, filed a brief, and participated in oral argument.

A four to four memorandum decision of the Supreme Court, one Justice abstaining, had the effect of permitting the decision of the lower Federal court to stand.[6]

Mr. Young said to me after the Supreme Court's brief "tie" memorandum decision in the Pullman case, "No one could have done more than you have done to win this case."

Nevertheless, I felt that this was an unsatisfactory outcome of a great effort by Mr. Young and his associates to modernize essential segments of railroad transportation, segments that had deteriorated so tragically and had been so costly to the railroad industry and the public under the many years of monopolistic control by Pullman Incorporated and its wholly-owned subsidiaries, aided by interlocking directorates with the larger railroads and their bankers.

It was after the Supreme Court decision in the Pullman case that Mr. Young asked me if I would be interested in his effort to establish a transcontinental railroad system. I answered in the affirmative. Soon thereafter, Mr. Young became interested in acquiring control of the New York Central Railroad Company. At the time I assumed that this new interest had much to do with his plans for a transcontinental railroad system.

Railroad managements, generally, were opposed to Mr. Young's efforts to modernize the industry's operations and services and thus, as he put it, "bring the railroads into the Twentieth Century," efforts which they and their bankers considered "unorthodox." Mr. Young's success in the financial reorganization of the Chesapeake and Ohio, Nickel Plate, and Wabash railroads on a voluntary basis, an accomplishment praised by the Interstate Commerce Commission in its approving report[7] did little to overcome the hostility of railroad managements and their bankers. This was evident during the hearings on the Otis-

[6] 330 U.S. 806 (1947).
[7] 261 I.C.C. 239 (1945).

Young-Kirby offer in the Pullman case and undoubtedly was a factor in the outcome.

The organized railroad industry overlooked a great opportunity when it opposed Mr. Young's efforts to determine, through the acquisition of The Pullman Company's sleeping car business, the areas of the United States in which the railroads could profitably modernize their passenger-train equipment and operations, including the sleeping car business, and, conversely, in what areas such operations could not be profitably operated despite gigantic strides forward in science and technology. Thus, Mr. Young could have served the railroad industry well by widening its horizons to a point where it might have made a meaningful effort to determine whether modern, comfortable, high-speed passenger equipment, efficiently operated, replacing obsolete, inefficient, and costly-to-operate equipment and slow and costly service, would be publicly accepted in important areas of the country, as they have been and are increasingly being accepted in other industrial countries.

With the conclusion of the Pullman case, I decided to devote myself wholly to transportation matters and accordingly withdrew from the firm of Arnold and Wiprud.

In addition to Mr. Young and the Chesapeake and Ohio Railway Company, my other clients included Hans Isbrandtsen, President of The Isbrandtsen Company, Inc. Like Mr. Young, Mr. Isbrandtsen was a rugged individualist. Hans, as his friends affectionately called him, had followed the sea all his life. A master seaman, he had also acquired over the years a thorough knowledge of the complex subject of foreign trade. These accomplishments, plus integrity, a self-reliant and forthright manner, were a combination that enabled him to conduct his business successfully without government subsidy for his steamship operations in competition with subsidized United States and foreign steamship lines.

A strong believer in private enterprise, Mr. Isbrandtsen refused to permit his steamship company to join the international steamship conferences of his competitors. Among other activities, these conferences agreed upon uniform rates to be charged ship-

pers. The weapon which these conferences used against independent steamship lines, such as Isbrandtsen Company's steamship
line, was a provision in their conference agreements for the making of dual rates. Under this provision, if a shipper did business
with a steamship line not a member of the conference, he would
have to pay a 9½ per cent higher rate to the conference lines
than a shipper who refused to do business with an independent
line. Thus the conferences, which were in fact international cartels to which the subsidized United States steamship companies
were parties, sought to force independent steamship companies
out of business. Some of the larger shippers in the United States,
however, continued to give the Isbrandtsen Company a substantial part of their foreign business because they liked Hans Isbrandtsen, the steamship services his company provided, and,
further, they wanted to keep a real competitor in the field.

I was retained by Mr. Isbrandtsen to work with John J.
O'Conner, the Washington, D. C. attorney for the Isbrandtsen
Company, in his legal battle against dual rate-making agreements and the practices of the international steamship conferences, which included as members the subsidized United States
steamship companies. Following extended hearings before the
United States Maritime Commission on complaint of the Isbrandtsen Lines, the Commission's decision was carried through
the lower Federal courts to the Supreme Court of the United
States. The Supreme Court held the dual rate-making provision
of the steamship conferences, designed and used to prevent shippers from patronizing independent steamship lines, to be illegal—
a signal victory for Hans Isbrandtsen and his independent
steamship company.[8]

In the years that followed the ending of the Pullman case,
the railroads, members of the combine that purchased The Pullman Company, have virtually abandoned the sleeping car business and most of their passenger business. The reasons given by
railroad managements for abandoning so much of their passenger services include such statements as "the passengers have left
the railroads; they have gone to the private automobile, motor

[8] 356 U.S. 481 (1958).

buses, and the airplane"; "the government has taken away mail from our passenger trains which has deprived us of needed revenue to operate these trains profitably"; and "we cannot compete with subsidized motorbus and airline companies in the transportation of passengers." Let us briefly examine the first and third of these contentions in the light of the opportunities, the attitude, and the program of the organized railroad industry. The other contention will be considered later.

In 1926, an able and respected railroad executive, Ralph Budd, then President of the Great Northern Railway Company, made a notable address in Des Moines, Iowa. His theme was that railroad executives should consider themselves "transportation men" and as such provide the public with whatever form of transportation would best meet its needs, including transportation by motor vehicle, by barges on inland waterways, and even by aircraft. None of these newer forms of transportation were under regulations at that time and the railroads could have entered these fields at will.

Mr. Budd elaborated on the point that the then extensive and costly program of the organized railroad industry to hinder and delay, in an effort to stop the development of these newer forms of transporation "would not return one cent to the treasuries of the railroads." He stated that the new and rapidly growing automobile industry had been a boon to the railroads in the form of rail transportation of vast quantities of raw materials and finished products to all parts of the United States. He documented his facts and concluded with a plea that the industry abandon its negative program and actively participate in these new and changing transportation developments in the interest of the railroads and the nation. But Mr. Budd's masterful effort went unheeded. The railroads' program to suppress newer forms of transportation proceeded to its inevitable defeat. The organized railroad industry was not at this time interested in becoming "transportation men" to better serve the public.

Despite all obstacles, these newer forms of transportation developed and grew to meet the increasing public demand. The government, as is well known, helped mightily in the form of rights-of-way for motor transport, airlanes and terminals for airlines, dams for waterways, and in other related matters, including, most importantly, research into new and better equipment and ways of performing these alternative services. But railroad managements remained aloof. With the state of mind that they appeared to have at the time, it is doubtful whether these newer forms of transportation under Mr. Budd's concept, even with government assistance, could have developed to the degree that they have in the intervening years.

Thus the railroads lost a real opportunity to enter new fields of public transportation, so greatly encouraged by government, which they now complain has been so successfully undertaken by others. But that was not all—by subsequent action they practically foreclosed themselves from another such opportunity.

In what it believed was in furtherance of its program against newer modes of transportation, the organized railroad industry turned to Congress and sponsored legislation to regulate them "as we are regulated." Congress obliged, but included restrictions which prevented the railroads from freely entering these newer forms of transportation.[9]

Thereafter, the policy of the organized railroad industry changed. With the Transportation Association of America, which it had sponsored and with which it was closely allied, the organized railroad industry announced a "plan to establish regional integrated transportation systems which would control and operate all rail, motor, water and air transport facilities and services throughout large geographic areas." Thus the railroads would convert themselves into regional "transportation" corporations. To achieve this objective, the announced intention was to immediately seek the following:

1. Congressional declaration of policy in favor of such regional integrated transportation systems.

2. The revision of the Transportation Act of 1940 with respect to pooling and mergers.

[9] Interstate Commerce Act, Secs. 5 (2) (b) and 207.

3. The repeal of the Sherman Antitrust Act as it applies to transportation companies.

4. The repeal of the Panama Canal Act to the extent that it prevents common ownership of rail and water carriers.

5. The modification of all other statutory provisions which have the effect of encouraging "unnecessary and destructive competition."

The organized railroad industry also announced its intention to seek legislation providing, among other things, for the establishment of a single regulatory body with responsibility over all forms of transportation and with power to control the expenditure of public moneys for the construction of additional transportation facilities.

One of the numerous public letters of the Transportation Association of America on the "plan" to establish regional integrated transportation systems, stated:[10] "They (the railroad owners) are not concerned whether their returns come from water, rail, bus, or air services."

Many prominent persons in public and private life opposed this grandiose scheme to monopolize public transportation in the United States. The Brotherhood of Railroad Trainmen, with understandable concern over the policies of those who guided the destinies of the railroads, stated the prevailing view that the accomplishment of this scheme would "put across the most gigantic utility monopoly this Nation has ever seen."[11]

Since the "power to control transportation rates is a power to influence the competitive success or failure of other businesses," such power in a gigantic utility monopoly of all forms of public transportation could be the end of our free, competitive, private enterprise system. Such a development could force the Federal government to nationalize all public transportation in the United States. The early demise of this transportation monopoly proposal avoided, at least for the time being, this tragedy for the Nation.

---

[10] Monthly letter No. 6 of the Transportation Association of America, dated November 6, 1943.

[11] The Railroad Trainmen, January 1944, p. 11.

P A R T   T W O[1]

FOLLOWING SEVERAL YEARS dealing almost entirely with head-end passenger-train traffics—mail, express and baggage—Robert R. Young, in August, 1952, asked me to undertake a study of the Chesapeake and Ohio Railway's contract with the Railway Express Agency. Aside from the legal aspects of that contract, the task was to determine the extent to which operations thereunder contributed to the railroad's passenger-train deficits and to recommend to its management a businesslike solution.

Strange as it may seem, no such study of the Railway Express Agency contract had been made by the management of any railroad. Indeed, since each railroad had not kept books on the handling and transportation of express on its lines under that contract, no railroad knew the amount of the losses from its express traffic. The study initiated by Mr. Young would be the first to develop this important information for railroad management.

My previous study of the Railway Express Agency's uniform contract with the nation's railroads had revealed these equally amazing facts:

The basis for compensation for services performed by the railroads for the Railway Express Agency, a corporation owned by 68 railroads, was as follows: through uniform contracts, binding on the railroads for a period of 25 years from March 1, 1929, it was provided that the Railway Express Agency should take the gross express transportation revenues, deduct all its expenses, and turn the balance, if any (and at times, for many railroads there was no balance), under a complicated formula, over to the railroads for performing the line-haul express service. Thus, the agent, the express agency, controlled the funds of its principals, the railroads, and in addition had all its expenses underwritten by its principals.

[1] This Part is not in chronological order because of a desire to achieve a proper distribution of topic matter. Between the events related in Parts I and II of this chapter, at the request of President Truman and Postmaster General Donaldson, I served as an official in charge of transportation cases in the United States Post Office Department, as related in Chapter VIII.

Such an organizational and financial set-up was without parallel in any other industry. Dupont, General Motors, General Electric, or any other successful business, would not long survive if they gave their agents, even those they wholly or cooperatively owned, control of their funds and a "blank check" thereon for expenses. The railroads are no exception.

Admittedly, the losses to the railroads *as a group* from express traffice during the many years since their exclusive-dealing contracts with the Railway Express Agency were entered into, were huge. No one knows the exact amount of these losses since, as stated, each railroad had not kept books on the handling and transportation of express on its lines, but in no year since 1946 had the railroads *collectively* estimated in proceedings before the Interstate Commerce Commission that their losses were less than $125 million per year. They claimed a loss of $129 million in 1950 and the Commission estimated the loss in 1951 to be about $145 million. If these losses were figured at $100 million per year, then the losses to the railroads from their contracts with the Railway Express Agency over the period from March 1, 1929, to March 1, 1952, were more than $2 billion.

This huge deficit constituted a burden which fell almost entirely on the railroads' carload freight traffic. Obviously, it cut several ways in that it not only reduced the railroads' net revenues from all operations, but it impaired their ability to compete in performing modern passenger as well as freight services. If shippers of freight refused to carry this deficit burden any longer and turned to other forms of transport, and the railroads were unable to reduce rates to meet competition because of this deficit burden, then freight volume and revenues would decrease, thus adding to the railroads' financial difficulties. Clearly, then, railroad managements should no longer ignore their express deficit burden.

In accordance with arrangements made by Mr. Young for my study of the Chesapeake and Ohio Railway's contract with the Railway Express Agency, I called on the railroad's President, Walter J. Touhy. During our discussion, Mr. Tuohy expressed the opinion that my study should be independently made. He authorized me to retain such assistance as needed, with the understanding that the officers and employees of the railroad would cooperate in supplying pertinent information that was in the possession of the railroad. Further, Mr. Tuohy requested the President of the Railway Express Agency to provide data and information for the study that was wholly in the possession of the Agency.

Based on the comprehensive field study which William E. Turner, a long-time employee of Mr. Young, and I made of the Railway Express Agency's plant, operations and personnel on the Chesapeake and Ohio Railway Company's lines, the data supplied by the Railway Express Agency and the Chesapeake and Ohio Railway Company, the information obtained from the reports and records of the Interstate Commerce Commission, and the thorough analysis of costs and related data by Wilbur R. Warren, a cost expert familiar with the express business of the railroads, our report to the management of the Chesapeake and Ohio Railway was made on December 4, 1952.

The report showed that the railroad received from the Railway Express Agency, in the year 1951, $570,330, representing 19.82 per cent of gross express transportation revenues on the railroad, for performing line-haul express transportation service at a total cost of $4,545,044, or at a deficit of $3,955,044!

In the year 1946, the Chesapeake and Ohio Railway received only $322,331, or 6.99 per cent, out of $4,291,204 in gross express transportation revenues on its line. Over the years 1939 to 1951, the railroad received from the express agency an average of 20 per cent of the gross express transportation revenues on its lines; the express agency received 80 per cent.

Our report to the management of the Chesapeake and Ohio Railway Company recommended that it take over and operate its own express business. Since this railroad is a comparatively small express carrier, the management determined that leadership in the reorganization of the express business on the nation's railroads should be undertaken by one of the larger express-carrying railroads.

Some months after Mr. Young had acquired control of the

New York Central Railroad Company, I was invited to attend a luncheon meeting with him and members of his staff in New York City. Mr. Young presided at the meeting which was attended by the new president, Alfred E. Perlman, and other officials of the railroad, and the new president of the New York, New Haven and Hartford Railroad Company, Patrick B. McGinnis.

As I entered the room, Mr. Young asked me to take the seat at the end of the long table, and added: "You are going to do all the talking."

I knew that he wanted me to discuss the head-end passenger-train traffics of the railroads, with particular reference to their uniform contract with the Railway Express Agency. Since the New York Central was the largest carrier of express, I devoted most of my presentation to the express agency contract and the unbusinesslike and costly nature of that contract as developed in our pilot study of express on the Chesapeake and Ohio Railway Company.

When I had completed my presentation, Mr. McGinnis, who was seated next to me, made some remarks about express and the other head-end passenger-train traffics that prompted me to put my hand on his arm and say, "Mr. McGinnis, pardon me, but out of my experience I must say that you are quite mistaken, and I will tell you why."

When I concluded, he turned to Mr. Young and said, "Bob, if you can spare this young man for a few days, I would like to take him with me to New Haven this afternoon so that he can talk to my staff about this matter. Apparently, I have been misinformed."

After what seemed to be a full minute, Mr. Young said, "Go ahead."

When Mr. McGinnis and I arrived at his office in New Haven, his entire official staff was waiting for us. My presentation, which prompted many questions, was well received. Mr. McGinnis then asked me to undertake a study of the New Haven Railroad's contract with the Railway Express Agency. I agreed if Mr. Young would approve and if I could select a staff from the qualified experts within his organization. Mr. McGinnis obtained Mr. Young's approval and then told me to pick the men I needed for the task.

Upon my return to New York, I was told that New York Central's Vice President of Passenger Traffic, E. C. Nickerson, wanted to see me. I immediately went to his office. He asked if I would be willing to undertake a study of the Railway Express Agency's contract with the New York Central to be made under his general supervision. I answered that I would, for I knew that this was what Mr. Young wanted me to do. Mr. Nickerson said that I could select a staff outside the railroad or one from the railroad. I answered that I would prefer to select a staff from men on the railroad.

The selection of a staff for the express study on the New York Central was simplified for me by the complete cooperation and assistance of the official family of the railroad. The field work, which developed the basic data for the report, was the result of teamwork in which men experienced in this field in the offices of General Managers of the various districts of the railroad cooperated with members of the staff of W. M. Smith, Manager, Express and Mail, in Vice President Nickerson's department, and engineers on the staff of A. B. Pulliam, Chief Industrial Engineer of the Railroad. W. R. Main, Director, Passenger Service Economics, made the study of train savings.

Manager Smith, a recognized authority in this field, assisted with his knowledge, his active participation, and the resources of his office. He assigned R. J. Welsh, Mail and Express Agent in his office, to assist me as supervisor of the field force. Mr. Welsh also processed the vast amount of factual material, including the cost of data, and prepared the exhibits which contained the underlying and supporting material for the report. A. A. Burkhardt, General Supervisor, Stations and Motor Services, in the office of the Vice President-Operations, developed the material relating to station operations and trucking. The Railway Express Agency supplied all the information requested and cooperated in the field studies.

The task was long and arduous, but the sustained enthusiasm

of all those on the New York Central associated with the study was remarkable. Perhaps it was because they learned the facts about a branch of the railroad's business that had been ignored, if not forgotten, at great cost to all railroads. Obviously, the time for a complete reorganization of this segment of the railroads' business on a sound basis in accordance with modern methods, techniques, and skills, was long overdue.

For these reasons, and perhaps others, the men associated with the express study on the New York Central seemed proud to have a major part, and as it developed a decisive part, in the successful effort by the managements of the New York Central and other railroads in bringing about a reorganization of their express business. It was for me a real opportunity and a great experience to have been associated with such a dedicated group of men.

Our report to the President of the New York Central, Alfred E. Perlman, was submitted on December 21, 1955. The report showed that the railroad received from the Railway Express Agency in the year 1954, $12,765,304, representing 27.15 per cent of the gross express transportation revenues on the railroad of $47,021,451, for performing the line-haul express transportation service.

As reported by the Comptroller of the New York Central, the loss sustained by the railroad from its express traffic in 1954 was $7,525,433, based on its transportation expenses, including rents and taxes (excluding Federal income taxes). On a similar basis, the Comptroller stated the railroad's loss for 1952 to be $10,334,158 and for 1953, $9,033,550. Comparable figures for the years prior to 1952, when payments by the Railway Express Agency to the New York Central each year were approximately *one-half* of those received in the years 1952, 1953, and 1954, were not available.

For the years 1939-1954, the gross express transportation revenues produced by the express traffic on the New York Central were divided, $541,707,663 for the Railway Express Agency and $149,403,922 for the Central. The percentages were 78.38 for the Railway Express Agency and 21.62 per cent for the New York

To Arne
With warm
regards
Al Perlman

Alfred E. Perlman, president, the New York Central Railroad
Company

Central. For these years, New York Central's express traffic produced average earnings per car-mile of only 18.42 cents.

These huge losses on the New York Central from its express business, led, as in the study on the Chesapeake and Ohio Railway Company, to an appraisal of the net revenue results to the railroad of performing its own express business, separate and distinct from the Railway Express Agency.

The similarity of the express and the bulk of the mail traffic, plus the fact that the New York Central had government authority to conduct motor vehicle services in connection with its rail service, primarily for the transportation of L. C. L. freight, in two of its districts, and had applications pending before government agencies for such authority in two other districts, led to the concept that express, mail and L. C. L. freight could be advantageously combined for transportation in coordinated rail-truck service.

To carry out this new and enlarged role for its trucking service, the report recommended that the New York Central should establish its own trucking company. Even though the operating rights were restricted, they were adequate for the coordinated rail-truck service outlined in the report.

Our field study demonstrated that there was no longer need for the 168 salaried express offices or the 467 express commission agencies on the New York Central and that express work in these offices and agencies should be concentrated in 55 express rail-terminal points on the New York Central. Basic to this approach would be the coordination of New York Central's rail-truck services at these 55 rail-terminal points, to which points the express would move by rail and from which it would be transported by truck to intermediate points. Traffic originating at intermediate points would, of course, move in reverse sequence.

The report states that the net gain on an "above the rail" basis to the New York Central in 1954, if it had performed its own express business in coordinated rail-truck service with mail and L. C. L. freight, would be $5,252,555. Subsequent detailed cost studies, however, made following the inauguration of coordinated rail-truck services for express, mail and L. C. L. freight in the various districts of the New York Central, including terminal savings and salvage of discontinued trains, show the net gain to New York Central approximated $8,000,000.

Shortly after receiving our express report, President Perlman called a meeting of his top officials. After a discussion of the report, Mr. Perlman turned to three of his vice-presidents and said, "You are the first board of directors of the New York Central's new trucking company which will be called the New York Central Transport Company. It will take over and expand New York Central's existing trucking operations," adding, "and this I want done right away."

He then turned to me and said, "First things first,—before we can establish an effective coordinated rail-truck service, we must have a trucking subsidiary that can perform the trucking end of the service."

Thus was the report received by President Perlman and a beginning made to completely reorganize the handling and transportation of mail, express and L. C. L. freight on the New York Central Railroad.

I was able to direct the express study on the New Haven Railroad at the time I was directing the New York Central express study. This was made possible by the complete cooperation I received from the official staff of the railroad, the officials of the railroad's trucking company, the New England Transportation Company, and the officials of the Railway Express Agency.

Our report, submitted to the President of the New Haven Railroad, Patrick B. McGinnis, on June 1, 1955, disclosed that, for the years 1939-1954, the gross express transportation revenues on the railroad were divided 78.39 per cent to the Railway Express Agency and 21.61 per cent to the railroad, which resulted in substantial annual deficits to this comparatively small express carrier for performing the line-haul express service. *The loss in 1954, for example, was $491,255.* The losses for the years prior to 1954 were larger, particularly for the years prior to 1952 when

the Express Agency's payments to the New Haven Railroad
each year were from *one-third to one-half* less than those received
by it in the years 1952, 1953, and 1954.

The report made recommendations to the management of
the New Haven Railroad for the reorganization of its express
business similar to those made in the New York Central's express
report, namely, that the New Haven should take over and operate its own express business; that there was no longer need for
the 69 exclusive express offices and the 62 express commission
agencies on the railroad and that the work of these offices and
agencies should be concentrated in the 8 rail-terminal points
named in the report for coordinated rail-truck service of express,
mail and L. C. L. freight; that the extensive and duplicating
truck services performed by the Railway Express Agency should
be performed by the trucks of the New England Transportation
Company "fanning out" from the rail-terminal points, as well as
the over-the-road trucking services from the named common
points.

Such reorganization of the express business on the New Haven Railroad, made possible by the far-flung motor-carrier operating rights of the New England Transportation Company,
would improve service and materially reduce costs.

A few months after Mr. McGinnis resigned as President of
the New Haven Railroad and became President of the Boston
and Maine Railroad, I learned that he had telephoned Mr.
Perlman, President of the New York Central, and asked if I
could be made available to direct a study of express on The
Boston and Maine Railroad. Mr. Perlman agreed, if my time
permitted.

Despite my heavy schedule as consultant to the New York
Central Railroad, I undertook this task. Again, I was fortunate
in receiving the complete cooperation of the official family of the
Boston and Maine Railroad. Ralph G. Fritch, Manager of
Head-end Passenger-train Traffics of the railroad, was assigned
to supervise the study, particularly the field work. As in other
studies, the Railway Express Agency supplied all the informa-

tion requested, as did the Boston and Maine Transportation Company, the trucking subsidiary of the railroad.

Our report, submitted to President McGinnis on October 5, 1956, showed that, for the years 1939-1955, the gross express transportation revenues on the Boston and Maine Railroads were divided 78.06 per cent to the Railway Express Agency and 21.94 per cent to the railroad, which also resulted in substantial annual deficits for this small express carrier. *The loss in 1955, for example, was $645,051.* The losses for the years prior to 1955 were large, particularly for the years prior to 1952, when the Railway Express Agency's payments to the Boston and Maine Railroad each year were *one-half or less* than those received in the years 1952, 1953, and 1954.

The Railway Express Agency's plant on the Boston and Maine Railroad, as set forth in the report, consisted of 146 stations, of which 72 were exclusive express stations and 74 were express commission agencies, In addition to its extensive pickup and delivery services at the exclusive express stations and at 17 express commission agencies, the Express Agency operated 10 over-the-road truck routes in the Boston and Maine Railroad's territory. There were 5 exclusive express stations and 14 express commission agencies on these truck routes, other than those listed above. To the extent that these trucking services parallel or serve the same communities as do the trucking services of the Boston and Maine Transportation Company, they, of course, constituted a duplication of such services, the cost of which fell, in major part, on the railroad.

These and other facts developed by the field study led to the conclusion that there was no longer need for the 72 exclusive express offices and the 74 express commission agencies on the Boston and Maine Railroad and that express work at these offices and agencies should be concentrated at the 12 rail-terminal points on the railroad named in the report.

Basic to this approach was the coordination of Boston and Maine's rail-truck services at these rail-terminal points and from these points express, with mail and L. C. L. freight, would be transported by truck to intermediate points. Traffic originating at intermediate points would, of course, move in reverse sequence.

In summary, the recommendations in the express report on the Boston and Maine Railroad paralleled those made in prior studies on the Chesapeake and Ohio, the New York Central, and the New Haven railroads.

Before all of these studies were completed, the railroads' uniform contract with the Railway Express Agency, which terminated on February 28, 1954, was renewed. Aside from the studies of the results under that contract made at the direction of Mr. Young, Mr. Perlman, Mr. Tuohy and Mr. McGinnis, other railroad executives made no effort to appraise the physical plant of the Express Agency on their railroads to determine to what extent it was obsolete, or to make an appraisal of costs to determine whether they could materially increase express revenues to their railroads by changing their method of handling and transporting express. Instead, the same old concepts, proven so disastrous to the railroads over a quarter of a century, were churned over and perpetuated in the new contracts, with the principal result that the distribution of the *residue* of gross express revenues which the railroads receive for performing the line-haul express service was reshuffled on a regional basis.

In the then pending express case before the Interstate Commerce Commission, Commissioner Knudson, in referring to the new uniform express contract, observed that, "It is as if the railroads were giving aspirin to a patient that needs an electrocardiograph reading and a radical change in his way of life."

The new 20-year uniform express contract, patterned after the old contract, was subject to cancellation by any railroad after four years and 10 months from March 1, 1954. This right of cancellation provided sufficient time to complete all the studies and reports on the Railway Express Agency's contract as it affected the Chesapeake and Ohio, the New York Central, the New Haven, and the Boston and Maine railroads, and, based thereon, to obtain serious consideration by other railroad managements of this costly area of their business.

The cumulative effect of these express studies, which brought to the attention of railroad managements for the first time the true facts about their express business, was decisive. The leadership was taken by the President of the New York Central Railroad, Alfred E. Perlman, when he served notice of cancellation of his railroad's contract with the Railway Express Agency. He was accorded widespread support in the railroad industry which led to serious talks about what to do with the Express Agency.

The end result was the reorganization of the Railway Express Agency along the lines of the alternative suggested by the Interstate Commerce Commission, namely, that the Agency would compensate the railroads for the transportation of express as they are compensated for the transportation of mail, at fair and reasonable rates. On this basis, the Agency would be continued as a common carrier under the Interstate Commerce Act and as such it would continue to collect all the express revenues. Out of these revenues, as stated, the Agency would pay the railroads fair and reasonable rates for the line-haul and terminal switching of express, and operate on the remainder of the gross express revenues.

The express studies on the Chesapeake and Ohio, New York Central, New Haven and Boston and Maine railroads would not have been made except for Robert R. Young. While executives of other railroads were skeptical, he initiated the studies to learn how and to what extent this ancient method of conducting an all-but-forgotten segment of the railroads' business affected their revenues. As the result of the report of these studies, railroad managements learned for the first time of their unbelievably unbusinesslike, long-term contractual arrangement that cost the American railroads more than $2 billion during the second quarter of the twentieth century.

The reports on these studies did more—they outlined for railroad managements a new method of handling and transporting express, along with mail and other homologous traffics, expeditiously and at lower costs.

The owners and managers of the American railroads would have honored themselves if they had evidenced some appreciation to Mr. Young during his lifetime for his leadership towards removing this huge deficit burden from their railroads.

In relating the facts developed in studies of the railroads' uniform contract with their wholly-owned Railway Express Agency, I have noted the railroads' resistance to change in this area of their business over which they had sole control. Since the turn of the century, there were other areas in which the railroads resisted constructive change that also proved extremely costly to them.

The Transportation Act of 1920, sponsored by the railroads over widespread public opposition, and its implementation by the Interstate Commerce Commission and the railroads, substantially raised railroad rates, thus accelerating the public demand and support for the development of newer forms of transportation; the railroad cartel-monopoly set-up under the Western Railroad Agreement was as detrimental to the interests of the railroads as it was to the public; the program of the organized railroad industry to stop the development of newer forms of transportation was a costly and humiliating failure for the railroads; refusal of the organized railroad industry to heed the advice of one of the railroads' most respected and able presidents—that railroad executives should consider themselves transportation men—was an irretrievable error—for the railroads; the organized railroad industry sponsored the enactment of legislation to regulate the newer forms of transportation "as we are regulated," rather than taking the opportunity to obtain from Congress constructive revisions in outmoded railroad regulatory laws; and the cartel-monopoly concept of regional transportation corporations that would own or control and operate all rail, motor, water and air transport throughout large geographic areas of the United States, was another costly proposal of the organized railroad industry that was finally abandoned after it found no public support.

The legislation sponsored by the organized railroad industry, immunizing private corporations operating the railroads and other forms of public transportation from the antitrust laws for all their major non-competitive agreements and practices, may be the most costly of all the policy decisions for the railroads. This legislation was finally enacted by Congress over the veto of the President of the United States. His veto message concluded with the statement, "This bill carries serious potential harm to the public."

In this view, it is only a matter of time before the public will lose confidence in the ability of those who own and manage the railroads to operate them in the public interest under our private system of competitive enterprise.

All these activities and "achievements" of the organized railroad industry can only be characterized as Pyrrhic victories for the railroads of the United States.

Undoubtedly, those who ruled the railroad industry in making the policy decisions on the important matters referred to above, sincerely believed that they were advancing the interests of the railroads. But this can be said of those in any field of endeavor who are unwilling to meet the challenge of change and therefore resist change in an effort to maintain the *status quo*. The startling fact is that the leaders in the railroad industry were so consistently wrong in their policy decisions over a period of so many years. Obviously, in their zeal as railroad men they lost sight of their function, which is transportation to meet the changing needs of the public.

In the mid-1950s, a new group of railroad executives on many railroads began to take over with the result that different views appeared to prevail in the making of policies in areas of the railroad industry. Applying the latest developments in technology and electronics, with qualified staffs in traffic management and operations, these railroads are endeavoring to meet their competition in the transportation of carload freight. Some railroads have improved their personnel in the field of research—economic, marketing, and technical research—and in cost finding. The question remains, what are the policies of these executives in relation to the public's interest? These policies could determine whether private companies can continue the operation of public transportation in the United States. (See Chapter X).

Thus, it is evident that policy making by executives in railroad transportation, as in other fields of endeavor, requires sound judgment based on knowledge and experience, administrative ability, an understanding of the importance of traffic management guided by reliable economic, marketing, and technical research and cost finding, and a sense of the present and future needs of the American public. And it should be added that since it is within the framework of public policy that the management of transportation companies must carry on their activities, the adequacy of public policy to meet changing conditions in the transportation industry is as important as are the internal policies and operations of transportation companies.

Coordinated rail-truck service for express and mail, in addition to less-carload freight (L. C. L. freight), on the New York Central, as recommended in our express report to President Perlman on December 21, 1955, was first inaugurated in the railroad's Southern District between Cleveland and Cincinnati and a short time later between Cleveland and St. Louis.

The changeover from the old to the new operation took place at midnight on October 1, 1956, between Cleveland and Cincinnati. Representatives from the Post Office Department, the Railway Express Agency, and the railroad, all of whom had participated in the studies and preparations for the coordinated rail-truck service, were on each train, each truck, and at each rail-terminal point for one week from the time the new service was inaugurated. The changeover went smoothly and without a hitch.

With some shifting of forces, the efficient handling of mail in coordinated service at rail-terminal points, was made by the existing forces. The Railway Express Agency continued to handle the station work for express, shifting its manpower as the needs of the service dictated.

Further savings resulted from the transportation of mail by

New York Central trucks from rail-terminal points direct to post offices at intermediate points, and in like manner from the transportation of express direct to the freight stations at intermediate points. Where the passenger business at intermediate points did not justify operation of passenger stations, they were abandoned.

As the result of the successful inauguration of coordinated rail-truck service for mail, express and L. C. L. freight in New York Central's Southern District, I was directed by Vice President Nickerson to make similar studies in the railroad's other districts. The pattern of the studies and the preparation and procedures for the inauguration of the new service developed in the Southern District were followed with success in the other districts of the New York Central.

As the result of further studies, an addendum was added to the original New York Central express report which recommended that rail-terminal points, sometimes called rail-concentration centers, for coordinated rail-truck services on the System be reduced from 55, as originally proposed, to 14. Several years later, this recommendation was put into effect with substantial financial benefit to the New York Central Railroad.

On July 16, 1957, Mrs. Wiprud and I sailed from Montreal, Canada, on the liner Empress of Scotland, bound for Southampton, England. From there we proceeded by boat-train to London. I was a delegate to the annual meeting of the American Bar Association, which was held in that city on the invitation of the Bar of England and Wales.

The trip had another purpose: the study of the causes and consequences of the collapse of Britain's railways into nationalization. To aid me in this purpose, Judge R. F. Mitchell, Commissioner on the Interstate Commerce Commission, wrote a letter of introduction for me to present to the Right Honorable Harold Watkinson, M. P., Minister of Transport and Civil Aviation.

In discussing the latter purpose with Robert R. Young, I said that I had become concerned with the trends in our transportation industry. Despite rising prices on the stock exchanges during "the greatest prosperity our country has ever known," the railroads, the core of our transportation system, were at best barely earning their costs. Therefore, I stated that in my view we could learn much from the mistakes as well as the successes of others in the transportation field; hence, my proposal to make a study of transportation in Great Britain.

Mr. Young encouraged me in this effort and wished me a successful and pleasant journey.

On arrival in London, I made arrangements to begin my studies of the history of Britain's railways while attending certain meetings of the American Bar Association. In the scheduling of my time, I was fortunate in having the understanding of all concerned.

It was a bright afternoon in late July, 1957, when I left my hotel in London for Berkeley Square House to keep an appointment with the Right Honorable Harold Watkinson, M. P., Minister of Transport and Civil Aviation. I had presented my letter of introduction to the Minister's Secretary the day before, together with a list of ten items that I wanted to discuss with the Minister. These questions added up to an all-important query: What brought about the end of private ownership and operation of Britain's railways and other forms of transport, and what had been the economic consequences of their nationalization?

The Minister received me promptly. We first discussed two matters that obviously were uppermost in his mind—modernization of railways and the transport labor problem. Recent developments in equipment, facilities and methods of operation on railroads and other forms of transport in the United States interested the Minister and prompted him to describe the highlights of the modernization program for British railways that was then in progress. The labor problem, we agreed, could best be solved through an expanding economy in which all forms of transport participated under equal conditions. As we concluded our discussion of these matters, the Minister observed: "If we can get by the question of ownership, our transportation problems are really much the same."

The Minister then took up the list of items that I had submitted and in a questioning way remarked that perhaps some of the items might be considered political in nature. I replied that they were not intended to be and if he so considered them, these questions could be ignored. I explained that I merely sought the essential facts that would answer the question: In a great nation dedicated to the private enterprise system, what were the conditions and events that had compelled nationalization of the transportation industry. He made no immediate response, but my frankness evidently pleased him. After looking over the items again, he turned to his Under-Secretary, R. R. Goodison, who was present at our meeting, and directed him to obtain for me such factual materials as were available bearing on my question.

Mr. Goodison was most generous in his help. Not only did he provide facts and information relating to most of the items on my list, but he made it possible for me to meet officials in the British Railways, the British Transport Commission, civil aviation, and the trucking industry. All patiently answered many questions about their respective transportation situations and about nationalization.

How clearly these fine men traced the demise of private enterprise in public transport. They neatly put together the pieces of what was once the world's great example of a successful private enterprise economy, almost ignoring the fact that large interstices in that structure were now filled with government-owned and operated enterprises.

Were they attempting to rationalize a condition that the facts so conclusively demonstrated had resulted from past mistakes in government policies and industry practices, mistakes that had too long been neglected and which they now found impossible to correct? Or did they actually believe, to paraphrase Lincoln in reverse, that a national economy could continue to exist half state socialism and half free enterprise? Were they not concerned with the possibility that government monopoly of basic industries, particularly transportation, would eventually swallow up the free enterprise half of the economy? Was not this, then, the "capitalistic road" to state socialism?

I pondered these matters on the return trip from London to

New York. My thoughts, however, kept reverting to the Minister's observation: "If we get by the question of ownership, our transportation problems are really much the same."

Of course, I realized the Minister had reference to routine operating and technological problems and the problems of transport labor that were of deep concern to him. But was not "the question of ownership" the crux of it? And if that question of ownership becomes academic, could the problems in a fundamental sense ever be the same? Clearly, there were important lessons to be learned from Britain's venture into nationalization of its transport industry, particularly in view of the close parallels between American and British railway history.

Shortly after my return from London, I began the writing of my report. Against the background of the events that led to the collapse of Britain's railways into nationalization, I sought to review the major problems confronting the transportation industry of the United States and some of the proposals which had been advanced by both government and industry for a solution of these problems.

Mr. Young and I visited together over my report in his New York office at 230 Park Avenue on the morning of October 18, 1957. While I reviewed its contents, he listened patiently, making occasional comments. When I concluded, we discussed the highlights and recommendations in the report, and how most effectively to present them in furtherance of his concept "to return sanity, through public understanding, to transportation." When he had to leave for another appointment, he stated that he would talk to me later about the matter. Although I thereafter had several letters from Mr. Young, all written from his Florida home, I did not see him again before his untimely death on January 25, 1958.

The passing of Robert R. Young was a severe shock to his many friends and admirers. He was a gifted man who devoted his considerable financial and organizational talents to the benefit of a retrogressing railroad industry. He understood that those who controlled the railroads, and had continued to operate them as they had in the past, had harbored too long a false assumption of the permanence of the railroads, so operated, as one of our basic industries.

Mr. Young's impatience with the inefficient and costly methods, practices, and policies, and the obsolete plant and equipment of the railroads, led him to dramatize these conditions, to experiment with new ideas in the light of great strides forward in technology, and to advocate a larger, longer view that would restore the railroads to the role they should play as a basic industry in our private enterprise economy. This approach was considered "unorthodox" by the organized railroad industry, but Mr. Young persisted.

After his remarkable success in reorganizing the financial structure of the Chesapeake and Ohio, Nickel Plate, and Wabash railroads on a voluntary basis, without the help of the traditional railroad bankers, Mr. Young secured control of the New York Central Railroad. He selected Alfred E. Perlman, an able and seasoned railroad executive on the Denver and Rio Grande Western Railroad, with an engineering education and background, as the President of the New York Central. Mr. Perlman's achievements in reorganizing the operations and modernizing the plant and facilities of that railroad are well known. Mr. Young characterized his achievements as "miraculous."

For me, the passing of Mr. Young, who widened the horizons of so many in a great industry, was more than the loss of a gifted man who had given me major opportunities for meaningful achievements in transportation. While others may have known him as unbending in business matters, I knew him as a gentle, considerate, and at times a sentimental person. He was my friend.

On one occasion, I recall receiving the following advice from Mr. Young: "Arne, never lose your independence of thought and action—it's the bloom on the peach. If you remember this, coupled with good judgment, and your ability and imagination, you will never fail in whatever you do. In whatever circumstances you find yourself, remember that timing is very important to success." There was more which I took to heart and which has served me well.

After we parted, I reflected on the many opportunities I had to discuss transportation and related matters with Mr. Young, either at his office or his New York City apartment, and on one memorable occasion as a guest at his home in Newport, Rhode Island.

Mr. Young was a good listener, which encouraged me to state my views frankly. His comments were usually brief and to the point. On one occasion, he stated his view that the thinking of most railroad officials was so limited and confined to their immediate tasks that the larger view of their problems and those of the industry, and their solution, were left to others. By "others," he meant the hired help of the railroad associations who, he said, lacked an understanding of the present or future role of the railroads in the nation's economy. Mr. Young concluded: "There is so much to be done."

When I was a guest at Mr. Young's home in Newport, Rhode Island, we took a long walk in the morning along the shore. This was his time for relaxation. He had with him powerful binoculars through which we could observe passing ships in the distance. He also pointed out the huge mansions, down shore from his home, that had been built "before the days of the income tax" by men of great wealth, now unoccupied because the younger generation could not afford their upkeep. One owner, Mr. Young said, had offered to donate his mansion to the city as a museum. At a high point on the shore some distance from this mansion and its formal gardens, a tea house had been erected which had been brought over from Japan by sections. Other mansions, he said, could be purchased "for a song," but there were few buyers.

Mr. Young told me that he had acquired his home in Newport, a beautiful, large but not pretentious house, with gardens, to get away from the pressures he experienced while living on Long Island where he was too accessible to persons with business problems or proposals.

Upon our return from our interesting and invigorating walk, and promptly at eleven o'clock, Mr. Young received business telephone calls in his upstairs library. During this time, I relaxed in an adjoing room lined with books. About twelve o'clock, Mrs. Young, a most gracious lady, came in and visited with me until lunch time. After lunch and until my departure for New York at four o'clock in the afternoon, Mr. Young and I discussed transportation matters which I was handling for him.

In my relationship with Mr. Young, I had many opportunities to meet outstanding people in private and public life. On one such occasion I had the pleasure of visiting with him and his long-time friend, the Duke of Windsor, It was on a train between Washington, D. C., and New York City. When the Duke observed that Wiprud was an unusual name, I remarked that my folks were from Norway. He said that he had been to Norway many times, and that his aunt was Queen Maud of Norway. I learned much during our discussion about Norway's history and folklore, a country Mrs. Wiprud and I visited a few years later. When he asked if I had relatives in Norway, I told him we had but that we had not heard from them since the beginning of the war—World War II.

The Duke then spoke of the war, the events that lead up to the war, and postwar problems. It was evident that the Duke had a wide knowledge of economic, social, and cultural conditions and problems in many lands.

The Duke, who was then 52 years of age, recounted the years that he had known wars. The percentage was startling. And, as he put it, with each war the horrors of it all multiplied. With sadness, and I thought with some bitterness, he observed that it was the youth, the flower of the contending nations that bore the brunt of wars.

From these and other views he expressed, it was obvious that the Duke has a serious side not fully understood by Americans but appreciated by the people of Great Britain.

These are recollections of several of the many meetings I had with Mr. Young which I shall always remember.

The report I made to Mr. Young on October 18, 1957, on my first-hand study of conditions that brought about the nationalization of transport systems in Great Britain, and the conse-

quences therefrom, lay dormant for many months after his passing. I finally concluded that in view of the close parallels between
American and British railway history, and the disturbing
implications to private ownership of our transport systems, he
would have approved making this information available to the
transportation industry in the United States. Accordingly, I
wrote an article, titled "America's Stake in the Transportation
Crisis," which was published on July 5, 1958, in the *Traffic
World.* The article not only summarized the parallel between
American and British railroad history, but analyzed the major
transportation problems in the United States, and suggested solutions, with a view to determining the steps that must be taken
in this country to preserve private enterprise in transportation.
The article was widely read and requests were received for many
thousands of reprints.

On August 1, 1958, the President of the New York Central
Railroad, in a printed memorandum to New York Central management employees, wrote:

"I believe you will find that the attached reprint of "America's
Stake in the Transportation Crisis" from the July 5th issue
of the *Traffic World,* has great significance for our industry. Included in the reprint is an editorial which appeared in the same
issue of the magazine on the importance of Mr. Wiprud's article.

"The author, whom many of you know, is an outstanding
authority on United States transportation, and is presently retained as a consultant to the New York Central."

On July 22, 1958, I was in Kansas City on a business trip.
My former chief, Postmaster General Jesse M. Donaldson, who
had retired, lived in that city. He joined me for lunch, and
during our discussion suggested that we call on former President
Truman at his office in Independence, a short distance from
Kansas City. He telephoned President Truman, who said he
would be glad to see us at his office at 10 o'clock the next
morning.

When we were ushered into President Truman's private office in the Truman Library in Independence, General Donald-

son said: "Mr. President, you remember Mr. Wiprud, an expert on transportation."

As we shook hands, he answered: "Of course I know Mr. Wiprud, but he isn't the only expert around here, I was chairman of a number of committees in the Senate that had to do with transportation, so I am an expert, too!"

After this cheerful exchange, and after President Truman expressed his views on the transportation situation in the United States, he asked my views on the current transportation problems. This gave me an opportunity to summarize my study of the reasons for the collapse of Britain's railroads into nationalization and the close parallels between American and British railway history. He observed that the situation might be different because Great Britain was a small country compared with the United States. I ventured the thought that although railroad history in the United States, like its railroad plant, traffic and distances, is on a grand scale compared with that in Great Britain, the parallels are strikingly close, varying only in degree or size but not in principle or relative importance.

President Truman appeared to thoroughly enjoy our visit. On leaving, I thanked him for receiving me. He said he was glad I called on him and wished me "good luck." On the way back to Kansas City, I expressed my appreciation to General Donaldson for all that he had done to make my trip to Kansas City so pleasant and memorable.

During the express studies on the New York Central Railroad which led to the system-wide coordinated rail-truck service on that railroad, I observed in Chicago that some of its passenger trains used the Illinois Central Station, owned by the Illinois Central Railroad, while others used the LaSalle Street Station, owned by the New York Central. Since there were ample facilities, trackage and space for more passenger trains in the LaSalle Street Station, not only for passenger business, but for express and mail, I inquired of the superintendent in charge the reason for this situation. He told me that there was a contract between the New York Central and the Illinois Central railroads which,

he had been told, could not be cancelled. I asked for and received a copy of the contract. After a thorough reading, I discussed the contract with New York Central's General Attorney
in Chicago, Marvin A. Jersild. We agreed that the contract
could be cancelled on one year's notice.

A study was then made of the feasibility of moving New York
Central's passenger trains from the Illinois Central Station to the
LaSalle Street Station and of the savings that would accrue to
the Central from such a move. The study showed that the move
could be made and that the estimated savings to the Central
would exceed $1 million a year. When these facts were brought
to the attention of President Perlman, he ordered the cancellation of the contract. After some litigation with the Illinois Central Railroad, all passenger trains of Central were transferred to
its LaSalle Street Station.

In 1959, Dr. Detlev W. Bronk and I discussed at various
times the problems of the railroad industry from the standpoint
of scientific and technical research. Dr. Bronk was the head of
the National Academy of Sciences and of the National Science
Foundation (established by the Federal government), institutions
that had become interested in the scientific and engineering
problems of highway, water, and air transport. Railroad research, with few exceptions, had been performed largely by the
suppliers of the railroads. While this arrangement produced
some improvements in equipment and related items, it was a far
cry from what could have been done if the railroad industry had
worked closely with the Federal government and with scientific
and technical institutions throughout the land.

In an effort to act as a catalyst for the entire transportation
industry in the scientific and engineering fields; Dr. Bronk
arranged for a meeting with senior members of the transporata-
tion faculties of about 15 universities to meet with representatives from government, industry, and private life who had given
intensive consideration to the various aspects of transportation.
Thus it was hoped that a deeper, more comprehensive consideration of the sociological and economic factors, as well as those

which could be identified with science and engineering, would result.

This meeting was held at Woods Hole, Massachusetts, in July and August, 1960. Only the New York Central and the Rock Island railroads were represented, but the managements of other forms of transportation took advantage of this opportunity to meet with and to learn from others their ideas, their mistakes, and their successes.

As consultant to the New York Central, I was required under my contract to keep abreast of developments in the transportation field and make recommendations to management that would improve the railroad's operations and services. For this purpose, I traveled extensively throughout the United States and Canada, conferring with executives of fifteen of the larger railroads in the United States and the two railroads in Canada. I was accompanied on some of these trips by John B. Joynt, Vice President-Planning, of the New York Central, and at other times by W. M. Smith, Manager of Mail and Express, and R. J. Welsh, Mail and Express Agent in the office of Mr. Smith, two New York Central men who had played important roles in our express studies and in the establishment of the coordinated rail-truck services of the railroad.

These trips produced a number of constructive results. For example, I learned from my conferences with the officials of the Southern Pacific Railroad that they had instituted a fast merchandise-train service between San Francisco and Portland, Oregon, and between Los Angeles and El Paso, Texas, and beyond, which transported small shipments, including fresh fruits and vegetables, at speeds faster than their passenger trains. The Southern Pacific's Vice President-Traffic, R. E. Kriebel, supplied me with a manifest, the schedules, and the type of equipment used in these services.

Upon my return to New York, I submitted to President Perlman the information supplied by Mr. Kriebel, and somewhat similar information provided by officials of the Canadian Pacific Railroad, for consideration in his plans to establish a merchandise-train service between New York City and Chicago. This service was instituted at the direction of Mr. Perlman in April, 1958, between New York and Chicago, utilizing its modern and efficient Flexi-Van equipment.

My experience in handling transportation cases involving major cost studies, brought my attention to the shortcomings in cost finding in the railroad industry. When Mr. Joynt and I learned in conferences with officials of the Southern Pacific and Canadian Pacific railroads that they, like the New York Central, had cost-finding, cost-control, and research divisions in their organizations, staffed with outstanding talent in these fields, we suggested that much good could come from meetings of these experts for the purpose of exchanging information and views on common problems in these areas with which all were concerned.

With the approval of the managements of these three railroads, a seminar of these experts was held in New York City from October 7 to 14, 1959, which Mr. Joynt and I co-chaired, At our invitation, Dr. Detlev W. Bronk, President of the National Academy of Sciences and President of the National Research Foundation, made the opening address. The agenda included discussions on scientific and technical research, transportation and economic research, marketing research, cost finding, and cost control in railroad transportation. In the area of cost finding, the discussions on the utilization of electronic computers for determining transportation costs on a continuing basis were most interesting and instructive. The railroads had successfully used computers in the division of joint rates, but cost finding by the application of computers presented special and difficult problems. A "breakthrough" would be highly significant for the railroad industry.

In the various fields of research, the discussions of the experts from the three railroads were equally stimulating and valuable. Particular interest was shown in the presentation on Canadian Pacific's extensive research and cost-finding organization, functioning under its president, which serves the many diversified activities and interests of that railroad. Also, the experts showed particular interest in New York Central's Technical Research Center which President Perlman established at Collingwood, Ohio. Among its achievements were cited the following: the development of a method for transporting missiles in railroad cars; the construction of a weighing device which through the use of gamma rays could weigh a freight car in motion; the adaption of a jet engine for snow removal purposes; and the railroad's ability to utilize the cheapest types of fuel oil available.

The success of the seminar in New York City prompted further sessions which were held in San Francisco, where the Southern Pacific was host, and later in Montreal, Canada, where the Canadian Pacific was host. At the San Francisco session, a discussion was had about the need for a census of transportation in the United States. This information is essential to economic and market research in the transportation field, as it is for Congress in enacting transportation legislation, and government agencies that regulate transportation companies. Yet, no such census of transportation had been made in the United States. As a result of this discussion, I was designated to discuss the matter with the Bureau of Census in Washington, D. C., the Federal government's agency charged with such public tasks.

Upon my return to Washington, I called at the Bureau of Census and was informed by the Director that the Bureau was prepared to make a census of transportation, but funds were not available for this purpose. The provision of funds, he added, was a matter for the Secretary of Commerce. I immediately telephoned the Secretary's office with the result that I was able to obtain an appointment with the Secretary of Commerce, Frederick H. Mueller, the following morning. After I had presented to the Secretary the urgent national need for this information, he assured me that sufficient funds would be made available immediately for an adequate census of transportation—the first ever made in the United States. Over the years the Government's census of transportation has grown to serve the needs of Congress, Government regulatory agencies, and the transportation industry.

CHAPTER VIII

Modernizing the Transportation of the United States Mail

> Neither snow nor rain nor heat nor gloom
> of night stays these couriers from the swift
> completion of their appointed rounds.
>
> HERODOTUS—*a tribute to the postmen*
> *of Persia 2500 years ago.*

WHEN THE President of the United States, Harry S. Truman, appointed Jesse M. Donaldson to the office of Postmaster General in his Cabinet, he broke a long-standing precedent under which that post was filled by the political manager of the party in power who thereafter continued to devote considerable time to the party's political business. The President determined that there was an advantage in having the head of the Post Office Department—one of the world's big businesses—a career man who came up through the ranks. As he rose on his merits to higher positions in the Department, Mr. Donaldson learned about its widely ramifying business and its problems.

Immediately upon assuming office, Postmaster General Donaldson proceeded to put the Post Office Department on a business basis. He reorganized the Department in line with recommendations of the Hoover Commission. On his recommendation, Congress enacted additional reorganization legislation and increased all but the first-class mail rates, which reduced the De-

To Arne C. Wiprud,
with sincere regards & best wishes.
7/2-48.   [signature]

partment's annual deficit by $130,000,000. He then turned his attention to the ancient and costly system and method of paying for the transportation of mail. It was in this latter area of his program of reforms that Postmaster General Donaldson, in 1948, called me to service in the Department as Associate Solicitor in charge of its transportation cases.

On April 19, 1948, at a gathering of officers and employees of the Post Office Department in Washington, D. C., I was sworn in by Postmaster General Donaldson as the Associate Solicitor of the Department. Following this ceremony, I began a series of meetings with the principal members of the staff assigned to me in connection with the nationwide mail pay case instituted by 204 railroads on February 15, 1947. On December 4, 1947, over the objection of the Department. the Interstate Commerce Commission, pursuant to a motion by the railroads, had granted an interim increase in railway mail pay of 25 percent. The hearings on the case had been in recess for about six months, and the Commission was pressing the Department to appear and present its case.

For five days my staff and I examined all aspects of the case, including the proceedings before the Interstate Commerce Commission during the year and two months prior to my appointment, the staff's theory of the case as contrasted with that of the applicant railroads, and the nature of the evidence that was being prepared by the staff on their theory of the case and that which was being prepared to meet the different theory of the railroads.

The Interstate Commerce Commission had, shortly before my appointment, notified all parties to the proceeding that hearings in the case would be resumed on May 12, 1948. To determine the course I would pursue, I studied the provisions of law governing the case. In an Act supplementing the July 31, 1947 Act, Congress increased the appropriation for the conduct of the Department's case to $1,000,000. I found a provision in that Act which I concluded constituted a mandate to the Post Office Department to make a study of the cost to the 204 railroads of transporting mail. On this provision I felt that I could turn this case around to the Department's view that costs should be a basic factor for the making of mail pay rates.

At the hearing on May 12 and 13, 1948, the large hearing room at the Interstate Commerce Commission was packed with railroad and Post Office Department lawyers, officials, and others concerned or interested in the case. Apparently, this was to be the test of the new man in charge of the Department's case. Judge R. F. Mitchell, a member of the Commission, aided by the Commission's chief examiner, presided.

After a few preliminaries, Judge Mitchell asked if the Post Office Department was prepared to proceed with the case. I presented my view that the Act of Congress appropriating $1,000,000 for the Department to conduct its case placed a mandate on the Department to make a study of the cost of transporting mail by the railroads, parties to the proceeding, and that the Department would be prepared to present its case to the Commission just as soon as the mandate of Congress could be met. I added that this would require the cooperation of the railroads because they had sole control of the essential facts regarding train, station, and related railroad costs for the transportation and handling of mail. I then moved that the Commission direct the parties to the proceeding to make a joint field study of railroad operations to obtain essential data bearing on their costs of transporting mail.

Judge Mitchell got the message: the Department could not proceed without complying with the mandate of Congress. He said: "Mr. Wiprud, is it not a fact that this is the first time that a request to make a joint cost study has been presented to this Commission?"

Not knowing all that had transpired on this point prior to assuming charge of the case, I replied: "Your Honor, I have been in charge of this case for less than a month, and I am not informed on this point."

But Judge Mitchell persisted: "Well, now, from your study of the case, and from the presentation you have made in support of a joint cost study, have you found that a request has been submitted heretofore by the Department to this Commission for such a cost study?"

My answer was: "No, your Honor, I have not."

Counsel for the applicant railroads vigorously opposed the making of a joint cost study, but Judge Mitchell ruled that such a cost study was essential to the proper determination of the proceeding.

As soon as possible after the Commission's ruling, my cost-finding section, composed of about 60 employees under the direction of Frank L. Barton, prepared forms and instructions for the making of a joint cost study to be discussed with the railroads' mail pay committee which had been set up to handle the railroads' case. I invited the committee to come to Washington for a conference with a view to an agreement on these forms and instructions. After a long delay, a messenger from the committee's headquarters in Philadelphia, Pennsylvania, called on me and stated that he was told to bring back a copy of the forms and instructions which the Department had prepared. I gave him a complete set of the forms and the instructions. After another long delay, I called for a conference thereon with the railroads' mail pay committee to be held at the Post Office Department in Washington, fixing the date.

About 15 representatives of the railroads, in addition to the members of their mail pay committee, appeared. In addition to the principal members of my staff, I invited the Department officials directly concerned with the case. We met in the great hall in the Post Office Department. Long mahogany tables were arranged the full length of the hall, with the railroads' representatives on one side and the Department's representatives on the other. The conference, I thought, took on the appearance of contending parties at the signing of a major international treaty! I presided at the meeting.

There were ten major areas in the Department's proposed joint cost study. Each area was discussed in detail. The spokesman for the railroads' mail pay committee stated they agreed to the making of studies in the first five areas, but not in the last five areas which, in the Department's view, were also essential to an adequate cost study. I asked reasons for their refusal. The spokesman said the last five areas involved work by train conductors and other railroad personnel which they would not perform, and even if they agreed, the cost would be prohibitive, about $500,000. I answered that I had received letters, which I displayed, from the presidents of every railroad union stating that their organizations would be glad to cooperate with their government in the making of these studies and, further, that I had written authority from the Postmaster General, which I also displayed, to pay for the studies to which they objected, in an amount not to exceed $500,000. The spokesman for the railroads' mail pay committee then stated that they still refused to cooperate and would give no further reason for their refusal.

In this situation, I stated, "Gentleman, you have now heard that the organized railroad industry refuses to cooperate with their government in making the joint cost study for the transportation of mail by the applicant railroads which the Commission has ruled is essential to the proper determination of the railway mail pay case. Therefore, I have no other course than to adjourn this meeting. The meeting is adjourned."

I immediately reported on the situation to Postmaster General Donaldson. I suggested to him that if the attitude of the railroads' mail pay committee did not change to active cooperation, it would be necessary to invite the presidents of the twelve leading mail-carrying railroads to a conference with him in Washington to discuss whether they would cooperate with the Department in completing the cost study. But first, I added, I would like to discuss the situation with Judge Mitchell, the presiding Commissioner in the case, with a view to arranging for a meeting in his office with the railroads' mail pay committee and the members of my staff to compose our differences. Postmaster Donaldson approved.

The conference with Judge Mitchell, the presiding Commissioner, led to a hearing on August 30, 1948, which was held in Ft. Dodge, Iowa. As the result of Judge Mitchell's ruling, a stipulation was entered on the record as to the nature of the data which the railroads would collect and compile in cooperation with the Department, the procedures to be followed, and the forms and summaries which the Department would receive. Judge Mitchell ruled on the studies the railroad would make for which the Department would pay the actual and necessary expenses incurred.

If I harbored the thought that we were finally on our way towards the completion of an adequate joint cost study for the transportation of mail to be presented by the parties to the Commission at hearings before it rendered further orders in the case, I was in for some surprises. A few months after the stipulation was signed before the presiding Commissioner, Judge Mitchell, in Ft. Dodge, Iowa, and made a part of the record, the railroads' mail pay committee resumed tactics that can be characterized as a throwback to the policies of the days when the railroads had a monopoly of virtually all forms of traffic, including mail.

On March 31, 1949, while many of the stipulated field studies were in progress and before the information and data developed from any of the studies could be analyzed and placed in evidentiary form, applicant railroads filed a motion for additional interim increase in mail pay. The increase of 20 percent sought from June 24, 1948, to March 24, 1949, constituted a total interim increase to the latter date (including the 25 percent increase previously granted by the Commission) of 45 percent. An additional 35 percent increase, from March 24, 1949 until further order of the Commission, was requested, bringing total interim increases to 80 percent, "such increased rates to be subject to retroactive readjustment in accordance with the rates of pay and compensation that may be established by final order herein." This motion was held in abeyance at the request of the applicant railroads until December 5, 1949, when they asked that it be brought up for hearing.

The reason for the requested delay for hearings was soon apparent. To support their bold move, which was in total disregard not only of their stipulation with the Post Office Department but the ruling of the presiding Commissioner that the joint cost study was essential to the proper determination of the proceeding, the railroads had to first amend their original petition which sought a 45 percent increase in mail pay. The first amendment, dated June 24, 1948, sought an additional 20 percent increase; the second amendment, dated March 24, 1949, sought a further additional increase of 15 percent; and the third and final amendment, dated December 30, 1949, sought still a further additional increase of 15 percent; all of which, with the original request of 45 percent, would raise their total request for increased mail pay to 95 percent over rates in effect on February 18, 1947, when the proceeding was instituted.

Thus, the amazing scheme of the mail pay committee of the applicant railroads in this proceeding emerged in full view. It was a bold and ruthless move against one of their best customers, the Post Office Department, in complete disregard of their stipulations and agreements with the Department, the rulings of the presiding Commissioner, the specific provisions of the Railway Mail Pay Act, and the court decisions relating thereto. Having prevailed upon the Interstate Commerce Commission to approve a 25 percent interim increase in mail pay over the objection of the Post Office Department on December 4, 1947, five months before my appointment, and without giving the Department's counsel an opportunity to prepare his affirmative case or to complete cross-examination of the railroads' witnesses, the managements of the railroads determined, as the saying goes, to "go for broke." *This they would do by raising their formal request for increased mail pay rates to 95 percent over existing rates, and then call up its second request for an interim increase of 55 percent, which, if approved by the Commission, would give the applicant railroads a total increase of 80 percent in mail pay based solely upon their self-serving evidence.* Their reasoning seemed to be—it worked once, why shouldn't it, with the Commission's blessing, work again?

This wasn't the finest hour for the managements of the railroads or for the Interstate Commerce Commission.

It was at this point in the proceedings that the newspapers, which had been following the case with increasing interest, named it the Four Billion Dollar Mail Pay Case!

When the railroads' scheme became apparent and had sufficiently developed, Postmaster General Donaldson prepared to take firm action to protect the interests of the Post Office Department.

On July 2, 1948, the Comprehensive Plan of the Postmaster General for the Transportation of United States Mail by Railroad had been filed with the Commission, served upon all carriers subject to the Railway Mail Pay Act, and published as required by law. On October 16, 1950, the Postmaster General promulgated a revised Comprehensive Plan, to become effective on January 1, 1951, which was filed with the Commission and similarly served and published, and which superseded the Plan of July 2, 1948.

The promulgation of the Comprehensive Plan and the rules implementing the service requirements of that plan was an exercise by the Postmaster General of his statutory authority to prescribe the class of service, the frequency of service, the amount of space required in cars for mail, and changes in or discontinuance of service "as the needs of the Postal Service may require." The fixing of fair and reasonable rates and compensation to the railroads for the service performed under the Plan and the implementing rules is the duty of the Commission. These are mutually exclusive powers set forth in the Railway Mail Pay Act of 1916.

The railroads objected, challenging the Postmaster General's authority to promulgate the Plan which would give him better control and greater utilization of the space paid for in cars on trains used for the transportation of mail.

In April, 1949, Postmaster General Donaldson, in his further effort to protect the interests of the Department, requested legislation to repeal the round-trip provisions of the Railway Mail Pay Act of 1916. These provisions imposed upon the Post Office Department the wholly discriminatory requirement, imposed upon no other type of traffic, requiring the Department to pay the railroads at full rates for the movement in both directions, although mail was actually transported in only one direction, "unless the car be used by the Company in the return movement." The Postmaster General directed me to prepare and present the Department's case to Congress in support of legislation to repeal these provisions of the 1916 Act.

Senator Hubert H. Humphrey was chairman of a subcommittee of the Senate Committee on Post Office and Civil Service. Following a conference with him, hearings were held by his committee on the proposal of the Post OfficeDepartment to repeal the round-trip provisions of the 1916 Act. Following these hearings, Chairman Humphrey, on instructions of the committee, requested the Post Office Department, Interstate Commerce Commission, General Accounting Office, and the General Services Administration to make comprehensive studies of their own, supplementing those of the committee, and report thereon to the Committee. This was done, with the result that the agencies named, except the Interstate Commerce Commission, submitted reports, with supporting data, strongly recommending the repeal of the round-trip provisions of the Railway Mail Pay Act of 1916. The Interstate Commerce Commission submitted a letter on the subject.

Chairman Humphrey presented the amendment for repeal, with an explanatory statement, which, in part, read as follows:

These so-called round-trip provisions impose upon the United States an obligation to pay the railroads at full rates for the movement of mail in both directions, although mail is actually transported in only one direction. No private shipper, no other governmental agency is subject to such a requirement. It is wasteful of Government funds. It lends itself to tremendous abuses and as the Postmaster General so clearly brings out in his report, it is impossible to administer.

. . . . . .

The fact is that operation under these provisions requires public funds to be paid out of the United States Treasury without an adequate opportunity for complete verification of railroad claims. It has been estimated that $31,000,000 was paid by the Government for unused space in 1949. Yet, there is evidence which indicates that close to 20 percent of the claims filed are incorrect. The Postmaster General points out that this fact was uncovered in a nation-wide field study undertaken as a part of the pending railway-mail-pay case. In other words, this study, the first of its kind to be made in 20 years, brought to light the fact that claims were submitted by the railroads upon which adequate checks could not be made, and as a result payments have been made to the railroads under these provisions upon improperly filed claims.

. . . . . .

But there are other reasons why these provisions should be repealed. The Postmaster General points out that they encourage the railroads to operate empty equipment in the return direction in order to obtain dead-head-mail pay. The obvious reason is that they get more for running a car empty than they do in handling it full of commercial traffic. A railroad representative admitted as much. The evidence before our committee shows that the railroads have issued instructions not to load any other traffic in particular cars "in order to fully protect our return-mail pay," and to withhold other traffic if necessary in order to accomplish this. There is also evidence that empty refrigerator cars were transported east from the west coast as a basis for obtaining dead-head-mail revenue at a time when similar cars were needed in the West to bring the fruit crop east. This, of course, is feather-bedding in its simplest form. The only way to stop it is to remove the incentive, and that can be done here without depriving the railroads of any compensation to which they are justly entitled, merely by prescribing rates for mail service on the same basis as the rate prescribed for other traffic.

Under date of September 27, 1949, the Chairman of the Interstate Commerce Commission, Charles D. Mahaffie, advised the Chairman of the Senate Committee as follows:

It is our view that in exercising this authority to fix reasonable compensation and prescribing the methods of ascertaining it, we may eliminate from our orders the present provisions for compensation on a round-trip basis if we conclude after a hearing that the rates prescribed as reasonable should not be applied to round-trip mileage, and may disregard like provisions contained in the 1916 Act in so doing.

Thus, after lengthy hearings before the subcommittee of the Senate Committee on Post Office and Civil Service, the Interstate Commerce Commission decided that it had the power to eliminate the round-trip provisions of the Railway Mail Pay Act which found justification two decades prior thereto in the transportation of special equipment, such as railway postoffice cars in which mail was distributed en-route, cars that could not be used for any other traffic. On this latter point, the Chairman of the subcommittee stated:

The Postmaster General sets forth clearly and concisely the tremendous change that has taken place in the matter of mail movements in recent years. Parcel post has grown by leaps and bounds, so that today most of the mail traffic does not constitute letters and newspapers but small and large parcels which are transported in any type of railroad car that is available. Almost 75 percent of the mail is transported in baggage and express cars, horse cars, milk cars, regrigerator cars, converted freight cars, and coaches.

The Department's difficulties in obtaining cooperation from the applicant railroads through their mail pay committee in completing essential areas of the joint cost study increased to a point where delays and inaction threatened to jeopardize the over-all cost study. Further, on behalf of the Department, I was compelled to reject studies in such areas as the cost to the railroads of switching mail cars at terminals and the station handling of mail because they were inadequate and highly overstated. Thus new studies in these areas were required with resulting delays. Other studies were based on assumptions that found no support in the facts as they existed at the time the studies were made. It was clear that delays and inaction in developing the essential facts through non-cooperation served the purpose of advancing their scheme to obtain huge increases in mail pay without enabling the Department to obtain reliable information essential to an adequate presentation of its case to the Interstate Commerce Commission.

In this situation, I recommended to Postmaster General Donaldson that he invite the presidents of the twelve leading mail-carrying railroads for a conference to ascertain if they would cooperate with their government in completing all essential areas of the cost study as soon as possible. He agreed that the time had come for such action. His official invitation was accepted by the twelve railroad presidents.

The meeting was held at the Postmaster General's office in

Washington, D. C., on November 28, 1949. The Postmaster General presided at the meeting. He asked me to sit with him and answer questions by the presidents of a technical nature or that related to areas of the cost studies where cooperation was not forthcoming. The Postmaster General made the following opening statement to the railroad presidents:

"At the outset, I want to state that I am sympathetic with the problems of the railroads, but I also want you to know that the Post Office Department has problems too. Our respective problems arise from a similar cause—expenses exceed income. For the fiscal year 1949 the expenses of this Department exceeded its income by $551,059,036. Naturally, this situation has caused me great concern and you may be familiar with my efforts to change it. However, I know that you cannot change this situation for me, no more than I can for you, but we can and should work together to bring about a speedy adjustment of those matters in which we have a direct and common interest.

"The job of transporting the mail efficiently and economically is one which presents problems which we should, of course, deal with frankly and in a cooperative spirit. The Government has a right to expect from you a standard of service adequate for postal needs and you have a right to expect from the Government fair and reasonable compensation for the services you actually perform. That is not only sound business—it is the law.

"Some of you have asked me to accept your statement as to increased costs of handling mail. Others have urged me to agree to an order of the I. C. C. for another interim increase in mail pay rates. It is no reflection on you to state that Congress does not permit me to do this. Congress has provided that the I. C. C. shall fix the rates that this Department shall pay for the transportation of mail by railroad and that these rates shall be determined upon facts developed in a full hearing before the Commission. I cannot ignore Congress, which constitutes my board of directors, nor would you want me to.

"As a result of our last conference, we have jointly proceeded with a field study to obtain the facts, a study that is about completed. After the completion of the field study comes the task of analysis and preparation of material for trial. Congress has appropriated about $1,000,000 for these purposes, which is a mandate on me to complete this study and present it to the Commission. Mr. Wiprud assures me that with increased cooperation along the lines I am going to speak to you about, we can complete that study and go to trial in much less time than in any previous general railway mail pay case. Further, by such cooperation, the trial can be completed in a matter of weeks instead of one year as in the past.

"I want to be frank with you. If you want to speed up this case so that you can get fair and reasonable compensation for the transportation of mail as contemplated by law, it will be necessary for you to find areas of agreement with us on these matters vital to the Department. I cannot sacrifice the interests of the Department to expedite this case, but I can agree to expedite this case if you will come in and find a way to agree upon facts, procedures and principles which will adequately protect both our interests."

The Postmaster General then outlined a specific course of action to expedite the case.

The first point raised which the Postmaster General asked me to answer was made by the president of the Baltimore and Ohio Railroad Company, Roy B. White. He stated that the studies, which the Department had requested be made, required the cooperation of railroad employees, such as conductors, baggage men, station mail handlers, and other railroad employees concerned with handling mail, who, he said, refused to cooperate. I answered that the Department had received letters from the presidents of all railroad unions, which I displayed, stating that their members would be glad to cooperate with their government in obtaining data and information for the joint study of the railroads' cost for transporting and handling United States mail. The railroad presidents seemed surprised.

The next point was made by the president of the Pennsylvania Railroad Company, Walter Franklin. He stated that the cost to the railroads in making the studies sought by the Department would be about $500,000, which the railroads could not pay. I answered that I had written authority from the Postmaster General, which I also displayed, to pay for these studies in an amount not to exceed $500,000, and that the railroads' agreement to make such a study at the Department's expense was contained in a stipulation signed by the Department and the railroads' mail pay committee in the presence of the presiding

Commissioner, Judge Mitchell, on August 30, 1948, and was a matter of record in the case. This fact also seemed to surprise the railroad presidents.

There was further discussion which made it apparent that the railroads' mail pay committee had not accurately informed their superiors about developments in the mail pay case; indeed, the railroad presidents displayed a remarkable lack of knowledge or information about their mail traffic.

As a result of this conference, the railroad presidents agreed to instruct their committee to cooperate to the end that the joint cost study could be completed as soon as possible. However, when the Postmaster General asked them to withdraw their motion for a second interim increase in mail rates of 55 percent, the president of the Pennsylvania Railroad, Mr. Franklin, declined to do so. The other railroad presidents remained silent, Thus it appeared that the scheme of the managements of at least some of the major mail-carrying railroads to secure an 80 percent increase in mail pay without giving the Department an opportunity to adequately prepare and present its case to the Commission, would not be abandoned. This fact prompted vigorous action by Postmaster General Donaldson to protect the interests of the Department.

That Mr. Franklin's refusal to agree to the withdrawal of the railroads' motion before the Interstate Commerce Commission for a second interim increase may not have had the support of the managements of all the applicant railroads was indicated by the president of the Union Pacific Railroad Company, A. E. Stoddard, as the meeting closed. He asked if I would come to a meeting of the nation's railroad presidents to be held in Washington, D. C., in April, 1950, in order to discuss the railway mail pay case with them. I said I would do so, if Postmaster General Donaldson approved. He agreed, and I told Mr. Stoddard that I would be present at this meeting.

At the direction of Postmaster General Donaldson, I requested oral argument before the entire Interstate Commerce Commission on the railroads' motion for a second interim increase in mail pay of 55 per cent to be held on January 26, 1950. The Commission granted the request.

In opening the Department's argument in opposition to the railroads' motion for another interim increase in mail pay, I summarized the efforts the Department had made to cooperate with the railroads' representatives to complete the joint study of the costs to the applicant railroads for transporting mail, and its status, which study the presiding Commissioner in the case, Judge Mitchell, ruled was essential to the proper determination of the case.

I then turned to the question of the Commission's power to approve the railroads' motion. I argued that the Commission was without authority to enter an order granting an interim increase in mail pay under the Railway Mail Pay Act of 1916 which governs the proceeding; that under that Act the Commission must assign the railroads' application for an increase in mail pay rates for hearing; and that at the conclusion of the hearing, after the Post Office Department as well as the railroads have presented their evidence, the Commission would then be authorized to establish, by order, fair and reasonable rates to be received by the railroads for the transportation of mail. In short, the Commission's power to enter an order increasing mail pay rates is conditioned upon the statutory and constitutional right of the Post Office Department to a full hearing which had not been held in this case.

Thus, I argued, since the Commission is without authority to approve the railroads' motion for a second interim increase in mail pay rates, it follows that the Commission's order of December 4, 1947, approving the interim increase in mail pay rates of 25 percent, was also beyond the power of the Commission to approve.

I concluded my argument by stating that in this situation the Postmaster General had no other course than to ask the Attorney General of the United States to institute a court action to recover all sums paid by the Department to the applicant railroads under the unauthorized order of the Commission approving the first interim increase, or, in the alternative, deduct from the amounts thus paid to the applicant railroads the amount of future bills of such railroads for the transportation of mail until the total amount paid under the Commission's order granting the first interim increase in mail pay rates had been recovered. And I stated further, that if the Commission, by order, approved a further interim increase in mail pay, I was authorized to state to the Commission that the Department would refuse to pay out government funds under such an order until the question of its legality had been decided by the Supreme Court of the United States.

The Attorney General of the United States intervened in support of the position of the Department that the Commission was without power to enter an interim order under the provisions of the Railway Mail Pay Act of 1916. The Attorney General's Special Assistant, Morton Liftin, made the argument for the Attorney General and concluded with the statement that the Justice Department was considering a suit to vacate the original 25 percent interim increase of the Commission.

On March 13, 1950, the Commission entered its order denying the motion of the applicant railroads for an additional interim increase in mail pay rates. That ended that part of the scheme of the applicant railroads, through their mail pay committee, to obtain an 80 percent increase in mail pay before the Department could present its evidence in the proceeding.

On April 28, 1950, with two members of my staff, James O. Riley, Director, Railway Mail Pay Adjustment, and Morton Lifton, who, at my request, had been assigned by the Attorney General to assist me in the case, attended the meeting of the presidents of the nation's railroads at their meeting in Washington, D. C., on the invitation of the President of the Union Pacific Railroad, Mr. Stoddard.

To set the tone for a constructive meeting, I said, "We may not be the three wise men, but we are three men of good will, and in that spirit we will frankly discuss with you all aspects of the mail pay case, answering to the best of our ability any questions that you may ask in regard to the case."

I then proceeded to discuss briefly the status of the case, the reason for the elimination of the so-called round-trip provisions, the form of the Department's proposed new rate structure for the transportation of mail by railroad, which was the subject of the Postmaster General's letter to the railroad presidents of April 10, 1950, and how, with their cooperation in completing the remaining important areas of the joint cost study, the case, which had been unnecessarily protracted for almost four years, could be speedily completed.

I asked Mr. Riley to discuss the principles of the new rate structure which he had developed for the Department, and then I asked Mr. Lifton to discuss the more important areas of the cost studies that had not been completed.

The interest of the railroad presidents in learning more about their mail traffic extended the meeting far beyond the allotted time so that we could answer the many questions asked by them regarding the transportation of mail by railroad, particularly as they applied to the problems involved in the pending case.

On October 11, 1950, the applicant railroads and the Department entered into a stipulation and agreement providing for a new rate structure for the transportation of mail to be applied on and after January 1, 1951; for the elimination of the round-trip provisions for storage car service for mail; and for the settlement of all claims of the railroads for compensation during the so-called retroactive period from February 19, 1947 to and including December 31, 1950.

I did not participate in the negotiations between the Department and the railroads in arriving at a settlement of the claims of the railroads for compensation during the retroactive period, though such an agreement would have to be approved by the Interstate Commerce Commission. I asked the Postmaster General to be relieved of participation in these negotiations, suggesting that he appoint a committee of officials in the Department familiar with the case to represent the Department in such negotiations. I explained to him that since I had represented the Chesapeake and Ohio Railway Company prior to his appointment of me to take charge of the nationwide railway mail pay case, my participation might be misunderstood. I felt, also that any decision for rate increases or compensation in the case under my direction should be confined to those made solely by the Commission based on the evidence presented in public hearings. The Postmaster General said that he understood my position and that he would appoint the committee I suggested to conduct the negotiations on behalf of the Department.

The amount of the railroads' claim for retroactive pay for the period stated was $886,000,000. The Department's representatives rejected this claim. After protracted discussions, the amount finally agreed upon and stipulated to by the Department and the railroads totaled $312,000,000, an increase in mail pay to the applicant railroads for the retroactive period of 48 percent over rates in effect on February 19, 1947. Of this amount $160,000,000 had been paid by the Department under the 25 percent interim increase approved by order of the Commission on December 4, 1947, leaving $152,000,000 to be paid in full settlement of the claims of the applicant railroads for the retroactive period.

Hearings were held by the Commission on the stipulation and agreement on November 8, 1950, at which evidence was presented by the railroads and the Department. On December 4, 1950, the Commission issued its decision and order which approved the stipulation and agreement in accordance with its terms.

Hearings were resumed before the Commission on December 18, 1950, to receive evidence from the applicant railroads and the Department on proposed railway mail pay rates for the future. These hearings continued, with several recesses, to March 8, 1951.

Most of the evidence presented by the railroads and the Department related to their respective cost studies for the transportation and handling of mail. There were wide differences between the parties in arriving at such costs. There were other differences. To meet the oft-repeated contentions of railroad witnesses that mail is burdensome, that preferential service is given mail, and that extraordinary care and attention are given to mail, all of which is not present in the transportation by the railroads of other traffic, the Post Office Department presented documentary and photographic evidence through expert witnesses in the Department that completely refuted these contentions. The Department's evidence showed that the railroads' equipment for transporting and handling mail was very old and unsatisfactory. Counsel for the railroads did not cross-examine these witnesses nor offer evidence in rebuttal. And there was no evidence presented by the railroads that they intended to remedy this unsatisfactory situation.

Assistant Postmaster General Redding, in charge of the Bureau of Transportation, testified that mail service is normally performed by the railroads at stations where there are serious inadequacies which prevent efficient and economical handling of mail and that this results in delays in the movement and delivery of mail.

Other Department witnesses testified that in 1925 mail was transported on 19,404 trains, whereas, in 1950, the number of trains transporting mail was only 6,794; that this development required the Department to greatly expand its highway post office and motor carrier services in order to provide mail service previously furnished by the railroads; and that the Department has never opposed the discontinuance of railroad passenger service on branch lines. On the contrary, they added, in many proceedings before regulatory bodies, representatives of the Department have appeared and supported the railroads in their efforts in this direction. The Department has and is permitting the substitution of motor carrier service, much of which is operated by the railroads, for discontinued rail service.

Reductions in service by railroads, Department witnesses testified, reduce the frequency of mail movements performed on trains or lines prior to abandonments or discontinuances and contribute to delays in the mails. The number of railway post office trains was reduced 45 percent from 1925 to 1950; the number of closed-pouch trains was reduced 71 percent in the same period; and the total number of trains on which mail was authorized by the Department was reduced 65 percent.

The Department's evidence also showed the advantages of mail traffic to the railroads. Mail requires no solicitation; railroads do not have to advertise for business as in the case of their freight and passenger services or concern themselves with activities to promote good will and favorable public relations. Further, mail service provides special advantages in regularity and growth of traffic and the accompanying stability of revenues.

Assistant Postmaster General Redding testified that the extent of the diversion of mail traffic from the rails to the highways will depend on the level of rail rates, and any substantial increase in rail rates will expand considerably the many favorable opportunities for trucking at present rail rates. Other Department witnesses supplemented General Redding's testimony on the growing competition for mail traffic by airplanes as well as by trucks.

If railroad managements had good reason to be complacent about their competitive position with respect to mail traffic, it cannot be found in the record of the nationwide railway mail pay case. And that record should put to rest for all time the "tongue-in-cheek" contention of the organized railroad industry that "the Government has taken away mail from our passenger trains which has deprived us of needed revenue to operate those trains profitably!" as a justification for passenger train discontinuances.

At the final hearings in this proceeding, the rates proposed by the railroads in their standard rate scale would result in an increase in mail revenues for all the railroads, except the New England and the short-line railroads, of approximately 168 percent over those received under rates in effect on February 18, 1947. For the New England railroads, considered as a group, their proposed scale would result in an increase of about 218 percent. The short-line railroads requested rates from 87 percent to 160 percent over and above the 168 percent increase in mail pay rates proposed above!

The Department's proposed rate scale would produce an average increase in mail pay to all railroads of 42 percent over the rates in effect on February 18, 1947, when the proceeding was instituted before the Interstate Commerce Commission by

204 railroads. Due to the separation of the line-haul and the terminal factors in the proposed rate scale, which permitted the Interstate Commerce Commission to prescribe separate rates for those two factors, Department witnesses testified that the scale would fully compensate all railroads, including the New England and short-haul railroads, for the services performed.

The Department, which had endeavored to carry out its stipulations and agreements with the railroads, was taken by surprise when the railroads offered a proposed order to the Commission departing in material respects from the intent of the rules and instructions attached to the stipulation and agreement of October 11, 1950, which was the basis for the Commission's order of December 4, 1950, as amended December 11, 1950. Rather than being limited in accordance with the purpose of the conferences leading up to the stipulation and agreement, the questions for presentation to the Commission were compounded and confused. For these and other reasons, the Department objected to the receipt in evidence of the railroads' proposed order.

The Department submitted its proposed form of order in accordance with the stipulations and agreements between the Department and the railroads and in conformance with the mutually exclusive powers of the Postmaster General and the Commission as prescribed by Congress.

Oral argument was had before the entire Interstate Commerce Commission on June 7, 1951. Most of the argument of the parties dealt with the many intricate details of the cost studies. I directed my argument on these cost studies to the major issues involved in the many and great differences between the Department and the railroads.

The thrust of the railroads' case as reflected in their continuing effort to obtain astronomical increases in mail pay rates, regardless of the clear evidence that this was the road to pricing themselves out of the business of transporting mail, prompted me to begin my argument on that theme.

While the railroads' original application for a 45 percent increase in mail pay rates had been stepped up by amendments to 95 percent, the rates in their proposed rate scale would result in increases in revenues for all railroads, except the New England and short-line railroads, of 168 percent for the transportation of mail. Dollarwise, I continued, the proposed rate increases in the railroads' rate scale would mean an overall increase in mail pay of $340,828,000 over the revenues produced under the rates in effect when the case began, bringing the total rail transportation bill of the Department for the fiscal year 1952, for example, from $202,874,000 to $543,707,000. For the New England railroads, considered as a group, their proposed rate scale would result in an increase of 218 percent. For the short-line railroads, the increase would be from 87 to 160 percent over the 168 percent proposed by the majority of the railroads!

The Department was not unaware of the fact that the astronomical rate increases proposed by the railroads in the new mail pay rate scale submitted by them, may have been designed to make their requested increases of 95 percent in their formal applications, which by law would be the maximum the Commission could grant, look reasonable, Prior experience in the case would seem to indicate such a purpose. The Department, however, could not conceive that the Commission would be misled by such an obvious tactic.

I urged the Commission to consider the railroads' proposals, based on their highly inflated cost studies, coupled with and confused by its revenue case theory evidence, in the light of the substantially changed transportation conditions since the last railway mail pay case. It must be apparent, I stated, that the implications of the changed competitive situation were lost on the railroad managements. They were proceeding as though the transportation situation was the same as it was two decades ago when they had a virtual monopoly of public transportation.

I emphasized the evidence that the truck lines on the short hauls and the airlines on the long hauls were eager to transport mail, offering lower rates and improved service as contrasted with the higher rates, the sharp reduction in passenger trains, and the deteriorating equipment, facilities, and services of the railroads for transporting and handling mail.

What, I asked, do these changed conditions portend for the railroads as well as the Department should such astronomical increases in mail pay rates be granted? The Department would have no choice. The short-haul mail traffic, and the definition of short-haul could be quite extensive dependent upon the rate level, would be transferred to the trucks. The long-haul mail traffic would increasingly be transferred to the airlines. On these points, I detailed the evidence.

As for the New England and short-line railroads, I stated that the increases under their proposed rate scale, if granted by the Commission, would end their mail-carrying days immediately and forever.

For these and other reasons, I stated that the Postmaster General respectfully submits that in the light of the evidence adduced at the hearings, the Commission should make the findings requested by him, and thereupon enter an order fixing the rates of payment to the railroads for the transportation of United States mail matter and service connected therewith, on and after January 1, 1951, at not to exceed the rates proposed by the Department.

The Department's warnings went unheeded by railroad managements and in effect by the Commission which, in its decision and order of November 13, 1951, approved the amount of the increases sought by the railroads in their formal applications. Time has proven that inferior services and high rates of railroads have forced the diversion of mail traffic to other modes of transportation.

Now that the problems arising out of the ancient and costly rules, regulations, and practices governing the transportation of mail by railroad and the many and equally costly inequities in the outmoded method of paying the railroads therefor, had been solved, Postmaster General Donaldson turned his attention to another principal reform which he had long had in mind, the separation of subsidies to airline companies from pay for carrying mail. In November, 1951, he asked me to undertake the task of working out a formula and the necessary legislation for the separation of subsidy from airmail pay.

After six months of work with a small but competent staff in the Department, we developed a formula which we wrote into a proposed amendment to the Civil Aeronautics Act that would effectively separate subsidy from airmail pay. With the approval of Postmaster General Donaldson, our proposed formula in the form of a bill to amend the above Act was presented to Congress.

For eight days, Assistant Postmaster General Redding, in charge of the Bureau of Transportation, and I testified before the House Committee in support of the Department's proposed amendment. At the end of the fourth day, an attorney for the international airlines asked for an executive session on the ground that testimony of separating subsidy from airmail pay was a sensitive matter for those airlines operating in the international field. So the committee went into executive session for the remaining four days. On the eighth day, an official of the Civil Aeronautics Board appeared before the committee and stated that the formula worked out by the Post Office Department could be put into effect under existing law by an order of the Board without the necessity of amending the law. The committee then adjourned and within a few months thereafter the Civil Aeronautics Board, following a hearing, by order, adopted the Post Office Department's formula separating subsidies, which the Board would administer, from rates compensating the airlines for carrying mail, which the Post Office Department would pay.

An interesting and perhaps significant incident occurred at the conclusion of these hearings. As we left the hearing room on the last day, we met outside the building several Washington representatives of the railroads. I asked them why they had not appeared and testified at the hearings in support of the separation of subsidies from airmail pay, a proposal that they had long advocated as one of the solutions to their difficulties. The answer was, "We have other fish to fry now."

It appeared that they had lost another whipping boy!

The major tasks for which Postmaster General Donaldson had called me to serve as Associate Solicitor in charge of transportation matters for the Post Office Department having been completed, on July 8, 1952, I tendered my resignation, effective at the end of the month, to resume my private law practice.

In addition to the letter from Postmaster General Donaldson accepting my resignation, I received a letter from President Truman, both of which I deeply appreciated. They expressed their appreciation for undertaking the difficult public tasks assigned to me, adding "you have handled these tasks with great distinction and credit to yourself and the Post Office Department." They extended their good wishes for my future success.

Before my return to private practice, the employees of the Post Office Department in Washington gave a luncheon in my honor. This was a heartwarming occasion which I shall always remember.

Jesse M. Donaldson was a career man in the postal service who understood its problems. As Postmaster General of the United States he devoted his full time to the solution of these problems. His efforts to reorganize the Department, as hereinabove related, were successful. In dealing with the major problems relating to the transportation of mail, an area of his reforms where I was privileged to assist him, he faced strong opposition from those in the transportation industry who fought to maintain the *status quo*. But he persisted and in this area, too, he achieved major needed reforms.

Following Mr. Donaldson's administration as Postmaster General, there was a return to the old practice of appointing to that high post the political managers of the party in power. As in the past, these political managers devoted considerable time to the party's political business. To their credit, however, they recognized that the mounting deficit of the Post Office Department and the demands of a growing economy and an expanding population required a further reorganization and modernization of the Department. Among the proposals advanced was the establishment of a "non-political" government-owned corporation to operate the postal service.

Whatever reorganization of the Post Office Department is agreed upon, it should be clear from the account in this chapter that there must be a man as Postmaster General who has the ability, the courage, and the determination to solve its problems in modern terms, without fear or favor. The nation needs a man for this post who will devote his full time and all his energies to this important task for his country.

CHAPTER IX

The Empire State's
Transportation Problems

PART ONE

ON AUGUST 3, 1960, I met Governor Rockefeller for the first time. This meeting was held in his New York City office at his request for the purpose of discussing a post in the Governor's Cabinet as Director of the New York State Office of Transportation, an office that had been vacant for several months. A mutual friend, Robert W. Purcell, President of the International Basic Economy Corporation and former Vice President-Law of the Chesapeake and Ohio Railway Company, had recommended me for the post.

My appointment with the Governor was for 9 o'clock that August morning, but I was up at 5 o'clock, and dressed for a prebreakfast walk to determine what I should say to the Governor, for I had doubts, despite my high regard for him, about accepting such a post if it was offered to me. These doubts arose from what I understood to be the nature of the office, which was largely advisory, and also from the fact that I had family obligations that hardly justified the substantial monetary sacrifice that acceptance of the post would entail.

The Governor received me promptly at 9 o'clock. Also present were Lieutenant-Governor Malcolm Wilson and the Secretary to the Governor, Dr. William J. Ronan.

Dr. Ronan had arranged the meeting several days after we had discussed the matter at a luncheon with a mutual friend, John B. Joynt, a prominent management consultant in New York City. Mr. Wilson, with whom I visited briefly before the meeting, mentioned that I had been up since 5 o'clock that morning, so the Governor served coffee all around. He then asked me to outline my experience in the transportation field and my views on transportation matters. After an hour's discussion, the Governor rose and said he had a meeting to settle a labor strike on the Long Island Rail Road, and added: "Mr. Wiprud, I want you to come."

And I found myself answering, "Governor, if you want me to come, I will come." Perhaps it was the earnestness of his request, and his expressed interest in transportation problems that prompted me to accept.

After closing my offices in Washington, D. C., and New York City, and severing all connections with my other clients, on August 15, 1960, I was given an interim appointment and sworn in as the Director of the New York State Office of Transportation.

I immediately launched on an all-out effort to reactivate the New York State Office of Transportation, staff it, obtain adequate office space in New York City; reopen the Albany office and staff it; activate and staff, in cooperation with my New Jersey counterpart, Commissioner Dwight R. G. Palmer, the New York-New Jersey Transportation Agency, to which bi-State agency the Governor also appointed me as the New York member; devise constructive programs to meet the pressing transportation problems of the State; and, when authorized by the Governor, implement such programs.

I shall always remember the helpful assistance given me by Lieutenant-Governor Malcolm Wilson; General C. W. R. Schuyler, Commissioner of the Office of General Services; J. Burch McMorran, Superintendent of Public Works; Keith S. McHugh, Commissioner of the Department of Commerce; Mrs. Caroline Simon, Secretary of State; Dr. T. Norman Hurd, Director of the Budget; Austin J. Tobin, Executive Director of the Port of New York Authority; Dwight R. G. Palmer, Commissioner of the New Jersey State Highway Department and my counterpart on the New York-New Jersey Transportation Agency. The Secretary to the Governor, Dr. Ronan, appeared to be a most helpful friend.

As stated, on August 15, 1960, in an interim appointment, Governor Rockefeller had designated me as Director of the State Office of Transportation. The formal nomination was submitted on January 13, 1961, and was confirmed by the Senate on January 23, 1961. On January 9, Governor Rockefeller nominated me as New York State's member to activate the New York-New Jersey Transportation Agency. This nomination was also confirmed by the Senate on January 23, 1961. I was quite surprised that my nominations for these posts were submitted with an oral presentation of my previous experience in the transportation field, which concluded with the statement that, "Mr. Wiprud will achieve even greater heights in the work on transportation that he will do for New York State!" The Senate then gave me a rising vote of approval. This evidence of confidence certainly called for an all-out effort on my part in my new tasks.

On August 30, 1960, fifteen days after I had taken office, the President of the New Haven Railroad, George Alpert, telephoned me from New Haven, Connecticut, regarding the financial plight of his railroad. It was a Macedonian cry for help. Here, I thought, was a major problem affecting the state of New York, particularly the New York metropolitan area, that I could at least "get my teeth into" while carrying out the larger task that was before me. I invited Mr. Alpert to come to New York City and discuss the situation with me.

Mr. Alpert came to New York City the following day, accompanied by his financial vice president, A. G. Kubach. I asked Dr. Ronan to join us. We were advised by Mr. Alpert and Mr. Kubach that the railroad had about $3 million in the bank, that its payroll was $1.5 million a week, and that its losses were very substantial and increasing. Under these circumstances, Mr. Alpert stated, the railroad could not continue operations for more than a few months. A program grew out of this conference designed to "save the New Haven Railroad."

To develop such a program, Governor Rockefeller called a conference on October 24, 1960, of the Governors of the four states served by the New Haven Railroad. This conference, which was held in Governor Rockefeller's office in New York City, was attended by Governor Abraham Ribicoff of Connecticut, Mayor Robert F. Wagner of New York City, and County Executive Edwin G. Michaelian of Westchester County, New York, and members of their respective staffs. Governor Foster Furcolo of Massachusetts and Governor Christopher del Cesto of Rhode Island, who were unable to attend because of pressing official matters, were represented at the meeting and consulted by telephone. Governor Rockefeller presided at the conference.

After a thorough discussion of all the available facts, an agreement was reached on a state and local program of tax relief and other aid for the New Haven Railroad. The governors decided to appeal to the Interstate Commerce Commission for further financial assistance for the railroad, in the form of Commission approval of Federal guaranteed loans.

To implement this program, an Interstate Staff Committee on the New Haven Railroad was formed consisting of representatives of the four governors. I was designated as one of the members. On my motion, Dr. Ronan was named chairman. The Committee met in almost continuous session for six days to develop facts that later formed the basis of the four-state program of tax and other relief for the railroad.

On October 31, 1960, the Interstate Staff Committee met in an all-day session with the members of the Interstate Commerce Commission, in Washington, D. C. At this meeting, representatives of the four states, as instructed, pledged tax relief and other aid for the New Haven Railroad. On the basis of these assurances, the Commission on the same day approved the railroad's application for a Federal guaranteed loan in the amount of $4.5 million. Subsequently, the Commission approved the railroad's applications for additional loans totalling $7 million. The legislatures of the four states enacted legislation, on the recommendation of their Governors, for tax relief and other aid for the railroad.

The Interstate Staff Committee continued its efforts on behalf of the railroad. It conducted studies and met with interested parties, including labor leaders, interested financiers, officers of the railroad, and officials in the states and communities served by the railroad to explore the contributions each could make to the solution of the railroad's continuing problems.

Since any plan for the future of the New Haven Railroad must necessarily have an analytical base for determining the extent to which each class of transportation services performed by the railroad was responsible for the deficit, Governor Rockefeller authorized the Office of Transportation to make a comprehensive study of the costs and revenues of the New Haven's operations. The crucial issue in terms of the interests of New York State was of course whether or not the New York City suburban service (the commuter service) was compensatory, On my recommendation, the firm of Edwards and Peabody, of Washington, D. C., was retained to make this study. Later, the Governor authorized the Office of Transportation to make similar studies on the New York Central Railroad and on the Long Island Rail Road.

On June 4, 1961, President George Alpert and Vice President A. G. Kubach of the New Haven Railroad called on Dr. Ronan and me to advise us that despite the assistance of the states and the Federal government, the financial difficulties of the New Haven Railroad had worsened. They sought support for a proposal to obtain another $4.5 million Federal guaranteed loan which, they stated, was needed to continue the railroad in operation. During the conference, I asked them whether, as we had previously discussed, they had worked out a comprehensive plan for the rehabilitation and modernization of the railroad, including the cost of implementing such a plan, which would show whether the railroad could become a viable enterprise. Mr. Alpert said they had not. Lacking such a plan, I expressed doubt that further assistance would be forthcoming in the form of Interstate Commerce Commission approval of Federal guaranteed loans for the railroad. Chewing his ever-present cigar, Mr. Alpert finally said, "I believe that Wiprud is right. Kubach, proceed immediately with the development of such a plan." Mr. Kubach merely nodded his head—a response that was not reassuring.

The need for further operating capital for the railroad was apparently too great. An application for an additional $4.5 million Federal guaranteed loan was filed by the railroad with the Interstate Commerce Commission. The application was denied.

On July 7, 1961, the New Haven Railroad filed a petition for reorganization under Section 77 of the Bankruptcy Act in the United States District Court for the State of Connecticut which was accepted by the Court.

At this stage in our strenuous efforts to save the New Haven Railroad, I was in for a real surprise. On July 10, 1961, a few days after New Haven Railroad's petition for reorganization under the Bankruptcy Act had been filed, Dr. Ronan requested that I seek a conference with Judge Robert A. Anderson, then Chief Judge of the United States District Court for the State of Connecticut, the Court that had jurisdiction over the New Haven Railroad under the Bankruptcy Act, and recommend that the Court appoint him, Dr. Ronan, as Trustee of the Railroad. Dr. Ronan's growing interest and increasing activities in the transportation work of my office, particularly in the New York metropolitan area, were welcomed by me, but this was the first indication that he wanted to actively enter the transportation field. I said that if this was what he wanted, I would go to New Haven and speak to Judge Anderson on his behalf.

I called on Judge Anderson at his Chambers in New Haven, Connecticut, on July 13, 1961. The Judge, in response to my inquiry, assured me that it was all right to discuss the subject with him, adding that "everyone else has." I then presented the name of Dr. Ronan and answered the Judge's questions regarding his position and past experience. I had respect for Dr. Ronan's many remarkable qualities, including his ability as an administrator, his resourcefulness in dealing with men and problems in private and public life, and his recent outstanding work in the field of transportation as related to the New Haven Railroad. These qualities in the man I presented as objectively and forcibly as possible to Judge Anderson. They were qualities that I believed would make Dr. Ronan an able and successful Trustee of the Railroad. My presentation seemed to be well received. The Judge finally decided to appoint three Trustees for the New Haven Railroad. Dr. Ronan, however, was not included.

On August 4, 1961, the Court, with the approval of the Interstate Commerce Commission, authorized $5 million in trustee certificates as security for additional loans. The hope expressed was that these loans would enable the railroad to continue essential operations until a solution of its difficulties could be worked out through this Court proceeding.

The Interstate Staff Committee on the New Haven Railroad promptly offered its services to the Federal Court and the Trustees, urging that the public interest required that every resource be utilized to maintain the essential passenger and freight services of the New Haven Railroad. The committee suggested a joint meeting with key executives of other leading *eastern railroads* to obtain short-term expert "lend-lease" assistance for the New Haven to make a comprehensive review of its properties, equipment, finances, traffic management, and its traffic potential. It was in the interest of the other railroads in the east, the committee stated, to give such assistance.

The suggestion of the Interstate Staff Committee was not accepted. Instead, on March 22, 1962, a group of nine railroad executives from the *midwestern and western railroads,* with Frederic B. Whitman, President of the Western Pacific Railroad, as its chairman, was appointed by the Secretary of Commerce to make a study of the New Haven Railroad! Its report, long delayed, was inconclusive.

The Trustees of the New Haven Railroad contracted for two major studies. United Research, an economic analysis group, conducted an economic survey of the area served by the New Haven for the purpose of providing data on the market potential of the railroad, both on a long and short-term basis. The engineering firm of Coverdale and Colpitts studied the economic and engineering problems of the railroad. In addition, the firm of

Gibbs and Hill made a study of the railroad's electrification facilities. As stated, the firm of Edwards and Peabody was retained by the New York State Office of Transportation to make the analysis of New Haven's costs and revenues by classes of traffic. These reports were submitted during 1962 and 1963.

The Interstate Staff Committee on the New Haven Railroad submitted its Final Report, with findings and recommendations, to the governors of the states of Connecticut, Massachusetts, New York and Rhode Island on February 15, 1963.

While I worked closely with Dr. Ronan, particularly in his role as Chairman of the Interstate Staff Committee on the New Haven Railroad, which consumed much of our time, my primary task as Director was to administer, supervise and work with my staff in the Office of Transportation as well as with my New Jersey counterpart, Commissioner Palmer, and the staff of the New York-New Jersey Transportation Agency, in the development of programs and related studies for the improvement of transport services, not only in the New York metropolitan area, but, insofar as the Office of Transportation was concerned, in upstate New York.

In addition to the time-consuming problems of the New Haven Railroad, and later the equally time-consuming hearings in the eastern railroad merger proceedings before the Interstate Commerce Commission, the Office of Transportation during my tenure as its Director, initiated surveys, studies, and programs on other long-festering transportation problems affecting the state of New York which were the basis for corrective action in my recommendations to Governor Rockefeller. The reports on major surveys, studies and programs included the following:

Modernization of freight handling in New York Harbor.
Tax relief for commuter railroads.
The opportunity, under private ownership and management, to provide the finest, most modern commuter services for the New York metropolitan area.
Coordination and improvement of passenger services on

Long Island and between Long Island and New York
City.

Express commuter service on New York Central's Harlem
Division.

Up-state New York transportation studies.

Mass transportation between New York and New Jersey.

As the surveys, studies, and programs progressed, I had a
number of unusual and interesting experiences, one of which
occurred during our work on mass transportation problems between New York and New Jersey involving the proposed acquisition and modernization of the bankrupt Hudson and Manhattan
Railroad by The Port of New York Authority. The New York-
New Jersey Transportation Agency was required to make recommendations on this proposal.

Before the bi-state Agency made its recommendations to the
Governors of the two States regarding the take-over by The Port
of New York Authority of the Hudson and Manhattan Railroad,
Mr. Tobin, Mr. Palmer and I met at the Newark airport and
proceeded by plane for a conference in Albany. After the conference, we returned by plane to the Newark airport. En route,
Mr. Tobin asked if I would like to return to New York City in
his helicopter. I answered that I would. As we approached the
city in the helicopter, Mr. Tobin said, "Arne, see that building
over there? That is the Port Authority Building, Can you see
that little red dot on top of the building? That is where we will
land."

I remarked, "Austin, that is impossible. We'll never make
it."

"I should have told you," he continued, "we will land on the
black spot, which you cannot see from here, which is in the
center of that little red spot on top of the Port Authority
Building!"

Well, we landed all right, and Mr. Tobin had his fun with
me during my first helicopter flight. Thereafter, I was privileged
to make a number of trips on that helicopter to observe from the

air the transportation terminals, rail facilities, the port facilities, and the various airports in the New York metropolitan area. Seeing such structures and facilities from the air is a great advantage when one later inspects them on the ground.

Aside from the extensive preparation and participation on behalf of the State of New York in the eastern railroad merger proceedings before the Interstate Commerce Commission, these in essence were the major activities of the New York State Office of Transportation during the first half of my tenure as its Director and of the New York-New Jersey Transportation Agency as its New York member.

I enjoyed my work. Much of my attention, however, had to be given to the time-consuming task of office administration, with the consequent need for working long hours each day, and many evenings and week-ends, in order to carry forward the more important and creative tasks of supervising and directing the transportation surveys, studies and programs of my Office. Gradually this severe schedule produced extreme fatigue, which brought concern to my family and warnings from our family doctor.

I often reflected on the limitations on my authority in relation to the transportation programs developed by my Office, limitations that I had not experienced in all my previous public or private work. It remained for a friend, Thomas M. Goodfellow, President of the Long Island Rail Road, to spell out the source and center of my limitations, and consequently of my frustrations.

On November 21, 1961, Mr. Goodfellow called on me at my office at 270 Broadway, New York City. I had great respect for Mr. Goodfellow as an able railroad executive and as a man of character and common sense. I enjoyed visiting with him. His frankness was refreshing. On this occasion, he pulled two chairs in front of my desk, seated himself in one and stretched his long legs over the other, and then said, "Arne, the trouble with your job as Director of the Office of Transportation for this State is that you have no power to do anything except make recommendations. What kind of a power is that in government or in private business? There are too many men between your recommendations and the final decisions. I think you could do a great job if only you had the power of decision."

Well, as the saying goes, after we "kicked" that observation on my job as a Cabinet officer around for a while, I, too, came to the conclusion that the limitation imposed by the Act creating the Office of Transportation was the source of other limitations that materially circumscribed the effectiveness of my Office.

Before he left, Mr. Goodfellow assured me that I had his full cooperation in making whatever studies my office wanted to make of his railroad, even though I had no real power to implement them!

The regional nature of transportation operations in the New York metropolitan area soon became apparent to me as Director of the Office of Transportation. Therefore, it seemed logical to me that the State should support the proposal of the Regional Planning Association of New York City, which urged the establishment of a tri-state set-up to deal with the commuter operations in the New York metropolitan area. When I broached the desirability of giving the State's support to this proposal, Dr. Ronan indicated that the "Governor's office" frowned on the idea.

The Tri-State Transportation Committee, however, was established on August 30, 1961, by the coordinated action of Governor Rockefeller of New York, Governor Meyner of New Jersey, and Governor Dempsey of Connecticut. In their joint announcement, the Governors stated; "The expeditious movement of millions of persons and tons of goods through the region is essential for the continued economic growth of the area. . . . The three states have a vital concern in finding a solution to the critical transportation problems facing the nation."

With the establishment of the Tri-State Transportation Committee, to which I, as director of the Office of Transportation, was designated a member, my office worked closely with it in developing demonstration projects eligible for financing under the Housing Act of 1961. Further, the staff of the New York-New Jersey Transportation Agency was moved to the quarters of the

Tri-State Transportation Committee and thereafter the major projects of that agency and of my office were taken over by the Tri-State Transportation Committee. From this time on, aside from cooperating with the Tri-State Transportation Committee, my office dealt primarily with up-state transportation problems and the emerging major eastern railroad merger cases before the Interstate Commerce Commission as they affected the State of New York.

These developments in transportation planning for the New York metropolitan area were sound. However, the Tri-State Transportation Committee, too, was only a planning committee. The task of effective implementation of programs agreed upon by the Committee for the three states required the establishment, by compact, of a Tri-State Transportation Authority.

There remained also the coordination of the agencies of government concerned with different modes and aspects of the transportation industry. Those agencies concerned with administration and promotional activities should be consolidated under a department of transportation with Cabinet rank. Such a department should also coordinate a simplified regulatory program, while still preserving independent and objective rule-making and adjudication in the regulation of carriers. These views I expressed in several articles in the national industry magazine.[1] I concluded that the multiplicity of uncoordinated and often conflicting governmental agencies is a virtual guarantee of the chaos which has come to characterize the relations of the government to the transportation industry.

These articles dealt primarily with conditions in the Federal government affecting transportation, but obviously they applied equally to state governments. In 1967, a beginning was made by the establishment of a United States Department of Transportation and departments of transportation in the states of New York and Florida. Whether private enterprise can survive in common carrier transport depends largely upon the adoption by the Fed-

---

[1] *The Traffic World,* July, 1958, and article titled "America's Stake in the Transportation Crisis," and June, 1960, an article titled, "Transportation and the Free Enterprise System," and in April, 1964, an article titled "WANTED: A National Policy to Invigorate Transportation in U.S. under Free Enterprise."

eral and state governments of sound transportation policies effectively implemented by such centralization of responsibility.

The problems of my Office were at times multiplied by the activities of young assistants to Dr. Ronan, whom he called "program associates." These "program associates" were sent by the secretary to "assist" some departments and agencies of the State in their official duties, whether they were wanted or not. They had no experience in transportation matters, however gifted these young men may have been in other fields. On one occasion, because of their activities, it was necessary for me to take bold action to save the Governor's transportation program for the New York metropolitan area.

On this occasion, when the 1961 commuter tax relief bill was before the Legislature, a bill that on October 7, 1960, I, as director of the Office of Transportation, had recommended to the Governor, the "program associates" of Dr. Ronan had without my knowledge caused an amendment to be introduced in the Legislature, so drawn that the bill granted tax relief to the New Haven Railroad, but not to the New York Central Railroad, on commuter operations of both railroads entering the Grand Central Terminal in New York City.

After this was done, on March 8, 1961, I was called to the office of Dr. Ronan in New York City, where several of his "program associates" were present, and told, "We have found a way to exclude the New York Central from the tax relief bill."

I was more amazed at the lighthearted attitude regarding this important matter than at the failure to consult me about a subject that was obviously the business of my Office.

The reaction to this "accomplishment" of Dr. Ronan's "program associates" was immediate. The next morning, Alfred E. Perlman, President of the New York Central Railroad, telephoned Dr. Ronan in Albany, where he had gone the evening before, stating that he was getting out a press release "blasting" the Governor's rail commuter tax relief program as discriminatory and "a fake," and further that under the circumstances he would not sign the contract with The Port of New York Authority for the lease by his railroad of new commuter cars to be built by the Authority under the state's program for the improvement of rail commuter facilities and services.

Dr. Ronan immediately telephoned me the substance of Mr. Perlman's call and asked my help. Since the Governor's rail commuter program for the New York Metropolitan area, for which the people of the State had voted a bond issue in the amount of $100,000,000, was imperiled I said I would do what I could and would see him in New York the next morning.

The next morning at our conference, I told Dr. Ronan that Mr. Perlman had a grievance and that he had better make peace with him since the New York Central was a commuter railroad entitled to tax relief just as much as the New Haven Railroad. A "program associate" was present. Dr. Ronan replied, "I will not be intimidated."

I answered, "This is not a case of intimidation. The Governor's entire program to improve rail commuter services in the New York metropolitan area is at stake. The New York Central is the only railroad at this time that has agreed to the new commuter-car program. If the Central pulls out, the Governor's program is dead," and I added, "Mr. Perlman is right. This amendment is discrimination against his railroad's commuter services."

I then urged Dr. Ronan to 'phone Mr. Perlman without delay and arrange for a meeting. He finally agreed. As a result, a meeting was arranged for the next morning, March 10, 1961, in Mr. Perlman's office.

Those present at this meeting were Mr. Perlman and officers of his staff, Dr. Ronan and one of the "program associates," and myself. Dr. Ronan immediately asked his "program associate" to tell Mr. Perlman how much the state had done for the New York Central Railroad. Before the "program associate" could utter a word, Mr. Perlman, a no-nonsense railroad executive, said, with characteristic emphasis, "The state has not done a damn thing for my railroad. What it is trying to do now is for the people of the metropolitan area. Let's get that straight."

Then, patting copies of the press release before him, Mr. Perlman expounded upon the duplicity of the State's amendment, particularly in the light of his cooperation with the State in carrying out the Governor's program to improve rail commuter services in the New York metropolitan area. Mr. Perlman left no doubt that he would give out his press release criticizing the Governor and his transportation program and that he would refuse to sign a lease with The New York Port Authority for new commuter cars if the State persisted with "this discriminatory amendment" against his railroad.

At this point, fearful that the Governor's program for the improvement of rail commuter services in the New York metropolitan area was in jeopardy, I urged the immediate and favorable resolution of the matter by removing the obvious source of discrimination against the New York Central. Thereupon, Dr. Ronan agreed to withdraw the offending amendment. When this was done, my office was able to proceed without further incident in carrying out its responsibilities for the Governor's program.

I naturally wondered if this type of interference with the duties of a Cabinet officer ever came to the Governor's attention. It seemed incomprehensible that he would condone such actions. For the time being, however, I was free from intrusions by "programs associates," but it was a difficult and frustrating experience for me as I am sure it would have been for other Cabinet officers.

Out of such experiences and the heavy schedule of my official duties, an illness which our family doctor, Dr. Wallace M. Yater,[2] a prominent physician in Washington, D. C., diagnosed as tension that produced extreme exhaustion, gradually seemed to overtake me and periodically recur with increasing force. He warned me against the possible consequences, but there seemed to be no relief from the strain of long hours of work, without adequate rest, if my commitments to Governor Rockefeller and the Legislature of the State of New York were to be met.

During those strenuous days, I missed my favorite form of exercise, golf. Often I thought, rather wistfully, of the most inter-

[2] Master of the American College of Physicians.

esting and unusual golf game for me, a game that came to the attention of President Dwight D. Eisenhower.

On one Saturday in November, I was a member of a foursome at Manor Country Club, near Washington, D. C., with Colonel Gynther Storaasli, Judge Luther W. Youngdahl, and Judge Bolitha J. Laws. Our starting time was 8:30 a. m. The fog was as thick "as a London pea-souper," but with two of the best caddies at the Club the game began. Strange as it may seem, the game was completed—all 18 holes—with respectable scores and not a ball was lost!

The story of this "saga," written with great style by John Gondella, appeared in the Washington D. C. *Post* on November 22, 1953. The story came to the attention of President Eisenhower, an ardent golfer. It apparently gave him a relaxing smile, for in a letter to our foursome he concluded with this speculative observation: "I wonder if it would help my game to try a round under similar conditions!"

In May, 1961, I mentioned to Dr. Ronan that I intended to discuss with the Governor the importance of the rail merger proceedings pending or in prospect before the Interstate Commerce Commission, from the standpoint of their impact on the economic welfare of the State of New York. I did not have that conference, but apparently Dr. Ronan did, for thereafter the Attorney General of the State, Louis K. Lefkowitz, and I, as Director of the Office of Transportation, received authority from the Governor to intervene in the rail merger proceeding then before the Commission involving the Chesapeake and Ohio, Baltimore and Ohio, and the New York Central railroads "as the interests of the State may appear."

The Assistant Solicitor General, Dunton F. Tynan, who had been assigned to the case, was taken ill, and I was asked to take over, set up a trial staff, and obtain witnesses; in short, to take charge of the case for the State of New York. With my other work, I had little time, before the hearings in this rail merger proceeding began, to set up a trial staff, so for the first few days

For: Arne C. Wiprud

With best wishes,

Dwight Eisenhower

of the hearings I handled the State's case with the assistance of Dr. Irston R. Barnes, my consulting economist, and Eric C. Halberg, my traffic consultant. After several days, Walter J. Myskowski, whom I had met several years before when he was on the legal staff of the New Haven Railroad, approached me and said he understood that I was looking for the assistance of another transportation lawyer. I knew of his reputation as a competent lawyer in this field. On my recommendation, State Attorney General Lefkowitz appointed Mr. Myskowski to assist me in this proceeding. Shortly thereafter I was able to obtain the services of Robert W. Alvord, a prominent tax attorney in Washington, D. C., to handle tax matters of special concern to my office.

Governor Rockefeller soon became concerned about the implications to the economy of the State of New York of these proposed railroad merger proceedings. He decided to appear personally and testify at the hearings involving the Chesapeake and Ohio, Baltimore and Ohio, and New York Central railroads before the Interstate Commerce Commission. The Governor's concern was that the consummation of the controls and mergers proposed in this and other emerging railroad mergers in the eastern part of the United States would change the flow of traffic of these railroads, with harmful impact upon the economy of the State of New York.

It was during the preparation of the Governor's testimony, and particularly during his careful study of the pertinent facts and the best method of their presentation, that I had the opportunity to discuss with him the policy considerations involved in the pending merger proceeding, the beginning of several major rail merger proceedings affecting New York State. And it was during this period that I felt that I had begun to know the man—the warmth of his personality, his broad and understanding approach to the economic problems involved, the keenness of his mind, and his obvious dedication to the public welfare.

On September 10, 1961, our discussions continued on the Governor's plane en route that afternoon from New York to Washington, D. C. Other members of his staff were on the plane, including Dr. Ronan, and an attorney friend, Oscar Reubhausen, upon whose judgement Governor Rockefeller also relied. As we were fastening our seat belts preparatory to landing in Washington, the Governor turned to me, and, with a smile, said: "Arne, you have got to get used to the way I work."

Apparently I had been somewhat vigorous in setting forth my views. I answered that I was sure I could.

Even at this late hour, the Governor was not satisfied with the draft of his testimony. Discussions continued in Washington that night after a dinner which the Governor gave for mayors and other prominent public officials from New York State who came to testify before the Interstate Commerce Commission following the testimony of the Governor. The final draft was completed early the next morning, September 11, and the Governor testified before the Commission's hearing examiners in a packed hearing room at 9:30 that morning.

The Governor, the mayors and other prominent officials from New York State urged the Commission to authorize only sound railroad mergers in the public interest and supported inclusion of the New York Central Railroad in the proposed affiliation of the Chesapeake and Ohio and the Baltimore and Ohio railroads. The Central, it was pointed out, serves many states and is the backbone of New York's transportation system, serving thousands of industries employing hundreds of thousands of people.

In urging upon the Commission a coordinated approach to railroad consolidations, acquisitions and mergers, the Governor testified as follows:

The proposed mergers of major railroads operating between the Atlantic Coast and the Mississippi River are the beginning of what will certainly develop into a basic reorganization of the railroad map for all the Eastern Territory.

The determination of the future pattern of the railroad network for the eastern half of the United States cannot be handled piecemeal. It must not be left to chance or to the struggle of competing carriers for temporary strategic advantages. Natural economic forces and personal initiatives cannot be allowed to run their course uncontrolled when the interest of the public is so vitally involved as it is in the existence of efficient railroad service.

Consolidations or mergers are not necessarily a solution to the problems of the railroads.

Soundly conceived consolidations can strengthen management, provide cash for modernization of equipment and facilities, permit reductions in costs, curtail reductions in service, provide more frequent and faster service at lower rates, eliminate overlapping and duplicating facilities, make more efficient use of plant and personnel, make possible the use of the most efficient and direct routes, and create balanced railroad systems capable of competing effectively with all other forms of transportation. . . .

On the other hand, unwise consolidations or mergers—while perhaps giving immediate corporate, tax or financial advantage to one or more of the carriers involved—could seriously weaken or bankrupt other railroads serving in the same or adjacent territories, thus materially jeopardizing not only the public interest in efficient transportation but the nation's interest in a healthy and growing economy.

If consolidations or mergers which are both sound and in the public interest are not proposed by the carriers themselves, then some other approach must be devised to bring about a coordinated restructuring of the railroad transportation industry.

Although the New York Central withdrew from this particular proceeding because of the Chesapeake and Ohio's opposition, and renewed its discussions for a merger with the Pennsylvania Railroad Company, subsequent developments not only sustained Governor Rockefeller's views on transportation policy in railroad merger cases, but established the fact that the Governor's testimony had (1) raised rail merger proceedings before the Commission to a high level of public concern, and (2) led to an active and constructive interest in developing competitively balanced railroad systems that are sound and in the public interest.

The Governor seemed pleased with the outcome of his testimony before the Commission on September 11, 1961. Thereafter, we discussed further efforts on behalf of the State of New York in other major merger proceedings pending or proposed in the eastern part of the United States.

The Governor's son, Michael, was on the plane from New

York to Washington on September 10, 1961. I had an opportunity to visit with him, though the discussions of the Governor's forthcoming testimony before the Interstate Commerce Commission required most of my attention. Michael impressed me as a modest, intelligent and extremely likeable young man. His tragic death a few weeks thereafter in New Guinea was a great shock to all of us. The Governor's long and anguished but fruitless search for his boy touched the hearts of all Americans.

As time went on, Governor Rockefeller became increasingly active on the national political scene and this of course made greater demands on his time. From this time on during my tenure as Director of the Office of Transportation, my meetings with Governor Rockefeller were necessarily infrequent.

At this point in my service for the State of New York, and with my over-taxed energies at a low ebb, I felt that I had met my commitments to Governor Rockefeller and the Legislature of the State of New York. I had reactivated the New York State Office of Transportation and developed a meaningful transportation program, where there had been none, upon which others could build to meet the growing needs of the State. Further, my counterpart in New Jersey, Dwight R. G. Palmer, a truly remarkable gentleman whose achievements in the transportation field for the State of New Jersey have been outstanding, and I activated the New York-New Jersey Transportation Agency to serve the common transportation problems of the two States. In this view, I could find the true compensation that comes to any man who undertakes important public tasks, the satisfaction of achievements in the public interest that laid the foundation for wider horizons for the people of New York State.

I resigned my post as Director of the New York State Office of Transportation in a letter to Governor Rockefeller, dated April 23, 1962, which I delivered to the Governor personally. We talked for a half hour, He seemed genuinely sorry that I had resigned. I showed him a plaque that I had just received from the Capital District Traffic Association naming me Traffic Man of the Year 1962 "for outstanding service in the field of transportation." The Governor said, "This reflects great credit on you and the staff you have built for your Office." In his letter accepting my resignation, dated April 30, 1962, the Governor stated:

> Your decision to resign as director of the Office of Transportation is the source of the keenest regret to me.
>
> I can hardly overestimate the value of the job you have done or the critical conditions in the transportation field which made your task so vitally important.
>
> Under your knowledgeable and devoted leadership, we have dealt with our transportation problems at all levels—federal-state, interstate, and intrastate—with creative imagination and at the same time, hardheaded realism.
>
> On behalf of the people of the Empire State, I extend immeasurable thanks for the great contribution you have made. I know I speak for them also in wishing you every success in your future undertakings.

PART   TWO

> A healthy, efficent and economical transportation system, including adequate commuter service, is vital to the expansion of the State's economy. To provide such a transportation system, the State must have an overall transportation policy developed in cooperation with the Federal Government, neighboring states, and our own communities.
>
> GOVERNOR ROCKEFELLER, *in his message to the Legislature on January 7, 1959, recommending the creation of the Office of Transportation.*

SEVERAL DAYS after receiving Governor Rockefeller's letter of April 30, 1962, accepting my resignation as Director of the New York State Office of Transportation in his Cabinet, I had a call from the Secretary to the Governor, Dr. Ronan, asking to see me. When I arrived at his office, he said that the Governor wanted me to stay in office for another year. I was greatly surprised, for no particular reason was given; but Dr. Ronan said it would be appreciated and that I could take it a little easier. I said that I would talk to my wife and family doctor before commiting myself to another year. We finally agreed to the Governor's request if the demands upon me were not too great.

Realizing the overriding importance to the economic welfare to the State of New York, and particularly to the port of New York, of the eastern railroad merger proceedings before the Interstate Commerce Commission, I immediately turned my attention almost exclusively to directing the State's case before the Commission and stating its position in testimony within the guidelines set forth by Governor Rockefeller in the Chesapeake and Ohio-Baltimore and Ohio-New York Central merger proceeding.

The series of rail merger proceedings instituted before the Interstate Commerce Commission beginning in 1960, involving major railroads operating between the Atlantic Coast and the Mississippi River, continued to be one of the most significant developments in transportation affecting New York State, as well as the entire northeastern part of the United States.

On the basis of developments in 1961, it appeared that there would emerge in the eastern part of the United States, outside New England, three railroad systems—one centered around the Chesapeake and Ohio and Baltimore and Ohio railroads and the railroads they controlled, the Western Maryland, the Reading, the Central of New Jersey, and the Lehigh Valley; another around the Norfolk and Western-Nickel Plate-Wabash railroads; and one centering around the Pennsylvania-New York Central railroads and their "family lines," the Pittsburgh and Lake Erie, the Detroit, Toledo and Ironton, and the Ann Arbor. The fate of the remaining railroads in the East, notably the Erie-Lackawanna, the New Haven, the Delaware and Hudson, and the Boston and Maine, would then depend upon their inclusion in one of the three systems since there appeared to be no possibility of combining them into a fourth system.

Within the State of New York, the Erie-Lackawanna is second in importance only to the New York Central. In 1961, its track mileage within New York State was about 20 percent of the total for all railroads in the State, and more than 40 percent of its total miles of road was within New York State. It serves most of the larger cities in the State. Within the New York metropolitan area, the Erie-Lackawanna operated 286 suburban and commutation trains each day, carrying about 35,700 commuters daily. It handled about one-third of the total import-export traffic which moved by rail between the Midwest and the port of New York.

The Erie-Lackawanna was in very poor financial condition in 1961. If it were forced to remain independent and to try to compete with the three large systems in the making, its survival would be in doubt and many communities would be deprived of rail services.

Against the background of these and other facts, as presented in the testimony and exhibits of New York State witnesses in the Norfolk and Western-Nickel Plate-Wabash merger proceeding, I testified in the proceeding on February 26, 1962, as follows:

"The State of New York would support the proposed transaction as being in the public interest, if provision were made for the inclusion of the Erie-Lackawanna in the Norfolk and Western system. Since, however, the Erie-Lackawanna has withdrawn its petition for inclusion, after the Norfolk and Western's agreement to negotiate in good faith with the Erie-Lackawanna if and when the pending applications are approved, it would seem that the Commission cannot now require the inclusion of the Erie-Lackawanna as a condition to its approval of the present applications. In the circumstances, the Commission should disapprove the pending applications, without prejudice to the refiling of an application or applications which would include the Erie-Lacka-wanna in the Norfolk and Western system. In the alternative, the Commission should withhold any action on the pending applications until studies and negotiations as to a possible affiliation between the Norfolk and Western and Erie-Lackawanna have been completed and the results made known."

In my testimony, I pointed out that a delay in the disposition of the proposed Norfolk and Western system applications would cause little or no damage. The Norfolk and Western, Nickel Plate and Wabash railroads, I continued, are among the most prosperous lines in the East and are not in urgent need of the contemplated merger savings in order to insure their survival. The additional merger savings resulting from the inclusion of the Erie-Lackawanna might well exceed any savings lost by delay in approval of the pending Norfolk and Western-Nickel Plate-Wabash merger applications.

On behalf of the State of New York, on October 4, 1962, I filed a petition jointly with The Port of New York Authority and the City of New York, requesting that the three major rail merger proceedings be consolidated by the Commission for decision. The consolidation of these three proceedings would permit the Commission to consider the three applications together, and in the light of each other, and thus would enable the Commission to determine whether any one or all three would be consistent with the public interest. On December 17, 1962, the Commission denied the joint petition insofar as it sought consolidation of the Chesapeake and Ohio-Baltimore and Ohio application with the other two proceedings, but reserved decision as to consolidating the Norfolk and Western-Nickel Plate-Wabash and the Pennsylvania-New York Central proceedings.

After the hearings in the Norfolk and Western merger proceedings were concluded, the Delaware and Hudson filed a petition for reopening and for inclusion in the transaction. Although the Delaware and Hudson was allowed to intervene, its petition for reopening and for inclusion was denied by the Commission. Should the Erie-Lackawanna be included in the Norfolk and Western system, it appeared incontrovertible that the Delaware and Hudson should also be included.

From our studies of the eastern railroad merger proposals, it was clear that the key to competitively balanced railroad systems in the northeastern part of the United States was the ownership by the Pennsylvania Railroad and its wholly-owned subsidiary, the Pennsylvania Company, of 33.7 percent of Norfolk and Western Railroad stock, which constituted effective control of that railroad. Without the complete divestiture of Pennsylvania's stock interest in Norfolk and Western, there would be no possibility of establishing competitively balance railroad systems in this great region of the United States.

Further, except for the New York Central, none of the main railroads serving New York State were included in the railroad merger applications pending before or approved by the Interstate Commerce Commission. And from our studies of the record in these merger proceedings, it also became clear that the inclusion of the New York Central Railroad in one of the proposed railroad systems was not assured.

For the purpose of discussing with Governor Rockefeller the position the State should take in the Pennsylvania-New York Central merger proceedings, and receiving his approval, a conference was held in the Governor's office in Albany on January 14, 1963, at which the Governor, the Attorney General, several other State officials and I were present. My office had prepared several maps showing the three major railroad systems proposed by the railroads directly concerned for the eastern part of the United States, as well as the railroads that were not included in these proposed systems. These maps, being large, were spread on the floor, and chairs were arranged around them for everyone present.

Referring repeatedly to these maps, I explained the major changes these proposed railroad mergers would make in railroad services for New York State, the effect these changes would have on the economy of the State, and the broad public issues involved. Thereafter, I outlined the position which my Office recommended the State should take in the testimony of the State's witnesses in the Pennsylvania-New York Central merger proceeding. Following an extended discussion, the Governor approved the position the State should take in this merger proceeding as recommended by my Office. Shaking my hand, the Governor added: "Arne, you and your staff are doing an outstanding job. I appreciate it very much." I thanked him and said that I had an excellent staff working on these railroad merger proceedings.

On January 21, 1963, I testified in the Pennsylvania-New

York Central merger proceeding at a hearing held by the Interstate Commerce Commission in New York City. I stated the position of the State as follows:

"The State of New York would favor the merger of the Pennsylvania and New York Central Railroads as part of the formation of three competitive systems within Official Territory, provided that as a condition to its approval of the Norfolk and Western-Nickel Plate-Wabash merger, the Commission required the divestiture by the Pennsylvania Railroad and the Pennsylvania Company of its large and probably controlling interest in the Norfolk and Western. Without the imposition of this condition, the pending joint application should be disapproved as not consistent with the public interest."

My statement of the position of the State of New York was made against the background of the following facts of record: The Pennsylvania Railroad is a party to both the Norfolk and Western-Nickel Plate-Wabash merger proceeding and the Pennsylvania-New York Central merger proceeding. The Pennsylvania Railroad agreed to divestiture of its Norfolk and Western Stock as a condition to the approval of the Pennsylvania-New York Central merger but did not agree to do so in the Norfolk and Western merger proceeding. In his testimony, James M. Symes, Chairman of the Board of Directors of the Pennsylvania Railroad, stated that the Commission should consider the Chesapeake and Ohio-Baltimore and Ohio application, the Norfolk and Western-Nickel Plate-Wabash application, and the Pennsylvania-New York Central application separately and in that order. In light of these facts and Mr. Symes' statement, I testified as follows:

"If the Commission were to approve the Norfolk and Western application without requiring divestiture by the Pennsylvania of its Norfolk and Western stock, the Pennsylvania might well decide not to go through with the merger with the New York Central, particularly if the Commission attaches any conditions which the Pennsylvania considers onerous. A Pennsylvania-Norfolk and Western-Nickel Plate-Wabash system would be a monopoly so powerful as to prevent effective competition by any other carrier within Official Territory, except possibly the recently approved Chesapeake and Ohio-Baltimore and Ohio combination. If the major lines providing substantial service within the State of New York are forced to remain independent and try to compete with the Chesapeake and Ohio-Baltimore and Ohio and the Pennsylvania-Norfolk and Western-Nickel Plate-Wabash combination, the results would be catastrophic. Mr. Alfred E. Perlman, President of the New York Central, has testified in this proceeding that the approval of the Chesapeake and Ohio-Baltimore and Ohio application, which has already been granted, and of the Norfolk and Western application, without approval of the Pennsylvania-New York Central merger application, would bankrupt the New York Central.

"The New York Central and the Erie-Lackawanna, the two largest railroads serving the State, have worked to improve the economic welfare of the State and have fostered the movement of import and export traffic through the port of New York. The Delaware and Hudson is also an important carrier serving the State. The future fate of the Erie-Lackawanna and New York Central is presently questionable. The bankruptcy of these two roads would likely result if their railroad competitors were allowed to strengthen themselves by mergers or affiliations, while the New York lines were forced to remain independent and try to go it alone. The serious effects upon the State of New York, and indeed upon the Nation, if this were allowed to happen, cannot be over-emphasized. Nationalization of the financially weak New York lines and indeed eventual nationalization of all the railroads could well result."

. . . . .

"Mr. Symes' position is that the Commission should consider the Chesapeake and Ohio, the Norfolk and Western and the Pennsylvania-New York Central applications separately and in that order. He opposed consolidation of the three applications for decision or simultaneous disposition, which was urged by Mr. Perlman. If the Norfolk and Western applications are approved before the Pennsylvania-New York Central application is decided, the Pennsylvania will have an opportunity to re-examine its position. At that point it would be in a position to exercise more directly its present power to control the Norfolk and Western system and drop the proposed merger with the New York Central."

In my testimony, I stated that New York State was gravely concerned about the future of the New Haven Railroad. I expressed the view that the survival of the New Haven could most effectively be assured by its inclusion in the proposed Pennsylvania-New York Central system. In this regard, I testified:

"The inclusion of the New Haven in the proposed Pennsylvania-New York Central system could result in a more efficient suburban passenger service to and from New York City. The Long Island Railroad, which is owned by the Pennsylvania, is presently being operated as a redevelopment corporation under a special New York State statute which expires in 1966. At that time, the Long Island will presumably return to the Pennsylvania control. A single system, including the Pennsylvania, New York Central, Long Island and New Haven, would undoubtedly provide a coordinated, more efficient suburban service in the New York metropolitan area, which is so vitally needed."[3]

On behalf of the State, I urged in my testimony that the Pennsylvania and New York Central railroads make studies similar to those made by the Norfolk and Western which resulted in agreement that reductions in force resulting from the merger be accomplished by attrition, thus avoiding the tremendous hardships to individuals which would otherwise result. I also testified that the State wholeheartedly supported the proposal that employees whose jobs would be eliminated as a result of the merger be given the opportunity to take advantage of a re-training program, thereby preparing them for work in some other field of endeavor. Thus they would be able to make a transition which the changing railroad industry seems to require. In this connection, I testified:

"It should be pointed out that if, by mergers or affiliations, the railroads serving the State of New York can improve their financial condition, their service, and their ability to compete with other modes of transportation, and thereby attract new industries to the State, this would undoubtedly help to stabilize and even increase railroad em-

[3] Following extensive surveys and studies of the operating, costs, and the legal problems involved, on October 30, 1962, I submitted an official report entitled "The Opportunity, under private ownership and operation, to provide the finest, most modern rail commuter services for the New York metropolitan area." On February 15, 1963, many principles in this report were adopted by the newly-formed Tri-State Transportation Committee. As I testified in the Penn-Central merger case for the State of New York, the Pennsylvania Railroad should be required to improve and continue the operation of the Long Island Rail Road.

ployment in the State. The railroad industry is today a sick industry. If it can be made healthy and viable, it would be in a position to stop the drastic reductions in employment which have taken place in recent years and maintain a steady and increasing level of employment.

"The State of New York, like most people in industry, is very desirous of having the railroads of the country continue under private ownership. It is the most basic industry in our private enterprise system. The present plight of the railroad industry is due to a lack, on the part of both railroad officials and government at all levels, of a sense of the future. Sound mergers may be of substantial help in keeping railroads under private ownership, particularly if coupled with more enlightened regulatory and taxing policies by government at the local, state, and national levels. Unwise mergers, on the other hand, will increase the prospect of nationalization. The Commission has a wonderful opportunity in the pending proceedings to help the railroads and the country, but the proposed reorganization of the railroad system must be done right. This may be our last chance."

On July 13, 1964, the Interstate Commerce Commission approved the merger of the Norfolk and Western, Nickel Plate and Wabash railroads, and on April 6, 1966, the Commission approved the merger of the Pennsylvania and New York Central railroads. The Commission required, and so conditioned its approvals, that the Pennsylvania Railroad divest itself of its stock holdings in the Norfolk and Western, and that the Pennsylvania-New York Central merger include the New Haven Railroad, but in neither decision did the Commission require the immediate inclusion of the Erie-Lackawanna, the Delaware and Hudson, or the Boston and Maine Railroads.

The Interstate Commerce Commission adhered strictly to its case-by-case approach of the past, notably in dealing with the Chesapeake and Ohio-Baltimore and Ohio-New York Central merger proceeding. This generated a flood of petitions filed with the Commission seeking consolidation for hearing and decision of the various merger applications, the reopening of hearings for further testimony that bore on the broad public issues involved, the inclusion of the smaller railroads in one of the emerging major eastern railroad systems, and for many other purposes. While the Commission modified its views somewhat in response to these petitions, notably in relation to the smaller railroads in the area, this "change of heart" proved to be inadequate.

The Supreme Court of the United States, in an appeal from the order of the Interstate Commerce Commission approving the merger of the Pennsylvania Railroad Company and the New York Central Railroad Company, held on March 27, 1967,[4] that under the Commission's findings in that case it was a mistake for the Commission to permit consummation of the merger until it had determined the future of the three comparatively small railroads in the area—the Erie-Lackawanna, Delaware and Hudson and the Boston and Maine railroads. Noting that the Pennsylvania-New York Central merger was the largest railroad merger in history, the Court said,

"If not handled properly, (the merger) could seriously disrupt and irreparably injure the entire rail system in the northeastern section of the country—to the great detriment not only of the parties here but to the public convenience and necessity of the entire nation."

The Court ordered the case remanded for a final decision on the "ultimate fate" of the three smaller eastern railroads.

Thereafter, on June 12, 1967, the Interstate Commerce Commission announced its decision imposing adequate protective conditions for the Erie-Lackawanna, Delaware and Hudson, and Boston and Maine railroads pending their inclusion in the Norfolk and Western-Nickel Plate-Wabash railroad system.

Thus, six years after Governor Rockefeller's forthright policy statement on rail merger proceedings before the Interstate Commerce Commission, his views found support in a decision of the Nation's highest court.

Further, the Chairman of the Commission, William H. Tucker, against the background of the Court's decision, urged in a public address in Chicago before the Western Railway Club, on April 17, 1967, that each railroad in the western railroad merger picture should "review its own proposal with a view to amending or modifying it to meet its realistic needs in a tough-minded assessment of the overall public considerations." Without such a

[4] 386 U.S., 372.

basic assessment, Chairman Tucker said, "it may well be that the entire merger movement in the west may become just an exercise in futility." Then, emphasizing that he was speaking personally and not as a spokesman for the Commission, Mr. Tucker, in referring to the western railroad merger situation, stated:

"The majority of railroads appear to be merely maximizing their own special position in the projected merger transactions, without any real regard for the public interest or for the interests of other railroads and the vital services that such roads perform."

He added that the provisions of the Interstate Commerce Act relating to mergers were designed to provide the framework for establishing soundly conceived rail consolidations that would improve the nation's transportation system.

"They were not enacted to serve as the main competitive battle-ground for any group of railroads. Unless some of the parties do an abrupt about-face from their present positions, they may be in for a rude awakening."

What a tremendous endorsement of Governor Rockefeller's views on the public policy considerations that should govern the Interstate Commerce Commission in rail merger proceedings! The end result was that, in all its broad sweep, the Commission finally sustained the position taken by the State of New York in the eastern railroad merger proceedings. Only a man in high position, with the character, dedication, and determination of Governor Rockefeller, could have raised the basic public issues in these proceedings to a high level of public concern so that those who had the power of decision could not ignore them. This was truly an act of a statesman.

My responsibility as Director of the New York State Office of Transportation for the conduct of the State's intervention and my testimony for the State in these two major eastern railroad merger proceedings were my principal tasks during the year that followed my earlier resignation in April, 1962. The rest was largely routine.

In accordance with our understanding, Governor Rockefeller accepted my resignation in a letter, dated March 21, 1963, wherein he noted my need for "taking things just a little easier in the years ahead," and added:

"The Office of Transportation, under your leadership, has made tremendous progress. It has become a real force for improvement of transportation within our State and has had an important impact on transportation thinking and planning outside.

"It is reassuring for me to know that you are willing to continue to serve us on a part-time consulting basis and that in this manner we will have the continued benefit of your long experience in the field and your wisdom in transportation policy matters."

My respect for Governor Nelson A. Rockefeller as a man of strong political convictions, for which he consistently fought with great courage and determination, grew during my years as Director of the Office of Transportation in his Cabinet. His concern with the problems of transportation, so basic to the economic and social welfare of New York State and the nation, was an area of his interest with which I was most familiar and that I could serve best under his banner. From this account of my service as his Cabinet officer on transportation, it must be evident that my experience was not only a great opportunity for public service, an opportunity for which I shall always be grateful to Governor Rockefeller, but an experience that immeasurably widened my horizons. These indeed were memorable years that I shall always cherish.

After I had completed my consulting work for the State of New York, Mrs. Wiprud and I moved to Boca Raton, Florida, where we built a "retirement home" near the ocean. Time proved that it was to be an active "semi-retirement home."

As Adjunct Professor of Administration at the Florida Atlantic University in Boca Raton, I lectured on transportation and related subjects. At the presentation of the Federal Land Bank Golden Anniversary Medal at the University, as related in Chapter I, its President, Dr. Kenneth R. Williams, stated that he was "delighted that the University can participate in doing honor to Mr. Wiprud because of his considerable contribution to our teaching program."

As a consultant, I assisted the Florida Council of 100 in its efforts to improve and modernize its intercity passenger transportation between Miami and Jacksonville, Florida. The Florida Atlantic University and the University of Miami, supported by the Council, filed a joint application with the United States Department of Transportation for a contract and grant to make a survey and feasibility study for this purpose under the provisions of the High Speed Ground Transportation Act of 1965. The then Secretary of the Department of Transportation did not approve this joint application.

In May, 1966, enroute to Europe as a member of the United States Delegation to the meeting of the Governing Council of the United Nations Development Programme, held in Milan, Italy, as related in Chapter XI, I stopped in Washington, D. C., at the request of Thomas F. Fleming, Jr., a leader in the Florida Council of 100, for a conference with Dr. Robert A. Nelson, Director of the Office of High Speed Ground Transportation, in the United States Department of Transportation. At this conference, Dr. Nelson and I negotiated a contract between the Department of Transportation and the Florida Atlantic University for a grant, which totaled $37,000, to make a study of the public demand for auto-train passenger service between Washington, D. C., and Jacksonville, Florida.

CHAPTER X

Conglomerates and the Future of Private Enterprise in the United States

In previous chapters, I related my experiences as an attorney, administrator, and consultant in the field of transportation. In these capacities, I dealt with matters involving major transportation policies and actions of the Federal government and the railroads, as well as other modes of transportation, for almost a half century. In my discussion of these policies and actions, I do not question the sincerity of officials in government or the industry. However, time has proved that many of their programs and actions were unsound and extremely costly from the standpoint of the transportation industry and the country.

Thus far we have discussed transportation policies in the past, and if the past is prologue, what does the future hold? Have the Federal government and the industry learned from their past mistakes, mistakes that have brought the transportation industry to the most critical period in its history? How will responsible officials in government and industry meet the nation's present and future transportation needs? Will they insure the continuation of private enterprise in transportation or will their policies lead to nationalization of transportation in the United States? These are questions to which answers are being sought by Americans who are concerned with trends away from competitive private enterprise in our national economy, including the transportation industry.

Apparently spurred on by the success of the organized railroad industry in prevailing upon the Congress to override President Truman's veto of the Reed-Bulwinkle bill, which effectively repealed the antitrust laws concerned with preserving competition in the transportation industry, dominant private groups pressed their plans to extend their control over large segments of the nation's economy. While public attention is focused on the plight of the cities, the poor, health, education and welfare programs, wars abroad, violence at home, antiballistic missiles, achievements in outer space, many of these dominant private groups are converting their organizations into "conglomerates" to achieve their objective.

A conglomerate has been defined simply as a corporation that exists mainly to make money by owning other corporations which have little or no relationship to each other. For example, the International Telephone and Telegraph Corporation, a large, powerful and fast growing conglomerate, acquired or merged with at least 120 companies, including some industry leaders, in the years 1961 to 1968. Its sales increased from $900 million to $4 billion and its assets from $1 billion to $4 billion in the same period. It ranks as the eleventh among the nation's industrial corporations and the fourth largest employer with 307,000 employees.

In 1969, the board of directors of the International Telephone and Telegraph Corporation consummated or approved 33 more mergers. Again, some industry leaders were involved, including The Hartford Fire Insurance Company with assets of $1,891,700,000 and $400 million in excess of required surplus. The International Telephone and Telegraph Corporation–Hartford Fire Insurance Company proposed merger involves about $6 billion in total assets, an amount greater than that of any merger in recent times, and probably in the history of the country. As hereinafter discussed, the Department of Justice instituted an antitrust suit challenging the legality of this proposed merger.

The industry leaders acquired or merged or with agreements to merge with the International Telephone and Telegraph Corporation were or are engaged separately in one of the following businesses: home building, operating bakeries, building and operating hotels and motor inns, producing chemical cellulose and lumber, manufacturing automatic fire protection equipment, renting cars, selling insurance, operating vending machines, and airport parking.[1]

In those instances where negotiations for stock control of a company fails, an aggressive conglomerate makes a tender offer for the company's stock directly to the stockholders over the heads of management. This tender offer usually consists of a mixed package of securities that includes the conglomerate's stock, debentures which amount to long-term promissory notes, and stock-purchasing warrants, a package that appears to be worth far above the market value of the company's stock sought to be acquired. If it can induce enough stockholders to accept the tender offer to insure control, the company is merged into the conglomerate and the conglomerate usually moves the old management out and installs its own management. A hotly contested takeover has been recognized by some as a form of industrial warfare. This latter method of acquiring a company is called "raiding." The tender offer is an important force in the conglomerate movements.[2]

The trend toward mergers in the United States has developed to amazing proportions. In 1968 there were 4,462 mergers, up approximately 50 percent from 1967, and 300 percent more than in 1963. Conglomerate mergers have increased from 38.1 percent in 1948-51 to 88.6 percent of all mergers in 1968. Government and private experts predicted that 5,400 independent companies with assets that might reach $18 billion, including some of the oldest and most respected names in industry, would vanish in mergers in 1969.

In 1966, the acquisitions of large manufacturing and mining firms, those with assets of $10 million or more, numbered 100 with total assets of about $4 billion. The number of large firms

[1] See Appendix B.
[2] Hearings before the Ways and Means Committee, House of Representatives, 91st Cong., 1st Sess., 2365, 2382-2385, 2395.

acquired rose to 160 in 1967 with assets of $8 billion, and to 188 in 1968 with assets of $12.4 billion. The most significant effect of the accelerating merger activity in recent years has been to concentrate further the ownership of manufacturing resources in the hands of a few vast conglomerate enterprises. In 1968, two hundred of the largest industrial corporations held 60 percent of the assets of all manufacturing corporations in the United States. The head of one conglomerate predicts that in 10 years there will be only 200 major industrial companies in the United States, all conglomerates.[3]

Assistant Attorney General Richard W. McLaren, in charge of the Antitrust Division, Department of Justice, in testimony before the Senate Judiciary Committee hearing on his confirmation, noted that his predecessors at the Antitrust Division had taken the position that the "purer" forms of conglomerate mergers could not be reached under Section 7 of the Clayton Antitrust Act. This section of the Act proscribes corporate mergers and acquisitions whose effect "may be substantially to lessen competition, or tend to create a monopoly." They suggested that conglomerate mergers which threaten undue concentration of economic power should be dealt with through new legislation. Mr. McLaren testified that he was not persuaded that Section 7 will not reach "purer" types of conglomerate mergers than have been dealt with by the courts thus far. He also testified that he was not opposed to new legislation but that the matter was too pressing to wait. He added:

> We are willing to risk losing some cases to find out how far Section 7 will take us in halting the current accelerated trend toward concentration by merger and—as I see it—the severe economic and social dislocations attendant thereon.

These dislocations he described as follows:

> Aside from the competitive impact of increased economic concentration, I am concerned over the human dislocations which result from these mergers. When the headquarters of one or two large companies

[3] *Ibid.,* 2391, 2397, 2410-2412.

are removed from the Nation's smaller cities to New York or Chicago or Los Angeles, I think we all recognize that there is a serious impact upon the community. The loss is felt by its banks, its merchants, its professional and service people—accountants, lawyers, advertising agencies. The community loses some of its best educated, most energetic, and public spirited citizens. I am concerned that some of our larger centers may become "branch house cities" whose major business affairs are directed by absentee managers.

As I have indicated earlier, these are results which contravene the national policy as repeatedly expressed by Congress.

The Department of Justice under the direction of Assistant Attorney General McLaren has instituted antitrust suits against some of the largest conglomerates, several of which are mentioned herein, and is seeking legislation from Congress to eliminate the tax advantages of conglomerate mergers which he calls "this tax-propelled merger mania."[4]

On February 10, 1969, Congressman Wilbur D. Mills, Chairman of the House Committee on Ways and Means, in a press release, expressed his concern with the increasing trend in recent months towards conglomerate mergers, which reads in part as follows:

A recent study made by W. T. Grimm and Company of Chicago stated that of 66 surprise takeover bids which have occurred since the summer of 1967 the total dollar value of these offers amounted to nearly $12 billion. One of the side effects of this has been to artificially inflate stock prices—in the case of the 66 takeovers to the extent of $2.4 billion over prior stock prices.

Congressman Mills questioned whether it was good either for the stockholders or for the economy' as a whole for these conglomerate mergers to occur. From the standpoint of the economy, these mergers substantially decrease competition whether or not the mergers occur in similar lines of business because of the consolidation of financial power that results.

From the standpoint of the stockholders, many of the securities offered in these takeovers are highly speculative and could well result in substantial losses whenever there is a downturn in business conditions. The stockholders should also be concerned with the problems

[4] *Ibid.,* 2386-2394.

presented by the merger of wholly unrelated businesses. From a personal standpoint, it may well make investment in selective industries virtually impossible. It is difficult to see how mergers of this type can benefit either the economy or the stockholders involved.

The financing of these conglomerate mergers is top heavy with debt securities which not only can present serious problems for the new business structure if business conditions turn down but also will have a serious impact on Government revenues by converting what formerly were nondeductible dividend payments into tax deductible interest payments.

Congressman Mills pointed out that the Committee on Ways and Means had expressed its concern with the problem of conglomerate takeovers by specifically including this topic in its tax reform hearings. He warned "companies to go slow in conglomerate mergers if they are depending upon any of the tax provisions for the success of their merger."

Mr. Paul C. Cabot, Board Chairman of the State Street Investment Corporation, Boston, Massachusetts, in testimony before the Ways and Means Committee, stated:[5]

It seems that each generation is cursed with problems all born of greed and a lust for power. Many years ago there was the panic caused by speculation in tulip bulbs in Holland. In this country, we had the era of the robber barons—Jim Fiske, Jay Gould, and others. In my lifetime, we had the Florida land boom of the early '20s, more recently the utility holding company scandals, and now we have the conglomerates.

Conglomerate leaders say the fear of conglomerates is exaggerated. Instead of harm, they contend that conglomerates, among other claimed advantages hereinafter noted, will aid the economy by taking over companies that are limping along under shabby, myopic and outdated management and provide them with better managements. But it appears that conglomerates are endeavoring to take over some of the largest and most successfully managed corporations in the United States. For example, in 1968, the Jones & Laughlin Steel Company, a billion dollar

[5] *Ibid.*, 2385.

corporation, was taken over by Ling-Temco-Vought, Inc., one of the largest conglomerates, and was immediately confronted with an antitrust suit instituted by the Antitrust Division of the Department of Justice. Among other conglomerates that have acquired or seek to acquire industry leaders is the International Telephone and Telegraph Corporation. Its most ambitious proposal is its agreement to merge with The Hartford Fire Insurance Company, a two billion company that is financially sound, well managed, and widely respected. As has been noted, this proposed merger is challenged in an antitrust suit instituted by the Department of Justice.

Many prominent leaders in industry are appealing to the Department of Justice and the Congress for protection because it is evident that no company is big enough to be immune from an aggressive conglomerate. One adverse effect has been stated as follows:[6]

The targets of this aggression are some of the most upright, prudent, powerful, and self-assured corporations in the land. Self assurance is fading. Proud old names have already been taken over, and dozens of veteran executives have been sacked. Foreboding, frustration, and even fear are epidemic in perhaps three out of five big corporate headquarters. Anguished executives who should be minding the shop are instead behaving as if they were up to some underhanded adventure, spending long hours counseling with lawyers, management consultants, proxy specialists, and public-relations men skilled in the art of forefending takeovers.

The many problems created by the takeover methods and other practices of conglomerates involving security issues, inflation of stock prices, tax considerations, effect on Federal government revenues, accounting practices, among others, are being given careful study by government and industry officials and their experts. The overriding public issue, however, is the rapidly increasing control and power over the nation's economy by conglomerates in the hands of a few private groups which threaten the continued existence of the American free enterprise system.

[6] Article by Gilbert Burck, titled *The Merger Movement Rides High*, in Fortune magazine, February 1969.

Bank-based conglomerates

Banks are normally barred by law from engaging in nonbanking businesses, but under a loophole in the Bank Holding Company Act of 1956 they may form a one-bank holding company and transfer to it the ownership of the bank. Then the banks, through the device of the one-bank holding company which is exempt from Federal Reserve Board regulation, have acquired or propose to acquire nonbanking enterprises, thus forming so-called bank-based conglomerates.

By December 31, 1968, 783 banks, controlling $108.2 billion in bank deposits of the nation, organized unregulated holding companies for this purpose or announced plans to do so. They include 34 of the largest 100 commercial banks in the United States, with deposits of over $100 billion, that are preparing to move into trade, insurance and manufacturing by forming one-bank holding companies in the conglomerate pattern. They include 9 of the 12 largest banks in the United States.

Of the 684 unregulated one-bank holding companies identified as of September 1, 1968, 578 participated in 20 different financial nonbanking activities, including insurance agencies and companies, as well as various types of credit institutions. Among these same 684 one-bank holding companies, 397 are engaged in 99 different nonfinancial activities, ranging from agricultural, mining and petroleum operations to various types of manufacturing, as well as carrying on businesses in the transportation, real estate, and wholesale and retail sales fields.

Thus have these banks entered a large field of nonbanking businesses. "This," the Staff Report for the Committee on Banking and Currency, House of Representatives, states "is in direct conflict with the basic principle of public policy established in the Glass-Steagall Act of 1933 and the Bank Holding Company Act of 1956."[7]

The Staff Report, which should be read by every concerned American, continues and concludes with a final warning:

[7] *The Growth of Unregistered Bank Holding Companies—Problems and Prospects,* Staff Report for the Committee on Banking and Currency, House of Representatives, 91st Cong., 1st Sess., 1, 2, February 11, 1969.

The principles established in these laws is that the health of the American economy is vitally dependent upon keeping the business of banking completely separate from nonbanking business activity. *This principle was originally laid down by Congress during the depression partly because of the relationship established at that time between commercial banks' nonbanking activities and the stockmarket crash of 1929.* It has been felt by many since that time that the mixing of banking with nonbanking activities within the same corporate structure has three major adverse consequences:

(1) There is inevitably a strong temptation to have the banking subsidiary of a holding company extend large amounts of credit, perhaps unwisely, to other holding company subsidiaries, thus creating unsound financial conditions for the bank to the detriment of the bank's depositors, stockholders and the public at large. *This is the kind of activity in which some of the larger banks in the country were engaged in the 1920s.*

(2) Since banks are the principal suppliers of substantial credit to almost every industrial, commercial and other kind of business in the United States, banks should not be in a position to discriminate unfairly against these users of bank credit by establishing competing subsidiaries and then denying credit to the competitors of the bank's nonbanking subsidiaries. This is a particularly serious problem in the many cities and towns all over the United States where there are only one or two major banking institutions to which business can turn for substantial amounts of credit.

(3) Because many large and small businesses, as well as individuals, depend on bank credit for their economic existence, bank subsidiaries of one bank holding companies are in a position to insist or "strongly suggest" that if the borrower wants continued access to bank credit, it should also use the services of the holding company's other subsidiaries. These services might include insurance, equipment leasing, property management, accounting, computing, investment and travel sercices, or any other business the holding company might decide to undertake. This would create unfair competition for non-bank related competitors of these subsidiaries and could in the long run substantially reduce or eliminate competiton in many businesses to the detriment of the public interest.

The Staff Report warns—

The unquestionable potential for these kinds of practices continuing unabated under existing circumstances could radically change the entire economic structure of the United States by the creation of giant conglomerate cartels centered around large banking institutions. Congress will have to decide soon whether it wishes to see the basic principle of maintaining a separation between banking and nonbanking activities effectively continued by plugging loopholes in existing law, or whether it is willing, through inaction, to see this principle, in effect, abandoned. [italics supplied]

Railroad-based conglomerates

Railroads, which are limited by law from engaging in non-transportation businesses, have formed conglomerates or have plans to do so. By creating "parent" holding companies, which then reach out into other businesses, the railroads seek to free themselves from what they regard as crippling Interstate Commerce Commission supervision of their non-transportation activities. Their apprehension seems unwarranted, to say the least, in view of the decisions of the Commission in the 1960s in which it appears to have abandoned its half-century old policy of antipathy to outside financial activities of the railroads. Briefly, these are the facts.[8]

In 1913, as the result of the Commission's investigation of the New Haven Railroad Company's "outside financial operations," it stated:[9]

No student of the railroad problem can doubt that the most prolific source of financial disaster and complication to railroads in the past has been the desire and ability of railroad managers to engage in enterprises outside the legitimate operations of their railroads.

The evil which results, first to the investing public and finally to the general public, cannot be corrected after the transaction has taken place; it can be easily and effectively prohibited. [italics supplied]

The Commission concluded:

Every interstate railroad should be prohibited from expending money or incurring liability or acquiring property not in the operation of

[8] Article by Colin Barrett, "Conglomerates and Public Responsibility," published in *Traffic World*, March 1, 1969.
[9] 27 ICC 560.

its railroad or in the legitimate improvement, extension or development of that railroad.

In 1914, the Commission issued its report on the New Haven Railroad, in which it characterized the misconduct of the officials of that railroad as "one of the most glaring instances of maladiministration revealed in the history of American railroading." It estimated the loss to the New Haven Railroad "by reason of waste and mismanagement" would amount to between $60 million and $90 million.[10] This report was issued three months before Congress passed the Clayton Antitrust Act. Section 10 of that Act sought to protect the public interest against transportation officials and private interests that seek to use the property, the funds, and the credit of the railroads in outside financial activities as a means of exploiting the American people.

In 1920, Congress enacted legislation (Section 20a of the Interstate Commerce Act) to implement the Commission's policy suggestion made in its 1913 decision, by giving the Commission veto power over a railroad's issuance of securities or assumption of any financial obligation and liabilities and provided that, before approving such action, the Commission must find that "it is necessary or appropriate for or consistent with the performance by the carrier of service to the public as a common carrier, and . . . . will not impair its ability to perform that service."

In the early 1960s, the Commission rendered two decisions that together have been responsible for the railroads' move toward conglomerate form.[11]

The first decision involved the Bangor and Aroostock Railroad Company, a small railroad serving northern Maine. This railroad created the first of the modern conglomerate holding companies, the Bangor and Aroostock Company, then merged this holding company with the Punta Alegra Sugar Company to form the Bangor Punta Company. Mr. Barrett's article in the *Traffic World* states:

To understand the importance of this move, the observer must

[10] 31 ICC 32.
[11] See footnote 8.

remember that the Commission is empowered to impose both the securities provisions and certain reporting requirements (albeit in somewhat lessened form) on railroad holding companies, as well as on the railroad themselves. However, as a prerequisite to imposition of these obligations on the parent companies, the statute requires the ICC to first assert jurisdiction over the holding company's acquisition of control of the railroad, and it may not do so unless control of more than one carrier is involved.

In 1960, the Bangor and Aroostock Railroad controlled the Van Buren Bridge Co., another carrier. The Commission, however, found that these two companies "are constituents of a single integrated system." It eschewed jurisdiction over the Bangor and Aroostock Co., and, by extension, over the Bangor Punta.

The Bangor Punta is completely free from any ICC supervision of its activities, although the railroad subsidiary, of course, remains under Commission jurisdiction. The Commission's policy of sharply inhibiting railroad expansion into non-transportation endeavors, accordingly, was (and still is) inapplicable to Bangor Punta.

Bangor Punta has acquired and owns about 20 companies, only one of which is a railroad. It is the first in the nation in the manufacture of public security equipment and second in boat making. Its total sales in 1968 were about $258 million; of this, the railroad's total contribution was a $100,000 profit.

In October, 1969, an agreement between the Bangor Punta Company and the Amoskeag Company provided for the sale to the Amoskeag Company of the stock of the Bangor and Aroostock Railroad, owned by the Bangor Punta Company, for $5 million. This stock was carried on the books of the Bangor Punta Company at about $18 million.[12] Thus, Bangor Punta Company, the first railroad-based conglomerate, became the first such conglomerate to "spin off" its railroad subsidiary and become a conglomerate owning and operating only non-transportation companies.[13]

Mr. Barrett continues:

[12] *Traffic World,* October 11, 1969.

[13] Northwest Industries, Inc., a railroad-based conglomerate created by the Chicago and North Western Railway Company, has offered to get out of the railroad business by selling all the assests of the Chicago and North Western Railway Company. (*Traffic World,* March 21 and April 4, 1970.)

Two years later, in another context, the Commission issued a decision which financial analysts saw as virtually an open invitation to transportation firms to diversify. The landmark quality of this decision is indicated by the fact that five of the eleven ICC members dissented on the ground that the majority was proposing to vitiate, in a single blow, the Commission's 48-year old policy of antipathy toward such activities.

Before the Commission was an application of the Greyhound Corporation (at that time an active carrier, not the holding company it subsequently became) for authority to issue considerable amounts of stock. Purpose of the issue was to allow Greyhound to gain control of Boothe Leasing Corporation, an industrial machinery leasing company not involved in transportation in any way; furthermore, Boothe insisted on a stock exchange arrangement to protect its stockholders from tax liabilities, thus making the ICC's decision on the stock question determinative of the fate of the entire transaction.

The Commission approved the stock issuance in its report and order in that case.[14]

As the result of these decisions, railroad managements have formed parent holding companies, or have plans to do so in furtherance of their programs for diversification into non-transportation fields. Among others, the Illinois Central, Chicago & North Western, Missouri-Kansas-Texas, Atchison, Topeka & Santa Fe, Seaboard Coast Line, Kansas City Southern, Boston & Maine, and the Penn-Central railroads have entered the conglomerate movement.

The Interstate Commerce Commission has not assumed jurisdiction over the parent holding companies created by railroads for the purpose of entering the conglomerate movement, except in two cases. The cases involve Illinois Central Industries, established by the Illinois Central Railroad, and Northwestern Industries, created by the Chicago & North Western Railroad.

The Commission has limited its supervision over these two holding companies to the imposition of the minimum in reporting requirements, but it has made no effort to apply the all-important securities provisions of Section 20a of the Interstate

[14] 90 MCC 215.

Commerce Act in railroad merger proceedings. However, other parties to these proceedings have appeared and argued that a parent holding company of a railroad-based conglomerate should be required to seek Commission approval of any securities issurance by it, or any assumption of obligation or liabilities respecting others' securities, to avoid weakening through the parent holding company the financial position of the railroad. To this end, the Commission was urged to take effective jurisdiction over the parent holding company of railroad-based conglomerates.

In its reply, Northwestern Industries warned the Commission that any enforcement of the securities provisions of the Interstate Commerce Act on it, or on any of its fellow railroad parents, would have an enormously detrimental effect on their diversification programs. The reply continued:

> The delay that would attend a Section 20a proceeding [in connection with securities issuance by the holding company] would deprive Industries and all similarly situated companies of any hope of successfully competing for the acquisition of non-transportation companies. The purpose and effectiveness of all railroad holding companies created in recent years to bring to the transportation industry the benefits of diversification would be destroyed.

This argument, which does not deny the Interstate Commerce Commission's exclusive authority in this matter, is that the Commission must not look through form to substance in performing its clearly defined duties to protect the interest of the railroads and the public. In essence, it is a plea for unregulated railroad diversification into non-transportation businesses, a concept that overlooks the fact that *the railroads are public service companies,* subject to public regulation as such, not a vehicle for unrestricted expansion *by any device*[15] into outside financial ventures which Congress brought under regulation by the Commission in Section 20a of the Interstate Commerce Act.

[15] The device here (as in the case of bank-based conglomerates) is that the "child" of the railroad, the holding company, becomes the "parent" to which the ownership of the railroad is transferred, and if the Commission refrains from enforcing Section 20a against the holding company. the latter can then use the assets of the railroad, without restriction, as a base to enter into outside financial activities which the railroad cannot do without the approval of the Commission.

I agree with the following statement of Colin Barrett in his article:

Virtually no one—certainly no responsible person—is seeking to block all railroad expansion beyond the transportation industry. There are, however, many who are fearful that untrammeled expansion could bring railroads more trouble than benefits.

Advocates of railroad-based conglomerates contend that:

Diversification is vitally important to provide a broader financial base for railroad operations, and it can be achieved through the establishment of railroad-based conglomerates.

The conglomerate parent holding company can supply funds for needed capital expenditures of the railroad, funds that the railroad itself cannot afford.

Since banks make size a principal factor in their consideration of loan requests, by increasing its size through acquisition of non-transportation companies, the railroad is given another financial advantage.

Losses incurred by the railroad component can benefit the balance of the conglomerate's structure by providing tax shelters for profitable non-transportation companies, members of the complex. There could also be tax advantages for the railroad component.

The unfavorable financial condition of many railroads requires diversification through railroad-based conglomerates without interference from the Interstate Commerce Commission. As has been stated, this contention is that the delay attending the application of the securities provisions of the Interstate Commerce Act by the Commission to the parent holding company would effectively destroy the most efficient method by which the railroads can diversify.

Opponents of railroad-based conglomerates contend that:

Railroad managements as a whole are (1) inexperienced in the highly competitive and sophisticated acquisition business, usually managed by lawyers and investment bankers, and (2) most railroad managements have little ownership in their companies and therefore must have limited entrepreneurial incentive to take risks or make aggressive moves.

Unregulated diversification through conglomerates would afford a perfect opportunity for milking the railroad by siphoning off, via intercorporate transactions, most of the wealth and disposable non-transportation assets (such as real estate) of the railroad. It could then be cast adrift to fend for itself with greatly depleted resources.

Inexperienced railroad men, with the best of intentions but with questionable judgment, might enter into a series of ill-advised transactions which could dissipate the conglomerate's—and through it, the railroad's—assets to a point where serious financial problems might arise.

Even with relatively experienced managements in the conglomerate field, over-ambition may cause over-expansion in terms of obligations, followed by extensive retrenching in order to right itself.

The parent holding company may become so large, and so diversified, that the operations of the railroad subsidiary may suffer from inattention, if nothing else. The railroad's principal duty is to transportation, not to a complex multi-business conglomerate structure.

The financial problems are one aspect of the problems resulting from the formation of railroad-based conglomerates. Another difficulty arises from the "commodities clause" of Section 1 (8) of the Interstate Commerce Act. This section prohibits railroads from transporting "any article or commodity, other than timber and the manufactured products thereof, manufactured, mined or produced by it [i.e., the railroad], or under its authority, or which it may own in whole or in part, or in which it may have any interest, direct or indirect, except such articles or commodities as may be necessary and intended for its use in the conduct of its business as a common carrier." Railroad-based conglomerates would make the "commodities clause" virtually impossible to police. The failure of the Interstate Commerce Commission to assume any jurisdiction, even for reporting purposes, over the holding companies of railroad-based conglomerates means that the Commission may not even know when possible violations of the "commodities clause" were taking place, because of the lack of information about the railroad's non-transportation activities.

As one whose philosophy about transportation is grounded in the conviction that transportation is a basic industry in our private enterprise economy which can and must be preserved as such, I have been concerned and puzzled about the attitude of some of the principal owners and managers of the nation's railroads on a vital matter.

This matter concerns the refusal or the claimed inability of the managements of the nation's railroads to include in their annual reports to the Interstate Commerce Commission the names of *beneficial* owners of large blocks of stock in their railroads which are held in the names of brokerage firms or investment houses, generally termed "street names." A brokerage firm, for example, may be listed in a railroad's annual report to the Commission as one of the largest stockholders of any given railroad but may actually have title to only a few shares, or possibly none at all. Other arrangements to hide the identity of *beneficial* owners include the establishment of ficticious companies as nominees of brokers of banks. The Commission has accepted such "street names" and nominees in annual reports of stockholders made to it by the railroads of the country, although, under Section 5 (7) of the Interstate Commerce Act, it has the power to demand and receive from the brokers or other organizations the names of *beneficial* owners of the railroads, or it can go to court to obtain a decree authorizing it to examine the records of brokers or others to determine the actual ownership of railroads.

In the 1960s, considerable controversy arose in the public press, in the Congress, and in the United States Supreme Court over the fact that these "street names" and other arrangements "walled off" the Interstate Commerce Commission from knowledge of the real owners of large blocks of stock in most of the nation's railroads.

This situation raises a number of questions of public concern. Since the Commission has not obtained the names of the "invisible owners" of large blocks of stock in the nation's railroads, how can it properly perform its functions under the Interstate Commerce Act to protect the public interest? Are any of these "invisible owners" foreign countries or groups in such countries and, if so, are they friendly or unfriendly to our free private enterprise system? Are these "invisible owners" individuals or groups of individuals in the United States or abroad owners of large blocks of stocks in competing railroads which may constitute common control of these railroads contrary to law? Do these "invisible owners" exercise such control that they determine the major policies of the nation's railroads, such as programs to establish railroad-owned transportation cartels and railroad-based conglomerates? These and many other questions are being asked that can only be answered by a frank disclosure to the Interstate Commerce Commission of the *beneficial* owners of blocks of stock in the nation's railroads.

This incredible situation is a matter of public importance that calls for firm action by the Interstate Commerce Commission. If this proves ineffective, then the Federal government can seek court or Congressional action to compel the disclosure of those domestic or foreign interests which may control the railroads of the United States.

Ownership of a rail subsidiary by a conglomerate holding company, of course, is not in doubt, but ownership of the holding company may be. The Commission's considerable powers to study the ownership of railroads, which it has not thus far exercised, would be inoperative respecting the parent holding company of the conglomerate, unless these companies are subjected to the Commission's reporting requirements.

As to the argument of the advocates that the enforcement of the securities provisions of the Interstate Commerce Act against the parent holding company would "effectively destroy the most efficient method by which the railroads can diversify," the opponents reply:

This argument is (1) an admission that the Interstate Commerce Commission has the power and the duty to enforce Section 20a of the Interstate Commerce Act against the parent holding companies of railroad-based conglomerates, and (2) a plea that it should not perform its duty under this power because a public hearing by the Commission on the issuance of securities, or the assumption of obligations or liabilities, by the parent holding company in acquiring a non-transportation company would involve delay. This argument is, the opponents state, that the Commission should permit an illegality on a vital matter affecting the interests of the railroad and the public in order to enable the parent holding company to carry on its non-transportation company acquisitions in secret.

The views publicly expressed by men at the management and policy level in organizations directly concerned with the railroad-based conglomerate problem give an insight into how such conglomerates may affect their organizations. Four such men, representatives of a railroad, a shipper, an investment banking firm, and a regulatory agency, appeared in a panel discussion on this subject held on April 10, 1969, in Minneapolis, Minnesota, which was sponsored by the Traffic Club of that city. The panel moderator was Frank C. Rathje, Jr., Vice President of the Continental Illinois National Bank of Chicago.[16]

Mr. Jervis Langdon, Jr,. Chairman and President of the Rock Island Railroad, in opening the panel discussion, raised the question: "Is inclusion in a conglomerate good for railroads generally?" He then stated his views as follows:

> To begin with, the ordinary conglomerate is likely to include subsidiaries that are users of rail service—perhaps heavy users—and to have an operating railroad in the same corporate home, with users and railroad under the same management control, raises special problems under the provisions of the Interstate Commerce Act, and probably is at variance with sound public policy.
>
> But the real reason for my doubt is that railroads with earnings from conglomerates may find it easier to avoid the tough decisions that are necessary to solve the railroad service problem, and the service problem must come ahead of everything else, even earnings.

Citing the railroad car-supply problem, which is dependent on railroad cooperation and pooling of resources to improve fleet utilization and management, Mr. Langdon continued:

> The trouble is that earnings, whatever their source, produce a sense of well-being, and railroads that satisfy their shareholders in this manner are not likely to want to deal with tough service problems from an industry standpoint, particularly if they detect the slightest chance of a compromise of their own competitive standing. . . .
>
> What incentive would there be for a railroad in a prosperous conglomerate to work together with other lines in the development of merger patterns . . . in which special interest might have to be subordinated to the attainment of common goals? What incentive would there be for such a railroad to work together with other lines in the mainten-

---

[16] *Traffic World*, April 19, 1969.

ance and operation of through routes ... to help with the organization of an industry board where internal disputes, such as the proration
of revenues arising from joint rates, could be arbitrated? What incentive would there be to work cooperatively in the development and
marketing of railroad service in order to stop the erosion of traffic to
other modes ... to work together with other lines in a determined
effort to have removed those restraints—legislative or otherwise—
which operate to prevent the full development and economic use of the
rail form of transportation?

As to the contention that concerted industry cooperation in
solving common problems may not be demanded "in the American tradition of free enterprise," Mr. Langdon said:

The answer is the *railroads are public service companies,* and the assumed competitive rights of individual carrier must be responsive to
the needs of the public. If the railroads in their present form cannot
provide an efficient national system, then, obviously, the form will
have to be changed.

What this means, he continued, is nationalization, even
though nationalization "has not always been a satisfactory answer in other countries." He added:

Moreover, if the railroads in the meantime have become conglomerate subsidiaries, a government take-over might be highly welcome.
     In the history of our country there have been many instances of the
spinning-off by private enterprise of public-service undertakings, and
they have invariably ended up in public ownership. There is ample
precedent in our country for the public ownership of railroads.

Mr. Robert Alexander, Vice President of the Pillsbury Company, another panelist, expressed the view that shippers need
more knowledge of the real purpose behind the formation of
railroad-based conglomerates. He cautioned, if they are formed
solely for the purpose of taking advantage of tax considerations,
to manipulate capital flow away from the transportation operations, and to abandon unprofitable transport services and facilities, this would invite shipper opposition. A matter of concern, he
stated, lies in the area of possible discrimination, preferential
treatment and unfair competitive practices.

Mr. Alexander directed attention to the broad purpose of the "commodities clause" of the Interstate Commerce Act, which is "to prevent carriers from occupying the dual and inconsistent position of public carrier and private shipper." He continued, "In my opinion, the transportation conglomerates would appear to be approaching, if not operating within, this role."

Warning that America is facing perhaps the most critical stage of its railroad and transportation history, Mr. Alexander stated:

> Any judgment errors on the part of holding companies which would result in further depreciation of rail service could be absolutely disastrous to our industry.
>
> While none of us want to see nationalization of our railroads, there appears to be a ground-swell of comment indicating that improvement must be forthcoming to avoid it. Unfortunately, the many promises that have been made in connection with mergers simply have not developed, and the shipping public is wary of any new promises of the carriers in connection with their continued existence under the conglomerate wing.

Mr. Charles L. Bergmann, Vice President of Shearson, Hammill & Company, another panelist, said he found it difficult to form a firm opinion whether or not railroad-based conglomerates should be praised or condemned. He added:

> Stockholders of a diversified holding company are primarily interested in the over-all profitability of the entire conglomerate enterprise. While it is logical to assume that they would prefer every unit to be profitable, they are once removed from direct contact with the railroad subsidiary. Thus, they are less likely to take an active interest in promoting or being concerned about the welfare of the transportation subsidiary.

Mr. Bergman enumerated the advantages a holding company of a railroad-based conglomerate could bring a railroad and stated that if this device is necessary to accomplish the full benefits sought, it should be accepted. He continued:

> On the other hand, if the holding company concept results in

divestment and impairment of a carrier's ability to serve the public, it must either be condemned or properly controlled by government.

Commissioner Paul J. Tierney, of the Interstate Commerce Commission, another panelist, stated that from a regulator's standpoint, whether transportation conglomerates are to be considered as "friends" or "foes" simply boils down to the question of whether or not they are in the public interest.

Mr. Tierney recounted reasons advanced in support of the formation of railroad-based conglomerates as a "friend" of transportation, and then enumerated some of the potential dangers. These might include possible pressure on top management to reinvest income in "businesses which will produce a greater rate of return than the railroads;" the likelihood of channeling capital out of the carrier subsidiary into the more profitable non-transportation subsidiary, thus cutting to a minimum the capital-spending and maintenance programs of the railroad; the chance of disinvestment of the railroad partner; the chance of adverse parent-company policy respecting purchases to be made by the carrier from non-carrier subsidiaries; and the possibility of circumstances arising that would dictate against compensating the carrier for use by the holding company of railroad tax benefits.

Before the close of the panel discussion, Mr. Langdon repeated his "grave doubts" that railroads should be or should become partners in transportation conglomerates, adding:

> We can improve the financial condition of the railroad industry—and improve it markedly—if we can provide additional services.

The railroads' role—or fate—in the present "merger mania" was discussed by Robert S. Hamilton, Vice President of the Southern Railway System before the Railroad Transportation Institute in Washington, D. C., on October 15, 1969.[17] He stated:

> Let's be blunt about it. The rise in numbers of holding companies in the railroad field is a sign of weakness in the industry.
>
> Business diversification such as has been adopted and is being

[17] *Traffic World,* October 25, 1969.

considered by a large segment of the rail transporation industry is an alarming augury for the future, in my mind. The ultimate effects upon the national economy and the basic transportation system of the country are certain to prove very, very costly.

Noting that a conglomerate's purpose is to maximize return for the multi-company operations, he continued:

This clearly points to putting money in places where greatest returns can be realized. Nothing in the immediate future indicates that rail transportation can be brought to anything approaching a par with the rates of return in industry being acquired by the holding companies railroads have set up.

Arguing that the long-range view must consider that successive managements of the parent company may be less rail-oriented in their approaches, he added that "emphasis in use of capital will shift more and more to the non-transportation sectors of the multi-company opportunities."

Mr. Hamilton then foresaw a time when some of the conglomerates built around railroad holdings may ease their "aging" parents out the door, raising the question "whether the ousted railroads are so drained of strength—so devitalized—that they cannot perform adequately as common carriers."

The principal programs of the major forces in the railroad industry in the 1960s are four in number. They may be stated briefly as follows:

1. Mergers of railroads into larger rail transportation systems.
2. Reduction of services of the railroads principally to the transportation of carload freight.
3. Authorization for railroads to diversify into other modes of public transportation.
4. Formation of parent holding companies as a means of establishing railroad-based conglomerates for the purpose of acquiring and operating non-transportation businesses.

Let us consider each item separately and then colllectively:

Item 1. Sound railroad mergers are in the public interest. Governor Nelson A. Rockefeller, in testimony before the Interstate Commerce Commission at a hearing involving the Chesapeake and Ohio, Baltimore and Ohio, and the New York Central railroads (see Chapter IX, Part I), warned that "consolidations or mergers are not necessarily a solution to the problems of the railroads," and then added:

Soundly conceived consolidations can strengthen management, provide cash for modernization of equipment and facilities, permit reductions in costs, curtail reductions in service, provide more frequent and faster service at lower costs, eliminate overlapping and duplicating facilities, make more efficient use of plant and personnel, make possible for the use of the most efficient and direct routes, and create balanced railroad systems capable of competing effectively with all other modes of transportation.

On the other hand, unwise consolidations or mergers—while perhaps giving immediate corporate, tax or financial advantage to one or more of the carriers involved—could seriously weaken or bankrupt other railroads serving in the same or adjacent territories, thus materially jeopardizing not only the public interest in efficient transportation but the nation's interest in a healthy and growing economy.

If consolidations or mergers which are both sound and in the public interest are not proposed by the carriers themselves, then some other approach must be devised to bring about a coordinated restructuring of the railroad transportation industry.

Following the guidelines laid down by Governor Rockefeller, I testified before the Interstate Commerce Commission for the State of New York as Director of the New York State Office of Transportation in the merger proceedings involving the Norfolk and Western-Nickel Plate-Wabash railroads and, later, in the merger proceedings involving the Pennsylvania and New York Central railroads (see Chapter IX, Part II). All of the conditions advanced by the State of New York upon which it supported these two mergers were adopted by the Interstate Commerce Commission.

Item 2. Railroad managers are seemingly convinced that there is no profit for the railroads in transporting passengers, mail, and less-carload freight.

As to the program of some railroads to bring about the discontinuance of their passenger services, the following editorial in the *New York Times* of September 18, 1969, is revealing:

Missing the Train

In what could have been a landmark decision and a turning point in the decay of American railroads, the Interstate Commerce Commission has evaded its responsibility with a plea of impotence. Denying its power to regulate the quality of passenger service, it rejected a petition of five states that the Southern Pacific Railway be ordered to improve the service on its Sunset Limited by restoring a dining car, for example, for the 45-hour trip from New Orleans to Los Angeles, in place of the vending machine car it now carries.

The I.C.C. would be pleased, it said, if Congress were to give it authority it considers itself to lack. Since it has in fact the power to determine whether a passenger route may be discontinued for decline in patronage, it is hard to see how it can evade the duty of determining whether or not that decline was avoidable or willfully and culpably incurred. Indeed, its own examiner's finding in the case of the Sunset Limited that the cause of the decline lay with the railroad, not the passengers, urged that the Southern Pacific be censured and that the Commission require sleeping and dining cars on certain trains, along with provision for inspection of services.

Nobody, not even the I.C.C., can be under any illusion about the deliberate sabotage of their passenger trains by some railroads intent on more profitable aspects of their business on skimming the cream from their diversified interests rather than performing the public service for which they long ago received invaluable rights of way. Those vanishing Americans who still hopefully ride the rails have too frequently experienced monstrous indifference to schedule, wretched connections, surly personnel and outmoded equipment, inedible food and failures of lighting, water and air-conditioning. And the Commission itself knows that applications for dropping a passenger train are regularly preceded by months of just such deteriorating service, designed to discourage so many patrons that a case for discontinuance can be made.

Since the I.C.C., in its recent decision says it lacks the power to save the passenger lines from self-destruction, we hope Congress will spell out that power and require its use. With intercity passenger trains down to a little more than a third of the number that ran only ten years ago, the Commission could suspend applications for discontinuance at least until Congress has had a reasonable time to act.

The railroads will need widespread public support if their

announced programs are to be seriously considered. Therefore it is difficult to understand by what process of reasoning some railroad managements could resort to such methods in dealing with the public. The reaction appears to be—so this is the way they run the railroads, what consideration would the public get if they operated all modes of public transportation? Even a fraction of the amount which the railroads contribute to the nationwide advertising of their carload freight business, apparently for the edification of the public, would be adequate to provide the simplest human needs for their passengers. Such consideration would have convinced the American people that the managements of the railroads are sincerely interested in discharging their obligations as public service companies. And, it should be added, in this matter the failure of the Interstate Commerce Commission to protect the public interest was not its finest hour.

The public response to the modern, high-speed Metroliner rail passenger service between Washington, D. C., and New York City, initiated by the United States Department of Transportation with the cooperation of the Penn-Central Railroad, must have been somewhat embarrassing to many railroad managers. It is evident that there is an urgent public need for similar railroad passenger transportation services in many areas of the United States, including the area along the Atlantic seaboard between New York City and Miami, Florida. And this service will be greatly improved when adequate tracks on improved roadbeds are provided for modern, high-speed railroad transportation for both passengers and freight.

The organized railroad industry is seeking from Congress a cash subsidy if it is to continue to perform rail passenger services. This industry solution of the railroads' passenger problem might also be reexamined by railroad mangers for, in itself, it could lead to the nationalization of the railroads' passenger services, and eventually to the nationalization of all railroad services. *Perhaps railroad managers may conclude that the use of funds of the railroad which they are investing in outside businesses could more profitably be used to improve their plant, equipment, facilities, and services to adequately and safely serve the public.*

As to the railroads' transportation of United States mail, the answer can be found in the reading of Chapter VIII.

It was inevitable that the services of the trucking companies would attract less-carload traffic. However, a nationwide railroad program to establish coordinated rail-truck services for less-carload traffic, such as was successfully established on the New York Central Railroad for mail, express and less-carload freight as related in Chapter VII, Part II, might have convinced shippers that the railroads were interested in serving all their freight traffic needs, an attitude that could have aided the railroads in increasing their carload traffic.

Item 3. This railroad proposal to diversify into other modes of public transportation has been revived by the organized railroad industry (see Chapter VII, Part I) as the best means of establishing a coordinated national transportation system.

The concern of those who own and operate other modes of public transportation is that the integration program of the railroads, if adopted, would replace American competitive private enterprise system with railroad-owned "cartel-monopolies" so large and powerful that they would force independent motor, water, and air carriers out of business. The possibility of such a development would also concern the Federal and state governments, for transportation systems supply and control every industrial and commercial activity. The public's interest in transportation is principally concerned with rates, for rates, not distance, measure and circumscribe the trading area. President Truman stated in vetoing the Reed-Bulwinkle bill: "The power to control transportation rates is the power to influence the competitive success or failure of other businesses." Thus, there is presented a major policy issue for the Federal government and the states, as well as for the entire transportation industry.

Admittedly, coordination of the services of the various modes of public transportation is essential if the nation is to have an adequate, efficient, and economical national transportation system, which it does not have, but urgently needs. Therefore, in view of the announced program of the organized railroad industry to meet this need, the owners and operators of motor, water, and air transportation should announce their program to achieve effective coordination of the services of all modes of public transportation, a program that would convince the Federal government and the states that a truly coordinated national system can be achieved in the American tradition of competitive private enterprise. Then, if a coordinated program which is both sound and in the public interest is not proposed by the carriers, some other approach will have to be devised to bring about the coordination of public transportation services adequate to meet the urgent needs of the nation in a rapidly changing world.

Item 4. A stated purpose of the program to establish railroad-based conglomerates is to obtain needed funds from non-transportation companies for the improvement and operation of the railroad which the railroad itself cannot provide. This proposal, which burst suddenly upon the nation in the name of "private enterprise," seems to imply that the railroads are a dying industry because they cannot operate profitably as a private enterprise. Therefore, the assets of the railroad would be used, through the device of a "parent" holding company, to initiate the acquisition of non-transportation companies, from the profits of which the railroad would be subsidized.

The railroad-based conglomerates contend that the regulatory procedure in the Interstate Commerce Act, previously discussed, creates a practical problem for them in acquiring non-transportation companies. This they hope to avoid by prevailing upon the Interstate Commerce Commission not to assume jurisdiction over the parent holding company. Aside from the legal question involved, which the Commission, and perhaps the courts, must decide, there is the larger issue of national policy that concerns the Congress and, indeed, all Americans.

The arguments for and against the establishment of railroad-based conglomerates, previously summarized, must lead to the conclusion that, on balance, the potential dangers to the railroads and the national economy outweigh the claimed advantages. *In this view, the establishment of railroad-based conglomerates could be the capitalistic road to nationalization of the railroads of the United States.*

The overall program of major groups in the railroad industry for the restructuring of public transportation facilities and services in the United States is presented to the American people and their representatives in government for their consideration and approval.

To anyone who seeks to view the whole field of transportation from the standpoint of the public interest, this overall program, aside from sound mergers of railroads, is a disappointment. Something more constructive was to be hoped for. Government operation may be forced on the nation, but, if so, it will come from such programs of major groups in the railroad industry and from the failure of the Federal government to replace the outmoded, overlapping, and often conflicting accumulation of transportation policies of the nineteenth and early twentieth centuries with a comprehensive, sound national transportation policy for the entire transportation industry in the remaining years of the twentieth century,—*a policy that will invigorate private companies performing public transportation services.* It is within the framework of such a national policy that all segments of the transportation industry can, with confidence, formulate their internal policies and plans, and adequately perform their respective duties.

The transition period in any field of human endeavor is always difficult, calling as it does for the constant reassessment of relative values and frequently the complete abandonment of concepts long held by various groups. In the transportation industry, giant steps forward in technology and methods have accelerated the need for such reassessment. In such a time, a firm grip must be kept on essentials. One of these essentials is the railroad plant and its welfare. One may reject the counsel of those who control the railroads, or the associations through which they function, as too selfishly interested for general public acceptance. But no thoughtful public official or private citizen will do anything to weaken or destroy the essential railroad plant. Railroad managements must, however, recognize that they live in a changing world and must adapt their operations to the constantly changing transportation situation. The solution of their problems does not depend on deliberately avoiding their

responsibilities as public service companies, in establishing cartel-
monopolies of all forms of transportation, or in forming railroad-
based conglomerates. In time, such a "solution" would destroy
the railroads as private companies performing public transportation services.

The solution of the "transportation problem" depends on
whether the responsible officials in government and in the transportation industry will make themselves willing and able to
formulate new government and industry policies and programs
that will save transportation as a basic industry in our private
enterprise economy. The new technologies are available, the
means are at hand, the need is apparent,—the "will-to-do" is
the only essential that stands in the way of developing modern
public transportation services under the traditional American
private enterprise system.

From the standpoint of the nation's economy, the overall
transportation program of major groups in the railroad industry
is in concept a part of the awesome development of merger-
minded conglomerates in other industries, including bank-based
conglomerates. Federal government officials contend that such
giant conglomerate concentrations of economic power would
change the face of the American free enterprise system within a
decade. In this view, our country would become a nation of large
cartel-monopolies, which would eventually result in a single all-
embracing concentration of power. Such vast power over the
nation's economy, which would be accomplished in the name of
"private enterprise," would destroy freedom and private enterprise as we have known them from the foundation of our
country.

In a democracy, this is too great a power to be exercised by a
few groups in our society. Small businesses would rapidly dis-
appear. Thus, freedom of opportunity for all but a chosen few of
our citizens would vanish. If this is the "wave of the future," it
would compel the coming generation, regardless of their talents,
to become, at best, specialists in vast intercorporate enterprises
controlling our economy,—numbers in their computers. This
could force the people of the nation to turn to socialism or some

other alternative to such oligarchic concept of "private enterprise." This, in turn, would bring about a vast expansion of bureaucracy in the Federal government. In either eventuality, the search of our people for wider horizons to improve their economic, social and cultural conditions under free enterprise would come to an end.

History would then record that this end to our freedom of opportunity in a free society, a way of life that has been an example to all the world, need not have happened; that the ambitions of a few powerful groups in our country could not have prevailed against an *informed citizenry* on this basic and vital issue. My experiences, as related in this book, would sustain this verdict of history.

A frank examination of these developments adversely affecting our free enterprise system inescapably leads to the conclusion that our Nation has only two choices and that, if there is further delay in acting energetically and wisely, there may be no choice at all. The Nation, through the Congress and its regulatory agencies and the Executive Department of the Federal government, may choose to exercise their constitutional powers to preserve our free enterprise system, or they may, through failure to act or to inform our citizens of the facts or by equivocation or delays, lose that freedom for all Americans.

CHAPTER XI

The United Nations Development
Programme—A Practical Approach
to a Great Challenge

IN MARCH, 1966, Mrs. Wiprud and I made all arrangements to leave New York on May 25, 1966, on the liner Queen Elizabeth for Southampton, England, for a long-delayed trip through Europe. Late in April, 1966, I was notified that I had been appointed a member of the United States Delegation to the meeting of the Governing Council of the United Nations Development Programme, generally referred to as the UNDP, to be held in Milan, Italy, in June, 1966. Vice President Hubert H. Humphrey had nominated me for this assignment.

This development required a complete change in plans. On May 21, Mrs. Wiprud and I left New York on the S. S. Independence for Naples, Italy. After a week in Naples, we proceeded to Milan a few days in advance of the meeting of the Governing Council of the United Nations Development Programme. On arrival, we learned that some members of the United States Delegation had preceded us. The Chairman of our Delegation, Ambassador James Roosevelt, the United States Representative to the United Nations Economic and Social Council, arrived the following morning. This gave us an opportunity to become acquainted and to discuss the various items of the Governing Council's agenda.

The time for briefing on the organizational structure and functions of the UNDP, following my appointment by the State Department in late April, 1966, was limited, but enroute from New York to Naples, I had an opportunity to read the material supplied by the State Department which yielded a great deal of valuable information. What follows is a brief summary (with facts and figures updated to the latest now available.)

The UNDP was established by a resolution of the General Assembly of the United Nations which merged the previously existing Expanded Programme of Technical Assistance (established in 1950) and the Special Fund (established in 1959) into a single entity. The basic purpose of this decision of the General Assembly was to insure the more rational and more efficient organization and use of the principal resources of the United Nations system in order to provide to the developing countries the very wide range of expert services, training facilities, and pre-investment assistance in the economic, social and cultural fields which the United Nations and its associated agencies are capable of offering.

Inaugurating the work of the UNDP in January, 1966, the Secretary-General of the United Nations, U Thant, stated its functions were of "the greatest importance in helping the United Nations to fulfill its responsibilities under the Charter." Since the overriding responsibility of the United Nations is to maintain the peace, it is clear that what he was implying was that the UNDP is of the greatest importance in helping to prevent the outbreak of violence and war through alleviating such major causative factors as world-wide poverty and poverty of opportunity.

The UNDP is not a program for the rich nations to give to the poorer nations. On the contrary, it is a world-wide partnership among countries at all levels of development whose aim is to enable the low-income lands to help themselves effectively. Thus, the developing nations are required to cooperate with the UNDP by mobilizing their own resources, financial and otherwise, to the extent possible as "counterpart support" for the pre-investment projects assisted by the UNDP.

In fact, less than 50 percent of total project costs are met by the UNDP, which pays for internationally recruited experts, imported technical equipment, specialized contract services and fellowships. The remainder—more than half—is met by the recipient countries, which pay for wages of national staffs, buildings, local facilities and services. Specifically, by the end of 1969, thousands of large and smaller-scale projects were approved by the Governing Council of the UNDP, which when completed will cost $1,781 million to the UNDP and the equivalent of an estimated $1,870 million to more than 130 recipient countries and territories.

Financial support for the UNDP, as demonstrated at yearly pledging conferences held in October has increased from $55.2 million in 1959 to $225,127,338 contributed by 121 nations to finance programme activities in 1970. National and regional projects carried out with UNDP aid include:

Surveys to determine the availability and value of low-income country natural resources, and to assess other potentials for the increased production and marketing of goods and services.

Expansion and strengthening of educational systems from primary through university levels; a full spectrum of professional, vocational and technical instruction; work-oriented literacy training; and the provision of fellowships for specialized studies abroad.

Activities to improve rural and urban living conditions and to open new employment opportunities, particularly for young people.

Establishment of facilities for applying modern research methods to priority development problems, and for disseminating new discoveries and production techniques.

Feasibility studies and other measures to help increase the availability of development capital from domestic and external sources, private as well as public.

Planning for the expansion of road, rail, air and water transport, and of modern telecommunications facilities.

Advisory, operational and training services related to overall development planning and to other essential governmental activities.

Some indications of the measure of success being achieved by

Vice President Hubert H. Humphrey

this Programme are shown in the following figures. By the end of 1969:

Commitments of over $3,200 million in follow-up investment for sound development schemes have been stimulated, directly or otherwise, by the findings and recommendations of 63 UNDP-supported natural resource surveys and by 12 applied research projects.

Close to 600,000 people have up-graded their professional and technical skills through participation in the programmes of UNDP-assisted institutes, universities and seminars. Many more have improved their competency by working on projects with international experts. The list includes thousands of secondary school teachers; industrial, agricultural and vocational instructors; managers, supervisors, marketing specialists and skilled workers; public utilities specialists, engineers and technicians; and administrators and development planners.

543 permanent national and regional institutes have been, or are being, established or strengthened covering technical and advanced educational training, applied research for agriculture and industry and development planning.

55,000-60,000 fellowship awards have been made to enable nationals of developing countries to undertake study tours abroad.

The criteria which govern all projects proposed for UNDP assistance, as prescribed by the General Assembly of the United Nations, are as follows: governments requesting assistance have an obligation to demonstrate that their projects have been selected on the basis of priority needs; that they will have a direct influence on the economic and social development of the country; that they are designed, whenever possible, for early transfer to the supervision and management of the recipient country; that they are integrated into overall national development efforts; that they are coordinated with other assistance programs; and, that they are free from political considerations.

The procedures to aid in formulating requests for assistance to meet these requirements have been summarized as follows: the recipient governments may seek the advice of the UNDP's resident representatives, who direct field offices in over 90 developing countries, and of the specialized agencies within whose competence the proposed projects fall. By the time that requests have been prepared—on an individual basis for both pre-investment projects and smaller technical assistance missions—the chief needs of the recipient government have been clearly defined at the field level. Requests for assistance are then sent to the Administrator of the UNDP for review and evaluation. In accord with the funds available, he draws up his recommended program for project approval. In this task he has the assistance of an Inter-Agency Consultative Board, composed of the United Nations Secretary-General and the executive heads of the agencies participating in the program. The Board not only supplies advice and guidance to the UNDP; it also permits a productive exchange of views on program performance and on possible new directions and additional fields of activity.

Final approval of all projects rests with the UNDP's Governing Council, composed of the representatives of 37 nations, developed and developing. This Council meets twice a year and is being increasingly composed of representatives of ministerial level and other highly skilled experts in development and development problems.

Responsibility for the field implementation of projects supported by the UNDP rests with the United Nations and its family of related agencies.[1]

In addition to providing governments with technical and professional advice, the agencies also recruit experts, procure equipment, contract for specialized services and supervise day-to-day operations.

The task of administering the program, subject to review and

[1] The list of agencies and organizations executing projects on behalf of UNDP is as follows: United Nations, New York, N. Y.; International Labour Organization (ILO), Geneva, Switzerland; Food and Agriculture Organization (FAO), Rome, Italy; United Nations Educational, Scientific and Cultural Organization (UNESCO), Paris, France; World Health Organization (WHO), Geneva; International Bank for Reconstruction and Development (World Bank), Washington, D. C.,U.S.A.; International Civil Aviation Organization (ICAO), Montreal, Canada; International Telecommunication Union (ITU), Geneva; World Meteorological Organization (WMO), Geneva; International Atomic Energy Agency (IAEA), Vienna, Austria; Universal Postal Union (UPU), Berne, Switzerland; Inter-Governmental Maritime Consultative Organization (IMCO), London, United Kingdom; United Nations Industrial Development Organization (UNIDO), Vienna; Inter-American Development Bank (ADB), Washington, D. C.; African Development Bank, Abidjan, Ivory Coast; United Nations Conference on Trade and Development (UNCTAD), Geneva.

approval of the Governing Council, is lodged in an Administrator, Mr. Paul G. Hoffman, who was selected by the Secretary-General for this post and was confirmed by the United Nations General Assembly. Mr. Hoffman assumed this key role in the UNDP on January 1, 1966.

The UNDP functions under the authority of the United Nations General Assembly and the Economic and Social Council. UNDP field office staffs, each headed by a resident representative, are composed of men and women from nearly 70 countries.

This, in summary, was the basic information I obtained from the reading of the documents supplied by the State Department about the organization and functions of UNDP, with some amplification as the result of my experience in Milan as a member of the United States Delegation to the meeting of the Governing Council of the UNDP in that city and later to its meeting in New York City.

The opening of the June, 1966, session of the Governing Council in Milan, Italy, was most impressive. It was held in a large auditorium in the Fair Grounds in Milan. All the buildings on the Fair Grounds are of a permanent nature and are beautifully designed and maintained. They are used the year around by national and international organizations, and by business and industrial companies for meetings and the display of their products.

The large room in the auditorium where the Governing Council held its meetings reminded me of the large room in the United Nations building in New York where the General Assembly meets. This room was wired for head-phones at each seat, as at sessions of the United Nations, and all speeches and discussions were translated into six languages. This enabled us to follow the proceedings during the ensuing weeks without difficulty.

My reading of government documents on the UNDP and the conferences of our Delegation before the convening of the Governing Council hardly prepared me for the scope of its activities

Paul G. Hoffman, Administrator, United Nations Development Programme

and the significance of its approach to the solution of the economic and social problems of the developing countries.

Ambassador James Roosevelt, of course, spoke for the United States Delegation at the meetings of the Governing Council. His speeches were brief and to the point, as were those of most of the delegates. His voice, and many of his mannerisms so natural to him, reminded me of his father. The members of the United States Delegation and, indeed, all of the delegates at the Milan meeting had respect and liking for Ambassador Roosevelt.

The UNDP is, of course, concerned with transportation, for adequate and efficient transportation is basic to the economic, social, and cultural progress in developing countries as it has been and still is in the developed countries. It was in this field primarily that my 42 years of experience in private and public life as an attorney, administrator, and consultant dealing with legal, economic, and social problems in all fields of transportation qualified me, as a public member of the Delegation, to make a contribution to conferences.

In our informal discussions before and after the formal meetings, all members of the Delegation had an opportunity to express their views with the result that, under the patient guidance of Ambassador Roosevelt, problems were resolved amicably and constructively. In all my experience, never have I been associated with an abler or finer group of dedicated public men and women than those who made up the United States Delegation to the June, 1966, session of the Governing Council of the UNDP in Milan, Italy.

During the course of almost daily meetings of the Governing Council, I had several opportunities to meet and visit with Paul G. Hoffman. I had, of course, heard much about Mr. Hoffman, but to meet and see him in action as the Administrator of the UNDP evidenced his remarkable talent for leadership that so eminently qualified him for this important post. This talent emerged so clearly at the conclusion of debate on major problems of policy or on pending important actions by the Governing Council, when the President of the Council at the Milan meeting, Mario Franzi, of Italy, would call on Mr. Hoffman for his comments on the matter. In clear language that no one could misunderstand, Mr. Hoffman would state the facts, his views thereon, and his conclusion. So far as I can recall, that conclusion was more often than not accepted by all the delegates without further debate—a fine tribute to the man.

When I mentioned my observation to a member of Mr. Hoffman's staff, after a particularly long debate during which many divergent views were expressed, he told me that the delegates seemed to await eagerly Mr. Hoffman's views and conclusions and to accept them very frequently as the best of possible solutions. Even between sessions of the Governing Council, this staff member added, delegates often called on Mr. Hoffman at his New York office about a decision of the UNDP and would accept that decision only after he had assured them that the decision was fair and reasonable and in their best interest as well as the interest of the UNDP.

The career of Mr. Hoffman prepared him for the vital role of Administrator of the UNDP. Following a distinguished career in American industry, Mr. Hoffman became involved in international development when he was appointed by President Truman in 1948 as the first administrator of the Marshall Plan (ECA).

Over the years since Mr. Hoffman served as Administrator of the Marshall Plan to his selection as Administrator of the UNDP in January, 1966, he had become known throughout the world as an administrator of organizations whose work had affected the lives of more people—and involved more people in successful efforts to help themselves—than any secular program in history.

Resigning his Marshall Plan post in September 1950, Mr. Hoffman served for two years as President of the Ford Foundation, a period during which the Foundation undertook major new initiatives on both the domestic and international scene. He continued his interest in international development. In 1956, he was a member of the United States Delegation to the Eleventh Session of the United Nations General Assembly, concentrating his activity in the work of the Committee on Economic and Financial Questions.

Mr. Hoffman served three terms (March 1963-March 1966)

as President of the Society for International Development, a leading professional organization in the field.

For seven years before assuming his present post as Administrator of the UNDP in 1966, Mr. Hoffman served as Managing Director of the United Nations Special Fund, which was merged with the United Nations Expanded Programme of Technical Assistance to form the new UNDP.

The United Nations Development Programme is a concept that Mr. Hoffman envisaged and, with able lieutenents from many lands, brought to fruition by uniting the nations of the world into this great peaceful effort by the force of their own interests.

During the June, 1966 meeting of the Governing Council of the UNDP in Milan, and later at its meeting in New York City during January, 1967, I was greatly impressed by the harmonious and cooperative spirit that prevailed among its members in dealing with the many and difficult problems on its agenda. While this was due in substantial part to the able, wise, and dedicated leadership of the UNDP, a basic reason, I believe, is the nature of its organizational structure.

The UNDP is the most extensive multilateral endeavor ever undertaken, whose membership represents a coalition of nations that exceeds that of the United Nations itself. Unlike bilateral aid, which so often is considered to be motivated by political considerations, the UNDP, being a multilateral organization, is free from such suspicions and charges. (For example, the UNDP has approved a fisheries project for South Vietnam and a university project in Cuba, after a mild exchange of "pleasantries" between the USSR and the USA.) If there is to be any hope for peace in the world, then one of man's greatest contributions can come through such a multilateral approach by the developed nations cooperating with the developing countries to help them solve their critical economic and social needs.

It is difficult to convey, in this brief space, a real sense of the impact that the world-wide, UNDP-assisted projects have had on the human spirit in the underdeveloped but developing countries. Millions of people who had no hope—who barely eked out an uncertain existence with their bare hands—now have hope that they can rise above the bare subsistence level by productive work, be free of communicable diseases, and be given an opportunity to educate themselves and their children. The opportunity of these millions of people to work themselves out of their abject poverty into a meaningful life is one of the world's best hopes for a peaceful and prosperous future.

As Administrator of the UNDP, Mr. Hoffman has constantly stressed UNDP's continuing search for wider horizons for all peoples by strengthening the capabilities of UNDP to carry out the development assistance responsibilities assigned to it by the General Assembly of the United Nations. He put his thoughts in these words:

The peace-building development work of the United Nations is a war on poverty of opportunity. One of the main causes of present suffering and unrest in the world is the denial to hundreds of millions of persons of the opportunity to realize their full human potential.

Now we have a chance successfully to combat this poverty of opportunity. It is a chance such as we never had before and a chance such as may never come again. We are now in a position to correct today's great underutilization of natural and human resources in the developing countries, an underutilization which is the root cause of the lack of opportunity from which the peoples of these countries suffer.

This indeed, is the main objective of all the activities of the United Nations Development Programme.

Under the inspiration of leaders like Mr. Hoffman, the United Nations Development Programme will continue to be the most practical and effective approach to meet a great challenge of our time.

In the morning of June 27, 1966, following the meeting of the Governing Council of the United Nations Development Programme in Milan, Italy, Mrs. Wiprud and I traveled by train to

Rome. That evening we were guests of United States Ambassador and Mrs. Reinhardt at a reception and the showing of a documentary film on Michelangelo, titled "The Last Giant."

After a few days in Rome, during which we met many interesting people and visited numerous places of interest, we began our delayed tour of European countries by their finest railroads.

The Upper Mississippi River Nine-foot Channel

The Project

THE PROJECT, authorized by Congress in 1930, embraced the section of the river between the mouth of the Missouri River and Minneapolis, Minnesota. This legislation provided for a 9-foot channel depth and a minimum width of 400 feet, to be achieved by the construction of a system of 26 dams and locks, supplemented by dredging. The project was mostly completed by the Army Corps of Engineers in the decade 1930-1940.

In 1937, Congress authorized a 4.6 mile extension of the project at Minneapolis so as to ascend the Falls of St. Anthony, thus extending the benefits to the center of that city's industry and to the area of its harbor sites and railroad networks.

In order to insure the full use of the upper river, Congress, in 1945, authorized the construction of a 10-mile lateral canal and lock No. 27 on the Illinois side of the river near Granite City, which by-passed an obstruction immediately downstream from the mouth of the Missouri River, known as the Chain of Rocks. In addition, to insure an adequate river depth at low water over the lower miter sill of lock No. 26 at Alton, Illinois, a rock-fill dam was constructed across the river immediately below the Chain of Rocks Bridge at St. Louis, Missouri. Construction of this project was authorized by Congress in 1958.

The completion of the construction in the Falls of St. Anthony area of Minneapolis-St. Paul, Minnesota, and the rock-fill dam at St. Louis, Missouri, placed in operation all of the 29 locks and dams of the upper Mississippi 9-foot channel project.

The majority of the locks in the 9-foot channel project are of the same dimensions, namely, 110 feet wide and 600 feet long. Exceptions occur at the upper and lower locks of the Falls of St. Anthony, which are 56 feet by 400 feet each; at dam No. 1, the only twin locks in the system-both 56 by 400 feet; and at dams No. 19 and No. 27, 110 feet by 1200 feet.

The height that a vessel is lifted or lowered in a lock differs widely according to location. For example, the lift in the upper lock at the Falls of St. Anthony is 49.2 feet; at dam No. 5A the lift is 5.5 feet; and in dam No. 19 the lift is 38.2 feet. The locks fill and empty by gravity, no power being required except for the operation of the machinery controlling the valves and gates.

The dams of the project are low structures and, except for some power facilities at Minneapolis-St. Paul, Rock Island, and Keokuk, are primarily for navigation purposes. Their low heights, necessitated in order to minimize excessive flooding of adjacent lands, preclude economical waterpower development and any flood control benefits.

The types of gates in the dams—being movable, can be adjusted to control the amount of water passing through the dam, thus maintaining almost constant pool levels with a minimum 9-foot depth in times of normal and low flows. During flood periods the gates are lifted entirely above the water level, and the dam structure then causes only slight obstruction to the flow of the river.

In the 669 miles of river between the first lock at the Falls of St. Anthony and the last lock of the project, No. 27, the Mississippi has a fall of about 420 feet. The purpose of the locks and dams is to create a series of slackwater pools with adequate depths for modern river navigation. The locks, in effect, act as steps by which vessels are lifted and lowered from one pool to the next, while the pools remain practically level. The system is sometimes compared to a stairway, the locks and dams being the risers and the pools being the treads. (See chart)

A Part of the Nation's Inland Waterways System

The project on the upper Mississippi, although in itself an undertaking of great proportions and of far-reaching economic effect, is but one link in the Mississippi Valley's great system of inland waterways, which includes the Illinois Waterway, the Ohio, the Missouri, the middle and lower Mississippi, and many other waterways. The integration of all these streams into a single network makes possible the economical shipment of bulk commodities—to and from almost every part of the valley, and, indeed, by transshipment to ocean vessels, to and from the ports of the world. As other great navigation projects—the St. Lawrence Seaway, the Calumet-Sag Channel, the Great Lakes connecting channels—continue to carry a steadily increasing volume of shipping, the inland waterways system can be expected to make progressively greater contributions to the economy of the Nation.

Commercial Traffic on the Upper Mississippi

Many industries, particularly those engaged in shipping bulk products in great volume, have taken advantage of the low-cost transportation made possible by the completion of the upper Mississippi 9-foot channel project. The growth of commercial traffic on the upper river since the beginning of the operation of the project in 1939 has been rapid and steady. In that year only about 2,400,000 tons were moved on the upper Mississippi; by 1961 that tonnage had increased to 28,100,000, or an increase of nearly 1070 percent. The steady increase in traffic continued, as follows: in 1962, 30,526,626 tons; in 1963, 30,943,237 tons; in 1964, 34,108,482 tons; in 1965, 37,841,593 tons; and in 1966, 41,311,941 tons.

The largest single bulk items moved on the upper river are petroleum products—gasoline, kerosene, fuel oil, lubricating oil—upbound from the oil fields of Texas and Louisiana. Coal in great quantity is also shipped upstream, mainly from the coal fields of central and southern Illinois and western Kentucky. Grain—corn, wheat, oats, barley and rye—is the principal downbound product. It is usually hauled to any one of numerous riverside elevators, and loaded on barges for downstream shipment, much of it going to New Orleans where it is transshiped to ocean vessels for overseas points. Scrap iron ranks second to grain in downbound tonnage. Many other products in small volume are carried on the water—iron and steel products, fertilizers, sulfur, cement, aluminum ingots and plate, sugar, dehydrated molasses, and many others. Among the more unusual items has been a barge of 1,200 tons of salad oil, valued at ¾ million dollars, and a barge of grain alcohol valued at 4½ million dollars. (See chart).

On the upper river, one is accustomed to seeing open barges for coal, tank barges for petroleum products, and covered barges for grain and mixed cargo, but some highly specialized types of barges have been devised for unusual cargoes. There are some with foot-thick linings of specially treated balsa wood which carry liquefied methane gas at a temperature of minus 258 degrees Fahrenheit, and at the other end of the thermometer, barges built like huge vacuum bottles which carry molten sulfur at temperatures of 300 to 350 degrees. Some barges are built to carry bulk cement mixed with air, pumped into and out of barges, making bags unnecessary. Others are filled with collapsible plastic containers to hold carbon black, and a special tank barge costing over a quarter million dollars carries anhydrous ammonia under 250 pounds pressure.

The passing from the river scene of the picturesque old steamboats is sometimes mourned, but beautiful though they were and marvels of efficiency for their time, they would have been no match for the modern, powerful Diesel towboats plying the river. According to old records, one of the largest cargoes ever carried by a river steamer was that of the "Henry Frank" which arrived in New Orleans in 1881 with 9,226 bales of cotton weighing 2,300 tons, stacked so high and solidly that the vessel was barely visible. A tow of 20,000 tons of freight loaded on 12 or 15 barges, with a length greater than that of the "Queen Elizabeth," all powered by one sturdy Diesel towboat, scarcely

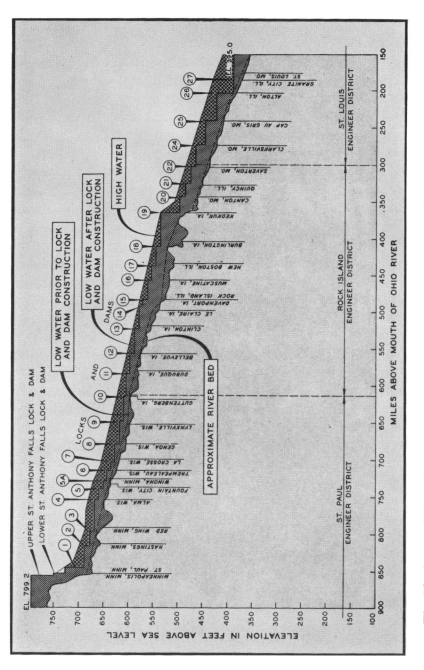

The "Stairway of Water" which makes navigation possible between Minneapolis and St. Louis
(Courtesy Office of Chief of Engineers, Department of the Army)

arouses a comment in a 1,500-mile trip from Baton Rouge to St. Paul.

The comforts and conveniences of the modern river towboat would also surprise many old rivermen—hydraulic steering, echo sounders, pneumatic hoists, air conditioning, electric refrigeration for food supplies, television, radio-telephone, and radar for operating in fog, all are standard equipment.

Recreational and Conservation Benefits

The series of lakes (pools) created by the locks and dams built for navigation purposes offer, as "extra dividends," a splendid potential for public recreation. Relatively stable water levels and the large water areas of the pools offer some of the finest outdoor recreation in the Nation. Each year hundreds of thousands visit the river to fish, hunt, or swim. During the summer months boating is particularly popular. Some may enjoy just a brief outing while others may be bound for the Gulf of Mexico or north to the Twin Cities of Minneapolis and St. Paul.

Congress, to facilitate pleasure boating, has authorized, and the Army Corps of Engineers has constructed, a number of small-boat harbors which have been turned over to local interests to operate and maintain. In addition a number of communities, individuals, and private companies have provided boat launching, docking, and servicing facilities which make boating on the river easier and pleasurable.

Although it may seem that boating reigns supreme, the pools and backwaters are unparalleled for other forms of outdoor recreation. Fishing for crappies, bass, catfish, walleyes, and many other species is excellent at varied locations in the pools and backwaters. Fishing is especially good immediately below the locks and dams. Not all fishing on the river is for fun—commercial fishing plays an important part in the river economy. Using modern equipment, professional fishermen ply their business of commercial fishing each year.

The stabilized water levels throughout the year has led to a remarkable improvement in wildlife habitat. The sloughs and backwaters abound in natural waterfowl foods. Thousands of acres of waterfowl habitat have been made available by the Corps of Engineers to the Bureau of Sport Fisheries and Wildlife, the United States Fish and Wildlife Service, and the five States bordering the river for wildlife management. These areas are managed as waterfowl refuges and for public hunting and fishing.

The recreational opportunities afforded by the upper Mississippi River Project are of inestimable economic value—above and beyond the economic values and benefits are those that contribute to the general welfare of the public through good, healthful outdoor recreation.

APPENDIX B

A Giant Conglomerate—
The International Telephone and
Telegraph Corporation

THE UNITED STATES DEPARTMENT OF JUSTICE, in an antitrust suit against the International Telephone and Telegraph Corporation instituted in the United States District Court for the District of Connecticut (Civil Action No. 13320), submitted to the Court the facts set forth in the text and, in addition, the following facts about the major companies of the 120 companies acquired by or merged with the International Telephone and Telegraph Corporation *prior to 1969.*

Continental Baking Company.—This company is the largest baking company in the country. It has 71 bakeries in 60 cities in 31 states with

300 distribution agencies and 6,500 driver-salesmen routes. Its total sales in 1968 were in excess of $620 million.

Sheraton Corporation of America.—This company is the largest owner and operator of guest rooms in the United States and Canada. It has more than 45,000 guest rooms in its hotels and motor inns here and abroad and employs 26,000 people. It has under construction or in the planning stage more than 30 hotels in the United States and abroad. Its 1967 revenues were $268,676,000.

Rayonier, Inc.—This company is an important producer of chemical cellulose and lumber. In 1967 it had sales of $150 million.

Airport Parking Company of America, Inc.—This company is the largest airport parking company in the country with parking facilities at 80 airports and numerous other locations.

Levitt & Sons, Inc.—This company is the largest home builder in the United States. It builds 6,000 homes per year. In 1968 its sales totaled $168 million. It has sold homes to 80,000 home owners. By 1974, it is expected to build new homes at the rate of 11,000 annually.

Avis, Inc.—This company is the second largest car rental company in the United States. It has 85,000 vehicles or about 25 percent of all United States rental cars.

The following facts were submitted by the Department of Justice to the United States District Court about major companies in the 33 mergers consummated or approved by the directors of the International Telephone and Telegraph Corporation *in 1969.*

The Hartford Fire Insurance Company.—This company has nine operating insurance company subsidiaries and two wholly-owned real estate subsidiaries. It sells a full line of insurance but specializes in property and liability insurance. Upon acquiring the Minnesota Life Insurance Company in 1968, The Hartford Fire Insurance Company (hereinafter Hartford) raised its life insurance in force to $2.1 billion. It collected premiums totaling $968 million and had an adjusted operating income of $53.3 million in 1968. The consolidated assets of Hartford totaled $1,891,700,000 on December 31, 1968, and it had $400 million in excess of its required surplus.

In 1964 the International Telephone and Telegraph Corporation (hereinafter ITT) entered the insurance business and, through its subsequently acquired insurance companies, expanded rapidly. By 1967 its life insurance companies had reached a world-wide level of insurance in force exceeding $1 billion.

The Department of Justice contends that (1) through reciprocity and vertical integration ITT-Hartford will have the power to foreclose Hartford's competitors from substantial insurance markets represented by ITT's suppliers, ITT's subsidiaries, ITT's employees and ITT's customers and (2) the addition of Hartford, with extensive financial resources and an established position in the insurance industry, will give ITT's subsidiaries undue competitive advantage over their competitors. The insurance markets affected by foreclosure are insurance generally, property and liability insurance, commercial property and liability insurance and workmen's compensation. ITT's subsidiaries will have undue competitive advantages in the following industries: home building, automatic sprinkler systems, hotels, baking, car rental, vending machines and airport parking.

Canteen Corporation.—This company is one of the largest vending machine companies in the United States, with sales and rentals of $320 million. In addition to over 210,000 vending machines, Canteen has inplant feeding operations, manages restaurants, and provides specialized food services.

Grinnell Corporation.—This company is the nation's largest manufacturer of automatic fire protection equipment. In 1968 it had revenues of $341 million.

INDEX

About the Author

Reverend Thorgrim T. Wiprud, a Lutheran minister, and his wife Dora emigrated from Norway to the United States before the turn of the century. They had three children—Theodore, the oldest, Arne, and Agnes, the youngest. With the passing of Reverend Wiprud in 1906, the task of providing for and educating the children, with such assistance as the children could give, was a difficult time for Mrs. Wiprud. She was a remarkable woman who lived to be 101 years of age.

The family was fortunate in having as administrator of the small estate and as guardian of the three children, J. A. O. Preus, then an attorney in Minneapolis. When Mr. Preus became Insurance Commissioner and later State Auditor of Minnesota, Arne Wiprud, who had become proficient as a stenographer, served as his private secretary. Mr. Preus encouraged him to study law. Completion of his law course led to many opportunities for service in public and private life.

Mr. Preus was elected Governor of Minnesota in 1921 and served until 1925.

An important opportunity came to Arne Wiprud with the organization of the Federal Land Bank of St. Paul, Minnesota, of which he became an official. This was one of twelve such banks established throughout the United States which developed into the largest rural credit system in the world.

There followed other important opportunities, including the long struggle of the shippers of the upper Mississippi valley, who Arne Wiprud represented, to unlock the land-locked midwest by improving the upper Mississippi River for reliable commercial navigation, thus making it an integral part of the nation's vast inland waterways system.

Reverend Thorgrim T. Wiprud and his wife, Dora

J. A. O. Preus, Governor of Minnesota 1921-25, painted by Carl Bohnen

Over the years, Arne Wiprud has known five Presidents of the United States—Calvin Coolidge, Herbert Hoover, Franklin D. Roosevelt, Harry S. Truman, and Dwight D. Eisenhower. He undertook difficult tasks in the transportation field for two Attorneys General of the United States, the Postmaster General of the United States, and two Governors, most recently as Director of Transportation for the State of New York in the Cabinet of Governor Nelson A. Rockefeller. In June, 1966, Arne Wiprud served as a member of the United States Delegation to the meeting of the Governing Council of the United Nations Development Programme, held in Milan, Italy. Over one-third of his active life has been devoted to public service.

Arne Wiprud speaks of the outstanding men in private life with whom he was associated as "giants of the earth," men who stood firm in major areas of public concern, no matter how powerful the opposition.

Arne C. Wiprud's home is in Williamsburg, Virginia. He is married to the former Beatha Mary Haugen.